# The Druze

# The Druze

## A New Cultural and Historical Appreciation

Abbas Halabi

ITHACA
PRESS

2015
www.ithacapress.co.uk

**The Druze**
**A New Cultural and Historical Appreciation**

*Published by*
Ithaca Press
8 Southern Court
South Street
Reading
RG1 4QS
UK

www.ithacapress.co.uk
www.twitter.com/Garnetpub
www.facebook.com/Garnetpub
blog.ithacapress.co.uk

Ithaca Press is an imprint of Garnet Publishing Ltd.



First Edition 2015

ISBN: 9781859643532

British Library Cataloguing-in-Publication Data
A catalogue record for this book is available from the British Library

*Typeset by* PHi Business Solution Ltd., India
*Jacket design by* Garnet Publishing
*Cover image* The Druze pilgrimage to Nabi Sabalan
© Hanan Isachar, courtesy of Corbis images

Printed and bound in Lebanon by International Press:
interpress@int-press.com

*To Karl-Abbas, my first grandson*
*and the future generation of my family*

# Contents

# Preface

This English edition of my book, the *Druze Muwahhidun,* completes a series published in three languages: French (2005), Arabic (2008) and, finally, English (2014).

I have encountered great difficulties in publishing the English edition. Since I do not claim the same ability to write in English as I do in French and Arabic, I requested the assistance of more than one informed person to help with the translation. My main concern was to avoid publishing texts containing words or sentences incompatible with the true meaning of the Arabic version. An outstanding knowledge of English was not sufficient for translating a work of this nature since its veracity and conformity to the original Arabic demanded an equal fluency in Arab culture, given that the Druze Muwahhidun are integral to this culture.

Consequently, I restrained my urge to go ahead with the publication of the English book, despite an offer by the publishing house of the newspaper *An-Nahar* to print it. I pondered who might be able to reproduce this book in what is considered to be the world's foremost spoken language.

My elder brother, Adnan, suggested recourse to a person who combined fluency in the English language and in the history and culture of the Druze. Therefore, I requested the good offices of an old friend, Walīd Abi-Mershed, a Druze from a notable family living and working as a Senior Editor at the London-based Saudi newspaper *As-Sharq Al-Aswsat.* In his younger years, Mr. Abi-Mershed was also active in Druze affairs and is thus familiar with both the English language and the content of my text.

Mr. Abi-Mershed's re-editing spanned approximately one year, during which time he sent me his revised chapters in succession. Once I had finalized my revisions of the text, I submitted the book to the publisher, thus completing my series as I had promised myself. I might also consider publishing in a fourth language – Spanish – should I succeed in finding the right editor.

In the introduction to my book, I refer to my early involvement in Druze affairs in Lebanon. I have progressively furthered my insight into the varied aspects of Druze life – be it on the confessional, religious, organizational, cultural or social and welfare levels. This endeavour was crowned by my election as Chairman of the Druze Endowments Committee, following my election to the membership of the Druze Community Council in April 2006 – a post that I still hold.

My long working experience of more than 40 years in Druze public affairs has enabled me to acquaint myself with the realities of the Druze, with the community's chronic problems and points of strength. It has also enabled me to forge strong relations with many elements of the Druze social strata in Lebanon – particularly its leadership, its elderly and youthful figures, and especially its civil society. Within the framework of this society, I constantly held a role or a position in all of its organizations or committees, either in my capacity as a founder or as a personal contributor to its activities and development. These relations enabled me to probe the points of strength and weakness of the Druze community, and induced me to ponder about its situation, concerns, needs and prospects.

In the course of this long experience, I reached certain convictions made possible by the freedom and independence of thought that I maintained throughout. From the onset, I did not commit myself to a political party or to any specific political trend. I was able to avoid the labels that categorize a Druze, wherever they are and wherever they come from.

I was close to the late Kamāl Jumblatt, and am still close to his son, Walīd. I knew Emir Majīd Arslān, and am now acquainted with his son, Emir Talāl. However, I was closer to His Eminence, the late Sheikh al-Akl Mohammed Abou-Chacra, who enabled me to found and consolidate the Druze Health Organization, which was one of his major achievements, in addition to the Druze Community Home in Beirut, an initiative with which were also associated Sheikh Toufīc Assāf (my father-in-law) and other prominent Druze.

I always strived to retain every small detail in everything I read. I was able to discern the positive influence of the Druze leaders without overlooking the negative. My assessment of their role remained generally positive, despite several criticisms I made in writing or orally in the media, or even in the presence of some of them.

Druze civil society is passing through a phase of weakness as a result of the overbearing influence of its leaders on its public activities. The main concern of prominent Druze figures has become to gain the approbation of one leader or another and the recognition of their role in one achievement or another. The long years of the civil war had already deterred this society from fulfilling its expected role as certain parties resorted to violent means to repress it, in the absence of any kind of protection from a state paralysed by feudal influence. The activities of civil society relented and, in the process, its elite lost its stature and left the field open to organizational entities connected to political leaders in Mount Lebanon. Clearly, had it not been for the persevering audacity of some Druze elites, all social activities would have been limited to whatever is affiliated with a political leader. This explains the absence of any significant cultural or social activity in the Mountain that is worthy of being considered a significant contribution to the resolution of the general issues affecting the constituents of the Druze Muwahhidun community.

The situation was made worse by the monopolization of Druze political representation and the stagnation of their political classes following the assassination of their leader Kamāl Jumblatt. Consequently, we rarely encounter nowadays an ex-Druze minister or deputy. In 2006, we witnessed the test of the election of the Community's Council, which, instead of promoting all-out support for the council, worsened the state of internal division. Then came the events of May 2007, which unified a number of political forces with the resulting increase in political pressures on the Druze community.

The Druze traditionally advocate diversity within unity, allowing for the expression and promotion of various points of view, thus granting all members of the community of choice between different positions.

The events of May 2007 put an end to this brand of diversity. Druze political forces united their ranks along a single project in an attempt to safeguard their community; they wished to spare it the scourge of a renewed civil war fomented by an arrogant force whose ambition extends beyond the control of Lebanon to encompass a regional axis that begins in Damascus and extends beyond it to Tehran. The outcome turned out to be the political condemnation of the very forces that had heroically opposed these attacks. This condemnation went so far as to accuse them of treason, even heresy. The diversity that provided the Druze community with a narrow margin of action and freedom was unquestionably eroded. The lesson we derive from this experience is that any agreement among the Druze leaders is a problem … and any disagreement, an even bigger problem.

The unification of the Druze political agenda did not generate unity in their internal agenda. Therefore, and parallel to the legally elected Sheikh al-Akl, we were presented with another Sheikh al-Akl whose main concern was to denounce the elected Sheikh al-Akl. The custodians of the Druze Endowments Committee were also subjected to wild accusations, and their numerous achievements were slandered by false accusations forged by turbaned men, wearing religious garb but devoid of any religious faith. This situation served the purposes of those who unjustifiably control the most important sector of Druze Endowments in Beirut. In an environment of contradiction and ambiguity, it becomes possible to circumvent the law, along with rights and order. Therefore, all the Endowments Committee's efforts to recuperate its properties in Beirut failed, which prevented it from developing and investing in a sizable asset capable of providing for the healthcare and educational needs of the Druze community at large.

Some observers consider the Druze Muwahhidun still to be living under the hegemony of a single leadership and single party in the era termed "The Arab Spring", which witnessed the Arab people's uprising against their longstanding oppressive rulers, their revolt against tyranny, clannish nepotism, hereditary succession, repression and persecution, and their determined demands for freedom, democracy, pluralism and the legitimate transfer of power. In their opinion, the Druze forfeited a "Spring" that had never blossomed at their doorstep nor at the doorsteps of their leaders. As to the phenomenon of hereditary succession, its customs have overburdened the Druze for hundreds of years – and still do – keeping them subjects of an ancient Lebanon despite being contemporaneous to ongoing events.

The Druze Muwahhidun may feel disappointed by the continuous relocation of political power from one party to another, having been in the vanguard of Lebanon's struggle for freedom, independence and sovereignty. They relinquished these aspirations for the sake of the "resistance", but the question remains: resistance to whom after the application of UN Council resolution 1701 ... unless its aim is to resist the Lebanese people and allow the advocates of "resistance" to control all aspects of the state? Today, everyone can see how a political repositioning is unfolding as a result of the weakening of the Syrian regime and the growing worries of the "resistance" *vis-à-vis* the findings of the International Tribunal investigating the assassination of the late Prime Minister Rafic Harīrī and several of his political colleagues ... and all of this in the avowed aim of preserving the Druze community and its role in Lebanon.

This is enough comment on the political level.

A more sensitive issue is the attempt to strengthen the trend claiming that Druze "particularity" resides in its esoterism, while the exoteric is the practice of the People of the Tradition and the Congregation (*ahl al-sunnah wa al-jamā'ah*). Some Druze hold the prayer rituals of *al-Jama'ah* on the occasions of the Feasts of the Fitr and the Adha, fast during the month of Ramadan, organize readings of Qur'anic verses in services taking place at the Druze Community Home in Beirut, and organize *Iftars* and prayers in one of its halls. Moreover, some brochures were published with instructions about the ways of washing the dead, conducting funeral prayers, teaching, praying and kneeling (*rak'āt*) to religious sheikhs, reciting Qur'anic verses and following Muslim rituals in marriage procedures .... Such practices only compound the Muwahhidun's confusion with regard to their religious affiliation and the worship of their faith, and raises the fear of an eventual loss of identity and the scattering of Druze particularity.

Any reader acquainted with my writings about the Druze Muwahhidun, as well as the many articles I have published on this topic, knows that I consider the Druze to be a Muslim Islamic denomination, belonging to the broader Islamic realm. The Druze are Muslim by affiliation and origin. However, they possess a doctrinal and religious particularity that should not be lost since they were brought up within its confines. It is worth mentioning that the bond that unites the Muwahhidun is due not solely to a religious factor – which accounts for their tolerance – but also to a minority sense of "togetherness" (*esprit de corps*) that brings them together in the face of adversities, as a natural reaction, to fend off eventual attacks that would deprive them of their identity, land or culture. The advocates of the new rituals clearly do not seem to comprehend the deep rift they might cause within the community, nor its devastating effects on the unity of its ranks and word.

Our brethren in the diaspora have experienced this confusion and rejected it. It may lead to an unsolicited schism within the Druze community.

I will not elaborate further on this sensitive issue.

This book targets primarily the Druze Muwahhidun who cannot afford, by reasons of upbringing and education, to read its Arabic version. I have resorted to this translation in order to allow them to become acquainted with their history, culture and the message of their religious community in the complicated Eastern Arabic language. The Druze have had a continuous near-millennial history since the initiation of Al-Hākim's call in Egypt. They were able to survive due to their historical role as guardians of Islam and Arabism, unimpeded by a minority complex in this vast world. In fact, they have always been part of the governing majorities. Their *esprit de corps* was heightened by their constant subjection to oppression and abuse on a political level, and to misinterpretations and distortions on the religious level. Their resilience proves that their *esprit de corps* has been stronger than the attempts to undermine them. As the saying goes: "Contentment disperses them and distress unites them." For this reason, the Druze are currently united in facing risks from all directions: a rise in religious extremism transcending Islamic currents to encompass Jewish religious fanaticism in Israel; Christian extremism in the West; and the dwindling role and numbers of the Christian minorities in the Middle East who are sometimes subjected to oppression and harassment. At the local Lebanese level, the Druze are faced with the display of an excessive means of might appropriated by the leadership of a single religious community, which might eventually prove harmful to the very essence of the Lebanon they have worked to preserve since they began to play a prominent role in its history – that is, since the sixteenth century AD.

The Druze consider Lebanon a unique experiment in the Middle East, based on a system of religious and sectarian diversity that recognizes individual rights and provides guaranties to its religious communities. Lebanon practises a democratic transfer of power and, regardless of its might, no political entity can monopolize the process of decision-making.

Lebanon adopted a system of equal power sharing between Christians and Muslims. It grants each religious community its share of the seats of power, whether in the executive, the judiciary or the military. Lebanon belongs culturally to the Arab world, but does not share its ideological definition: Islam is one, but not its exclusive, component. Lebanon also believes in the role of its Christian constituents regardless of their number and effectiveness. If there is any raison d'être for the existence of Lebanon it would be the Christian presence with which the Druze Muwahhidun share similar uncertainties and concerns and, above all, a common life in Mount Lebanon.

I have frequently emphasized (in the meetings of the Druze Communal Council) the necessity of organizing a Druze Conference – but one that, unlike the Expatriates' Conference that deviated from its aims for the sake of political expediencies, would be a cultural conference addressing the challenges of the present and the apprehensions of the future. (At the time of writing, and) within its current term of election, it is too late for the present council to sponsor such an event despite its importance for the revival of the cultural and educational life of the Druze community away from politics and politicians.

It may be that we still lack the proper vision to answer the questions of the new generation – rent by political division and blind partisanship – concerning its future as an essential component of its country, both in its role and message.

Readers of this book will find a preliminary vision of this message in Chapter 8 and its annex. However, regardless of how keen the ability of an individual, this vision should be formulated within the context of a general dialogue and as the result of an exchange of ideas within a community whose members are reputed for their culture, wisdom and faith, and who are known above all for their intellectual integrity and for probity unmarred by bowing to special interests, benefits or paybacks.

In the wake of this translation, I present my book to the reader as a personal point of view that does not commit anyone but myself. It is left to the reader to accept or refute it. However, I assure the reader that I have presented it with sincerity and objectivity, and as the result of the personal experience that I went through, hoping for fair judgement and uttering the Qur'anic verse: "Then to your Lord is your return so He will inform you of that in which you differed" (Q6:165).[1]

## Note

1 ثم إلى ربكم مرجعكم فينبئكم بما كنتم فيه تختلفون

# Foreword

The Druze have safeguarded the privacy and secrecy of their beliefs and customs as a natural reaction to the persecution they have experienced throughout their history. They have also ignored legitimate and inquisitive questions about their identity and discipline of life. This attitude has led to the propagation of a distorted picture of their monotheistic beliefs and customary mores.

This distorted picture was propagated by the works of many orientalists, whose perception of the Druze was as fighters armed only with daggers, ready to slaughter Christians at any opportunity. The time has come to correct this image.

When it comes to defending the interests of their community and their clan, the Druze are certainly fighters loyal to the command of their ancestors "to protect the brethren". But the Druze, just like other religious communities, have their difficulties and needs: they long for a comfortable and fair life, and stability in their relations with their fellow citizens.

They do not constitute an "island", isolated from the world. Rather, they suffer from all the problems of Lebanese society, just like any other Lebanese person, and are affected by the behaviour of the other religious communities. They have both strengths and weaknesses and, as followers of a monotheistic creed that focuses basically on reason and logic, they should not go astray or lose their way.

In this book, I will attempt to dissipate the ideas referred to above, break down the myths, remove the taboos and present an authentic picture of the Druze and other Lebanese communities devoid of hypocrisy and flattery, allowing the Druze to feel proud of their identity in relation to the "other". Some Lebanese have contributed to complicating this task by using opportunities arising from differences of political opinion to try and disfigure and confuse the situation, even inflicting harm by throwing false accusations and attempting to project a harmful image of their Druze fellow citizens.

However, what amazes me most is that the problems I encountered when I first became committed to Druze and national issues 38 years ago, are still present today, and with the same degree of intensity I realized, by following the historical development of these problems, that they tend to repeat themselves, year after year and even, without exaggeration, century after century. The issue is, more than anything else, a matter of the basic problems of upbringing, to which are added transitional issues that complicate the general picture.

It is easy to lay the complete responsibility of this state of affairs at the doorstep of the political leadership, and I do not deny their part in it. But I must say that the Druze cultural elite, which was granted by Kamāl Jumblatt an utmost importance, has become almost excluded from the search for a solution to these problems. Similarly, it is impossible to lay this burden upon Druze religious leaders alone, due to the particularity of their upbringing, formation, and their asceticism and piety.

We are thus all responsible, at various levels, for the current situation, although those in positions of power and the rank and file Druze may not carry equal responsibility since attaining any public post may hinder the credibility of any endeavour, and reaching any seat of prominence may justify subservience or even the loss of the prerequisites of any commitment.

This book is a new work, although some of its contents have been drawn from my previous work, *Les Druzes: vivre avec l'avenir*, published in French by Dār al-Nahār in 2005, which sold out so quickly that Dār al-Nahār issued a reprint in 2006.

The present volume targets a broader spectrum of readers than the French version. Moreover, this edition, translated from the Arabic, confronts me with the dual responsibility of, first, obtaining the approval and direct moral support of the Druze religious authorities involved in the cultural and religious heritage of their faith, and, second, to attract the attention of the "others" – Lebanese or Arab, Muslim or Christian.

Therefore, I have endeavoured, while working on the text, to benefit from observations and opinions previously expressed about my French book, and I particularly undertook to add a complete account of the new developments in the affairs and status of the community of the "Druze Monotheists" (Muwahhidun) – the new term used in a law promulgated on 9 June 2006. Much as I was grieved in my previous book by the lack of organization of the affairs of the community, this time I found myself witnessing a new organization, which may not be devoid of faults, but which, nevertheless, lays a new path and offers the Druze community a new opportunity to confront modernity through institutions.

I have thought at times that the Druze political leadership was reluctant to organize the affairs of its community, or at least unable to achieve it lest it loses its absolute control over the process of decision making. But today I find myself admiring it for taking the initiative to facilitate the creation of a new opportunity to organize Druze communal affairs. This may give rise, in time, to another opportunity to organize religious affairs in need of modernization, revision and renewal following a long period of stagnation, stirred from time to time by parties lacking the credibility of religious reformers or by over-reactionary attempts to bring the creed out of its historical captivity, without taking into consideration the fact that moving on from one stage to another, if it is to be achieved safely and peacefully, entails an intellectual and cultural journey that must be carefully undertaken by stages.

I have spoken about the lack of organization, the laxity of administration, the fragmentation in preserving the *awqāf*, the absence of the spiritual and mundane leadership, and other matters that escaped the attention of the new generations brought up in the midst of a tragedy, considering the difference between their history rich in heroic exploits and glorious deeds and their present gloomy situation.

In spite of attempts to bridge the gap between the new generations and their faith undertaken by a number of religious leaders aware of the danger of their alienation from their faith, there is still a great need to revive and renew the heritage in order to achieve a reconciliation between the Druze Muwahhidun and the period in which they live.

I have included in this book appendices containing writings, articles and quotations relating to prominent Druze personalities, whose lives and achievements I have had the opportunity to write about, and thanks to whom I have completed this task. I have particularly endeavoured to acquaint the reader with their work, personalities and achievements. Maybe we need, today, to enhance our knowledge of these distinguished personalities in the context of an institute or university concerned with Druze studies that could become a centre for clerical training based on true knowledge and grateful cognizance, which would also seek to revive the heritage of our pious forefathers and pave the way to progress and the future.

Following the publication of the French edition of my book I received some criticism which did not, regrettably, relate to its approach or contents, but restricted its concern to the omission of certain names that perhaps deserved to be mentioned. I tried in vain to persuade the inquirers that far from holding any negative attitude towards anyone, the purpose of the book was completely different. Similarly, the lack of in-depth coverage of doctrinal matters gave rise to criticism from others who were not satisfied with the fact that the aim of the book was to provide a brief essay on the Druze community and that it was not, in fact, a book about religious beliefs. When I looked into this aspect and investigated what was being written and published, I noticed that numerous works written by Druze and non-Druze alike had appeared during this period, and copiously dealt with these matters. I do not intend, here, to assess them.

From a political point of view, I tried my utmost to describe events without expressing a personal opinion – which I have done in my numerous published writings on these topics. However, I have tried to separate my opinions from the subject of this book in order to preserve the objectivity of my presentation, and retain the aim and purpose of the text.

I feel a sense of contempt and satisfaction while writing about *banu ma'rūf,*[1] the upholders of monotheism and truth, and I have dedicated and devoted my life to supporting their progress, the improvement of their standing and their reconciliation with modernity. I first became involved in this cause as a young man influenced by a liberal education, which I also tried to instil in my own small family, considering that misanthropy is a deadly disease, fanaticism a lethal sickness and narrow-mindedness an unnatural phenomenon in a world open to cultures, civilizations and creative interaction, without, however, denying my firm roots and primary allegiances.

Participating in conferences and seminars in Lebanon and abroad offered me an opportunity for openness without abandoning the religious and cultural basic beliefs I have adopted from a monotheistic creed, and my understanding of it as a revolution against blind traditions and rigid formalities. My distress increases when I see some of those entrusted with this revolution willing to submit to a painful current political and religious situation.

Having been an active Druze since 1969, I have become very attached to my community affairs and its legal, historical, political and cultural foundations. Since that time, my companions and I, full of the same fervour, became concerned about portraying the Druze community as a solid factor in guaranteeing the unity, independence and sovereignty of Lebanon and the stability of the Middle East, or at least the region historically known as Bilād al-Shām.

## Forty-Four Years of Activity

I am a former judge and currently hold the position of vice-president of the Board of Administration and legal adviser of the Bank of Beirut and the Arab Countries (SAL). I am also active in revitalizing public office in my capacity as member of the Board of Administration of the Lebanese National Institute for Administration (ENA-Lebanon). Additionally, I have participated in numerous activities and in the founding of several societies concerned with charities, culture, health, education and sport. There is no ongoing Druze association in whose establishment or activities I have not been involved and, in November 2006, my efforts were crowned by my election to the new Druze Communal Council and my appointment as Chairman of the Awqāf Council. Meanwhile I have not neglected my openness to the "other", through taking up responsibilities and undertaking activities in the realm of Muslim–Christian dialogue both at the Lebanese and Arab levels above and beyond the many tasks incurred by my banking and legal responsibilities.

As well as these positions and concerns, I am eager to remain aware of the affairs and needs of the Druze community, to maintain strong relations with its religious leaders, and to play an active role in civil society, trying always to preserve and support its activities in order to allow it to effectively play its part in it lest it becomes marginalized by the pressures of the traditional political leadership or its organized clans.

Faced with the existence of similar challenges to the role of other Lebanese confessional groups in our national life, and in the absence of the presumed role of the Druze cultural elite – marginalized by the influence and arrogance of its politicians – the Druze community needs to channel all its energy to bring to the fore its historical and national heritage.

The Druze need to contemplate with wisdom and discernment how to survive in the Middle East and secure their future in their area and in the world, where minorities, and even moderate majorities, are threatened by extremism.

I hope this book will be received with good will, a warm welcome and genuine understanding. I salute all those who have written before me about the Druze and do not, by any means, belittle their contribution, and I apologize in advance for any unintended shortcomings this book may contain.

Most of the chapters in the book were written with determination and courage emphasizing descriptive aspects drawn from other sources. However, I have added material drawn from my personal experience and perceptions that do not commit any other person than me alone. As to the analytical sections, they have been written in conjunction with the historical developments in an endeavour to foresee the future and present the issues in the way I, and the cultural elite, see them whenever their discussion takes place.

I also apologize in advance to all those individuals who contributed alongside me in joint activities for not mentioning them by name in this book. These omissions should not be taken as a personal choice, but rather within the context of the rationale of the book, which does not lend itself to mentioning all names, let alone the danger of overlooking some of them and the consequences that may entail. This is why I have tried to refrain from mentioning the names of particular individuals as much as possible, and reverted to it only in the process of establishing that the work I have undertaken in relation to the community was never an individual work, but a work shared with others.

I address my heartfelt greetings and sincere thanks to all those who have worked with me, and I call on the new generation to seize the initiative and never forget the roots and past we are proud of, nor the need to work for the welfare of their country – although within the context of a more complex atmosphere than before – without forgetting the communities to which they belong.

I also wish to salute the spirit of my late mother who raised me within the monotheistic values. I also acknowledge the patience of my wife, Randa, throughout the long years in which we have shared sweet and bitter times, and I thank her for all her observations and suggestions, drawing from her pure inner soul the necessary steadfastness, strength and determination to public services.

I also thank my children for the questions they asked me as they were growing up about their community's heritage and culture. I drew strength from their inquisitiveness and have often held "council" with them in Ra's al-Matn, my home, in the shade of the ancient pine trees, where I have arranged special sessions for them and their cousins with the Druze elders on the eve of 'Id al-Adha.

Last but not least, I recall the spirit of Kamāl Jumblatt, always supportive of any cultural activity not only among the Druze community but also throughout Lebanon and the wider Arab and Islamic world.

I place this book in the hands of those who have pure intentions, hoping they will receive it in good will.

Ra's al-Matn, 7 December 2012.

## Note

1 Banu ma'rūf is another appellation of the Druze or Muwahhidun.

# Introduction

The demographic make-up of the Druze community in Lebanon has not prevented its members from playing an important role throughout Lebanese history, notably in the political, economic, cultural, social and spiritual spheres. One of their most important contributions was their deep involvement in the founding vision for what Fr Joachim Mubarak has called "the Lebanese idea" – that is, the idea of an independent Lebanese state. The Druze have been outstanding throughout their history in their opposition to every form of colonialism, mandate and domination, particularly in the Arab East. Throughout the ages, they have resisted the Crusaders, the Mongols, the Mamluks, the Ottomans and the French Mandate and, at present, they have, with encouragement from the West, defied Syrian domination to the extent that they have been described as a war-like, rebellious and obstinate people.

But even if their resistance has been correctly described, the true history of this community is surrounded by profound ignorance. The reason for this ignorance goes back, on the one hand, to their enemies determination to distort the truth in order to discredit their beliefs, and, on the other, to the care of the religious authorities within the community to hide their beliefs both to prevent them being corrupted and to protect their followers from persecution.

Druze doctrine has a mystical character, different from traditional (that is, orthodox or official) Islam in many aspects, specifically in the rules of worship and conventions for initiation. This has led to the religious beliefs of the Druze being largely secret, or one may say esoteric, so that their truths are only made openly available to a select few wise initiates. This esotericism has made it possible to ward off all attempts to pervert the Druze creed and has kept it alive through successive ages in an environment that was intolerant and hostile towards any belief suspected of being different from its own, to the point of provoking accusations of false doctrine and heresy.

But this excessive concern to rely on the esoteric way, known as *taqiyya*, led to the spread of speculation, rumours and false accusations against the Druze, which built up in the minds of many a perception of them as belonging to a false religion confounded with a distorted historical portrayal. Consequently, the unique nature of their beliefs became impossible to justify with regard to questions raised about the extent of their belonging to the Muslim community, especially in view of the numerous misleading publications that have appeared about their identity and beliefs. These questions continue to be asked today, and to constitute a significant part of the records, which give rise to unjustifiable reactions towards them and is in itself enough to show the particular place the Druze occupy in the confessional landscape, not only of the Arab East but also across the world map.

Ignorance, partial information, distortions of reality, myths and unfounded rumours, as well as the select use of the records and historical controversy, have encumbered the Druze identity and they seriously need to lift the shroud of secrecy, refute the exaggerated fallacies and restore the truth by presenting a contemporary cultural approach.

Every attempt to undertake this approach needs to trace the whole historical, religious, cultural and social heritage of the Druze, without being restricted only to the Druze of Lebanon. Although it is practical to differentiate between the Druze of Lebanon and their brethren in Syria and Palestine at the present time, this differentiation need not necessarily apply, and indeed should not be applied, to earlier periods of history. Moreover, only a chronological perspective can make it possible to clearly grasp the true "spirit" of the Druze faith, and specifically their beliefs and practices, particularly since they have grown in gradual stages of conceptual development since the emergence of the sect in the Middle Ages and have taken shape in numerous geographical areas, including Lebanon. From this perspective, the Druze way appears to be the result of both a series of Islamic schisms and a chain of transmission of ancient and specific religious ideas. This requires a detailed explanation of these two factors by way of introduction.

## Schisms in Islam up to the Birth of Druze Doctrine

In the course of its history, Islam experienced divisions and trends, splits and tendencies, each of which, despite drawing from the same source, introduced a number of religious interpretations and new doctrines. The question of the rightful succession to the Prophet Muhammad (may God bless him and give him peace) has been the main cause of these divisions, which multiplied due to the numerous interpretations supporting the line of descent of one Imam or Caliph or another.

The introduction of new religious theories, along with oblique or even obscure formulations of some ancient beliefs, has made the legitimization of this or that line of succession possible. Apart from political considerations, the original message of Islam, and specifically the Druze doctrine, emerged through the complementarity of these trends and tendencies, until it reached its final form in the Druze way. So a review of these trends and tendencies, highlighting their differences and roles, will be useful, even if it can only be brief.

The Islamic state, according to the ideal vision left by the Prophet (may God bless him and give him peace), derived its sovereignty from God alone and is therefore submitted to the divine law above any other law. Thus, from the beginning, political authority in Islam was inseparable from religious authority, in complete contrast to Western and Christian concepts. As a result, every political dispute, whatever its causes or origins, became a religious dispute, and vice versa. Therefore every dissident faction took on a particular doctrinal and theological discourse and used this discourse to promote the possibility of overthrowing the established order, and was happy to organize the groups of its supporters along religious lines.

Thus the first four centuries of Islam witnessed the birth and establishment of numerous Islamic parties, each based on specific social, political and cultural factors. It should be noted that the declaration by each of these parties of a new doctrinal discourse, even though it derived from the original Islamic discourse and its first divisions, was in complete harmony with the historical environment and heritage that accompanied its birth. Druze doctrine, which was elaborated and elucidated between the end of the tenth and beginning of the eleventh centuries, contained within its context the consummation and final form of religious principles and ancient ideas that Islam contained or drew from, which matured and became more clearly defined with the rise of Shi'ism – and more particularly Fatimid Isma'ilism – and led to the preaching of the Druze doctrine.

The greatest and most important division in Islam took place in AH 11/632 AD, only a short time after the death of Prophet Muhammad (may God bless him and give him peace). As he had left no instructions regarding his succession, a disagreement emerged over the identity of the future leader. This crisis could have torn apart the still young and fragile community apart, if they had not all agreed (after some serious tension) to choose as their head the most senior and most respected of Muhammad's Companions, Abu Bakr.

He took on the title of Caliph (*khalīfa*) – that is to say the lieutenant, or deputy, of the Prophet, which conferred upon him both religious and political authority, and he became the "Prince of Believers". He was the master of the Muslim community, and the first to lay the foundations of the historic Islamic institution known as the caliphate. Abu Bakr ruled for only two years and three and a half months (AH 11–13/632–634 AD), but he was keen on appointing a successor before his death. His heir was 'Umar Ibn al-Khattab, who ruled until his assassination in 644 (AH 13–23/634–643 AD). He provided for the system of succession by creating the means of appointing his successor. He entrusted this responsibility to a council of six members chosen from among the most senior of the Prophet's Companions and those closest to him; they selected 'Uthman ibn 'Affan, an Umayyad, to be the new Caliph (AH 23–36/643–656 AD).

However, from the first days of the caliphate, a group of the believers held the opinion that it would have been more legitimate to assign this responsibility to the first convert to Islam, 'Alī ibn Abi Talib (Peace be upon him). 'Alī was related to the Prophet, being both his cousin and his son-in-law. He was pious and courageous in defending Islam. This group of believers was first given the name *Shī'at 'Alī* ('Alī's party), and later simply the *Shī'a*. Initially, they were just a political faction with no doctrinal or religious position. At first, 'Alī made no objection to the choice of others to be Caliph because of the justice and equality that had characterized the rule of Abu Bakr and 'Umar. 'Uthman's reign, on the other hand, was characterized by the appearance of injustices within the Muslim community resulting from the accumulation of wealth and privileges by the Umayyad clan thanks to the favours and partiality the Caliph bestowed upon his family. All this led to widespread protests and finally to 'Uthman's assassination in AH 36/656 AD allowing 'Alī to claim the title of Caliph. 'Alī's caliphate (AH 35–41/655–661 AD) saw an increase in disturbances and the outbreak of numerous political and religious divisions within the Muslim community. 'Alī notably came up against the hostility of the Umayyad clan, especially Mu'awiya ibn Abi Sufyan, the governor of Bilād al-Shām from 'Umar's time, and who had extended his power under 'Uthman. Mu'awiya had refused to recognize 'Alī as Caliph.

'Alī (PBUH) was assassinated in AD 41/661 AD and his death ended the period of the first four Caliphs, the *Rāshidūn* "Rightly Guided". The accession of Mu'awiya to power inaugurated the establishment of a hereditary monarchy which was to increase inequality and discord between the Muslims, and favour a privileged and dominant aristocracy and the spread of their dominance. In the eyes of many Muslims, the state had turned away from the true way of Islam. In a society governed by religion and whose leaders represented the official doctrine, it was inevitable that this kind of discontent would manifest itself in the formation of religious parties, which offered a safe refuge for the underprivileged. 'Alī's party, which continued after his death, made increasing political, social and religious demands, and Islam was divided into two factions. Over and against the Sunnis, who followed the "orthodox" faith and the official authority, the Shi'is gathered an increasing number of malcontents and opponents of the regime. At the Battle of Karbala in

680 AD, Husayn (PBUH), the youngest son of ʿAlī and Fatima (the Prophet's daughter) was killed, and a Shiʿi contingent was completely wiped out by the Umayyad army. Thus fell the first prominent martyrs of Al al-Bayt – the Prophet's family, and the Shiʿa movement arose with a power and religious fervour that sprang from suffering and oppression, and was reinforced by a determination to defend the true faith. From then on, the fierceness of the opposition and the bitterness towards the Umayyad dynasty increased, and the devotion of numerous believers to the descendants of ʿAlī grew stronger. Umayyad rule came to an end in 750 AD, making way for the ʿAbbasids, who came to power through the support of the Shiʿis, although they soon distanced themselves from them and chose to keep the Sunni tradition as the official religion. As a result, Shiʿism turned into a movement associated with both covert discontent and open rebellion. Later, numerous groups came into being within the Shiʿa, each gathering around one or another member of Al al-Bayt, feeding the resentments of its followers against the rulers and supporting the rise to power of its own members. At the end of the eighth century, Shiʿism was violently shaken by a decisive struggle concerning the person of the Imam.

In Shiʿi doctrine, the Imam is a central figure. He is a religious leader and the repository of theological knowledge entrusted to ʿAlī's descendants, members of Al al-Bayt. He also holds legal authority over the Muslim community which wrested from the Umayyads and the ʿAbbasids the power they had usurped. The Imams succeeded each other from father to son in the line of ʿAlī and Shiʿis agreed on the first six of them: ʿAlī (d. 661 AD), al-Hasan (d. 673 AD) and al-Husayn (d. 680 AD) (peace be upon them), ʿAlī Zayn al-ʿAbidin (d. 714 AD), Muhammad al-Baqir (d. 732 AD) and Jaʿfar al-Sadiq (d. 765 AD) (PBUH). But a disagreement arose over the succession following the last of them, Jaʿfar, having designated as his successor his son Ismaʿil al-Mubarak. However, the latter died while his father was still alive and Jaʿfar did not appoint a substitute (although the Twelver Shiʿis say that he appointed his second son Musa to be Imam after him). When al-Sadiq died, most of the Shiʿis recognized his other son, Musa al-Kazim, as their Imam, followed by his descendants up to

Muhammad ibn Hasan al-'Askari, the twelfth in the line of Imams after 'Alī, which is why this majority group is called the Twelvers. However, a small group of Shi'is continued to recognize the imamate of Ismā'īl, who had died, and maintained that, before his death, he had designated his son Muhammad to succeed him. This group was called "Isma'ilis" after the name of their Imam and the line they recognized became the dynasty of the Fatimid Caliphs.

The 'Abbasids pursued Muhammad ibn Isma'il and his companions and persecuted them, forcing them into hiding. This led his followers to practise their rites and live their lives clandestinely. In spite of the secrecy of their movement and the need to conceal their aims and ambitions, the Isma'ilis succeeded in forming a cohesive and well-organized religious movement. As for Ismā'īli doctrine, it developed in a complicated form, which allowed the establishment of numerous levels of exegesis and interpretation. This doctrine was spread through the Muslim world by preachers, who preached and articulated the message of the Imam.

The greatest success of the Isma'ili movement was the establishment in North Africa of an independent kingdom. Far removed from the heart of the 'Abbasid caliphate, and populated by Berbers ready to rebel against the established authorities, North Africa was fertile soil for dissident messages of opposition. The Ismā'īli preachers prepared the ground there until 'Ubayd Allāh al-Mahdī, who was from the Maghreb and a descendant of Ismā'īl, declared himself publicly as Imam at the beginning of the tenth century AD. He was proclaimed Caliph and Imam in 909 AD and inaugurated the era of the Fatimid dynasty in Tunisia after the Isma'ilis had gradually assumed complete control of North Africa, providing their faith and doctrine with the security of a state, which became their state. The Fatimids, in order to mark themselves out and vindicate the legitimacy of their struggle, added to the classical Islamic call to prayer the phrase "*hayya 'ala khayr al-'amal*" ("come to good works"). During the reign of al-Mu'izz li-Din Allah, the fourth Caliph descended from 'Ubayd Allah al-Mahdi, the conquest of Egypt took place and al-Mu'izz founded the city of Cairo, transferring the capital of the caliphate to Egypt. The city remained for two centuries the first city of the Islamic empire, the heart of the caliphate and the capital of a powerful and flourishing empire that rivalled the 'Abbasid caliphate in Baghdad; it was also an intellectual centre from which Isma'ili teaching spread.

Druze doctrine was developed in Egypt during the reign of the sixth Fatimid Caliph, al-Hakim bi-Amr Allāh (996–1021 AD), when a group of Ismā'īlis, going beyond the official Fatimid doctrine, declared that the Caliph and Imam al-Hākim was possessed of a nature superior to that normally conferred by the imamate. It even went as far as to attribute to him a divine nature, using the very preaching methods of the traditional official Isma'ili line. The preachers of this teaching spread their new doctrines everywhere, reaching as far as India. Although these new ideas met with a sympathetic response among some peoples, the official teaching of Cairo did not endorse them and indeed condemned them. After the disappearance of the Caliph al-Hakim, the followers of this new doctrine were persecuted and were called Druze after the name of one of their preachers, Nashtakin al-Darazi. They were forced to flee Egypt for countries more receptive to their ideas and their preaching.

## The Spiritual and Religious Heritage of Druze Doctrine

The Druze community found itself carrying the historical and religious heritage of the Shi'i and Isma'ili movements. However, the true roots and spiritual influences of this movement lie, according to some sources, in pre-Islamic religions and philosophical trends that go back to ancient times. Although successive schisms within Islam systematically introduced new religious formulations, some of these ancient concepts found their way to immortality by being absorbed into the core of Druze doctrines. This chain of intellectual transmission is easily explained. It must be borne in mind that, through a century of conquests, the Arabs were able to build an Islamic empire that extended from the Pyrenees in northern Spain to north-west China. The heart of this empire, which stretched around the eastern Mediterranean, was the crossroads of the most ancient civilizations and was subject to influences from India and Persia to the east and Greece to the west. The transfer of ideas took place freely across the whole Mediterranean basin, flowing with the movement of populations.

In the course of their expansion, the Arabs proved themselves to be full of curiosity and demonstrated a genuine desire to understand the newly conquered territories; they had no fear of assimilating new elements that were the product of their systems of thought and belief. In view of this cultural and intellectual opening demonstrated by the Arabs, people of all races, colours and civilizations adopted Islam and integrated themselves within the Muslim community and acquired the same privileges and rights as their Arab conquerors. The integration of these peoples was naturally accompanied by the understanding and assimilation of new ideas. Thus, elements of the pre-Islamic monotheistic religions (Judaism and Christianity), Persian religions, ancient myths and Greek philosophical speculation all found their way into Islamic civilization and the Islamic thought system, having various levels of importance and influence, and were expressed in Arabic.

Certain of these ancient, non-Islamic elements absorbed by Islam were then passed on through Isma'ili Shi'ism and lasted long enough for them to be found at the heart of the Druze doctrinal system. Although they had been formulated in such a way as to facilitate their absorption into these new doctrinal systems and the elaboration of an independent, coherent creed, their ancient roots remain easily identifiable. Alongside the most ancient influences inherited from Isma'ili Shi'ism, are Indian, Persian[1] and Hermetic[2] religious influences, as well as monotheistic elements. All these religious currents had a common theme, regardless of their doctrinal differences, and this is their syncretic nature. Their central figures, whether sages of ancient India, Egypt or Greece, or the prophets of the monotheistic religions, were seen as "lights emanating from the source … of all lights",[3] bearers of the divine message and, as such, guides to the true knowledge of almighty God.

The special nature of each of these figures undoubtedly prompts us to consider the particular role played by the Imam in the Shi'i and Isma'ili movements. Just as the monotheistic religions (Judaism, Christianity and Islam) see the prophets as deliverers of the divine message, so the Shiʿi doctrine, whether Isma'ili, Twelver or some other sect, holds that the Imam is the repository of these messages. This role is closely linked with the mystical, esoteric and syncretic aspects inspired by certain ancient religions, principally Gnosticism, whose essence, with its concentration on the duality of good and evil, may be considered to be true knowledge that gives access to the divine realities.

The tenets of Gnosticism are based on searching or striving towards the true knowledge of God, which can only be attained through a life of abstinence and asceticism that will free the soul from material and fleshly desires. Man's salvation is thus attained by gnosis – that is, true knowledge of the divine realities. Gnosis is different from and higher than what most people experience. In order to differentiate itself from Sunni Islam, which respects the outward or exoteric meaning of the Qur'an (*al-zāhir*), Shiʿi, and especially Ismaʿili, doctrines developed the idea that the true knowledge of the divine realities is contained in their hidden or esoteric meaning (*al-bātin*). This is the point of distinction between the Sunnis, who adhere to the literal meaning of the text and are called the people of the Shariʿa, and the Shi'is, who adhere to interpretation, and are called the people of the Way. From this perspective, the Imam, who alone is appointed by God and invested by Him with the ability to interpret the hidden meanings correctly, is qualified to explain the Qur'an in its many levels and ranks of reading and meaning. As spiritual leader – that is, a guide to the way to the true knowledge of God – it is his duty to transmit and explain this divine message to the disciples according to their spiritual maturity and ability to understand and receive it, given that to receive and understand the divine message depends on some pre-conditions and abilities in the believer. Therefore, most of the religious movements that have grown from Shiʿism or Ismaʿilism and have introduced some esoteric, mystical elements into their teachings require their followers to attain various degrees of moral self-preparation and spiritual achievement along the path by which they attain the truth.

Ismaʿilism, which was born out of Shiʿism, went to great lengths in its endeavour to introduce and absorb mystical, esoteric and disciplinary elements, which is what probably led to its being described as extreme or excessive Shi'ism. According to the doctrines of this movement, the imams and Fatimid Caliphs were the infallible leaders and guides of the whole of humanity, the interpreters and authors of the hidden meaning of the Qur'anic revelation, and the true guardians of Islam against the Sunni Caliphate in Baghdad. Since the Druze way was worked out at the core of Fatimid Isma'ilism, it built upon this specific spiritual heritage, preserving its esoteric and disciplinary mystical elements, and even attributing to them increased power and importance. This led to its gaining a reputation for being an extreme, syncretic, esoteric religion. In addition, the Druze did not direct their striving towards, and search for, divine truth on the hidden meaning of the Qur'an alone; they also relied on their own books, such as the *Books of Wisdom,* a collection of letters written by Druze preachers to their followers, containing explanations and interpretations of the Abrahamic heritage, based on both Sufism and Greek philosophy, according to the Islamic esoteric tradition. Only Druze believers are permitted to read the Books of Wisdom and only the initiated are allowed to interpret them. This is a relic of Sufi mysticism not restricted to esoteric Islam also extending to some Sunni thinkers such as al-Ghazali, who wrote in his *Lamp of Lights*: "The hearts of the free are the graves of the mysteries"[4] and initiates – that is, those who have entered, and have been accepted, into the special mystical way with all its demands, so that the "truths" contained in these books can be revealed to them little by little as they progress in their spiritual quest and advance in their level of initiation. The restrictions that determine who has the right to "enter" into initiation are especially inspired by the essential aspects of mysticism, and the fact that the rule followed by the great Sheikhs is based upon the unity of word and action – that is, the unity between knowledge and behaviour, and the fact that attainment is the fruit of the spiritual balance resulting from that unity.

In contrast to Shi'ism and Isma'ilism, every Sheikh has the right to interpret the religious texts written by the Imams, provided he relies on the text itself in his interpretation. For the Druze, the religious message is not restricted to the Imam; rather every Sheikh and every practising believer of sound mind may interpret it. Therefore, the Druze have only had imams in exceptional circumstances and the interpretative role of the Imam came to an end with the sixth Fatimid Imam. Only the first five ministers of the creed of al-Hakim bore this title (Hamza ibn ʻAlī, Ismaʻil ibn Muhammad al-Tamimi, Abu ʻAbdallah Muhammad al-Qurayshi, Abu al-Khayr ibn ʻAbd al-Wahhab al-Sabiq and Baha' al-Dīn al-Muqtana) throughout the whole initial period of the proliferation of Druze teaching at the beginning of the eleventh century. The title was also borne by al-Sayyid Jamal al-Dīn ʻAbdallah al-Tannukhi, in the fifteenth century, and the Druze inherited the rules of interpretation from these first five Imams as al-Hakim's representatives. The amir al-Tannukhi and other eminent Sheikhs explained Druze teachings only in order to clarify matters of practice, not to give interpretation for its own sake.

The fact that the Druze do not have Imams is explained by the religious precept that led to a definitive split between them and the Fatimid Ismaʻilis. Although appointed by divine power and free of all sin, the Fatimid Caliphs and Imams were not able to claim a divine nature. During the reign of al-Hākim, the group of disciples who would form the Druze distanced themselves from the official Fatimid teaching of Cairo by declaring that al-Hākim had a superior nature to that of the other imams and refused to believe in an imamate after him. According to some interpretations, this teaching went far beyond the established normal roles of the Imam as messenger and repository of the divine message. When the Caliph al-Hākim disappeared, the teaching of Shiʻism, and hence Ismaʻilism, and consequently the Druze, took on a new aspect known as "messianism", which is the teaching of the expectation of the coming of the messianic saviour at the end of time, equivalent to Mahdi-ism among the Shi'is.

The expectation of the return of the messiah, which has Judaeo–Christian origins, became a central idea in Shiʻi doctrine and revolved around the figure of the imam. This belief was built on the notion of the return of a spiritual leader with supernatural qualities, whom the believers would wait for until the day of salvation. Thus, most Shiʻi groups are expecting the coming of the Mahdī, the last imam from the Prophet's family, before the end of time, so that the world would be filled with justice instead of being full of injustice and oppression. This belief, which brought a degree of security and comfort to the Shi'is who were oppressed by the Umayyads and 'Abbasids, was integrated first into Isma'ilism and then, with some variations, into Druze doctrines. The Druze expectation of the messiah, or the mahdi, came to be centred around the Caliph al-Ḥākim, who, it was said, had not died nor been killed, but was in "occultation", which means departure from this world of the living but without passing into death or oblivion. His certain return, in expectation of which the Druze live to this day, would signal the end of time and salvation for all true believers.

Apart from religious elements based on ancient currents of belief, the Isma'ili and Druze movements integrated into their understanding of the universe some elements of Greek Platonic and Aristotelian philosophy and, to a certain extent, Neo-Platonism.[5] It represents God as absolutely transcendent above all that could be conceived by thought, reason or language; it declares that the unity of the divine being was absolute, and considered that the universe and creation were simply a series of principles emanating from God. The Isma'ilis, known for their strict monotheism, were very receptive to these ideas and this definition of God. As a result, they easily absorbed into their theology the idea of the ineffability of God and the impossibility of His being grasped by the human mind. It may be that the Platonism of the Isma'ilis was one of the reasons that led the Druze to split from them.

These ideas found a place in Druze beliefs, along with the terminology used by Plato, which often referred to God as the One or the Good – terms often found in Druze sources. The Druze retained in principle the Neoplatonic definition of the universe, although with some modifications to bring it into harmony with their own view of the origin of the universe, creation and existence. According to Druze beliefs, God created by his own will the Universal Intellect (*al-'Aql al-kullī*), which in turn begat the Universal Soul (*al-nafs al kulliyya*). A series of five great cosmic principles was thus created, each principle emanating from the preceding one. After the Universal Intellect and the Universal Soul, the Word (*al-kalima*) was born, and from it appeared the Preceder (*al-sābiq*) and the Follower (*al-tālī*). These emanations succeeded each other to end finally in the material world and the beings that inhabit it. Thus, creation is the manifestation of truth: "God refined his essence and called it truth and solidified his essence and called it creation".[6] The existential glory compares with the Unique One as the sphere compares with its central point. "When He decreeth a matter, He saith to it: 'Be' and it is" (Q2:117). The Universal Intellect is the command or the will to do something, and the source of the act of willing and the will itself are the Universal Soul, and the speaking of the decree is the Word, and "Be" is the Preceder, and "it is" is the Follower. In contrast with Islam and Christianity, and influenced by Greek philosophy, the Druze came to believe that the world was very ancient and that 343 million years had passed between the creation of these five first cosmic principles and the creation of mankind. They then identified these five principles with the five limits of existence and their proponents – that is, the great preacher Hamza and his assistant preachers al-Tamimi, al-Qurayshi, al-Sabiq and al-Muqtana.

Taking this definition of the universe as the starting point, Druze doctrine stated that the soul was immortal and it was only the material human body that dies. A particular interpretation of certain Qur'anic verses led some individuals to speak of reincarnation. And so Druze doctrines absorbed the notion of the transmigration of souls, originally an Asian concept, affirming that every human being is bound to be reincarnated immediately after death in the body of a new-born human being, and the Druze would be reincarnated within their own community, for they consider the spirit to be "by command of the Lord" (*amr rabbī*),[7] such that it is to the human being as the meaning is to a linguistic expression. Just as the meaning cannot be conveyed by any random expression, the Druze believe that this meaning – that is, the spirit – must be expressed in a body in order to be refined by knowledge. Every believer thus has a new opportunity to pursue his quest for divine truths throughout his successive lives until he attains his salvation at the end of time. And since the Druze [or the monotheists] believe that their teaching [or: monotheism] is the highest level of knowledge, those who believe in reincarnation have deduced that a Druze [or: a monotheist], if he wishes to be continually perfected, must be reborn as a Druze [or: as a monotheist]. As for the types of human nobility and the ability to receive the hidden truths – that is, the qualities that believers must be adorned with and which constitute the various degree of preparedness for entry into the way by the practice of mysticism – we find that they have been taken from Pythagorean philosophy.

Druze doctrine was essentially a Sufi, esoteric, mystical, messianic way, with monotheistic origins and foundations, in spite of containing elements derived from Greek philosophy. Its followers believe that their doctrine is the final crown of the ancient doctrines which had been taken up by Judaism and Christianity and then by Islam, further developed by Shi'i teaching and more closely defined by the Isma'ilis, in order to finally reach its perfection and culmination with the Druze. It is a doctrine orientated towards the search for the true knowledge of God, who is described in most Druze religious sources as "the Unique One". Because of all these indications of the very powerful monotheism expressed in their doctrine, the Druze always referred to themselves as *muwahhidūn* or *Unitarian,* "Believers in the One and Only", and this is the only term used to refer to them in the *Books of Wisdom*. Believing themselves to be the repository of the perfectly formed religious teaching and of the true faith, the Druze also refer to themselves as *ahl al-haqīqa,* "the people of the truth", in the same way as the Sunnis are referred to as *ahl al-sharī'a,* "the people of the law", and the Shi'is as *ahl al-tarīqa,* "the people of the way".

At the beginning of the eleventh century, the Fatimid preachers worked at spreading these doctrines throughout the Middle East, even as far as India. They found a favourable response in northern Syria and in the areas around Mount Lebanon, the Anti-Lebanon, Damascus and northern Palestine. However, the opportunity to join this new religious teaching lasted only for a limited period, from AH 408/1017 AD, the year Druze teachings were publicly proclaimed, to AH 434/1043 AD, when the last of the major Druze preachers ended his missionary activity and stopped sending messages to his followers. At the end of this period of active preaching, each believer committed himself to the Druze teaching by a pact (*mīthāq*, known as *'ahd* in the Shi'i tradition of interpretation), which was and would remain the symbol of his belonging to the community until the end of time – that is, until the return of al-Hākim.

## The Purpose of This Book

At the present time, any mention of the Druze makes the general public think of a number of stereotypes, preconceptions and baseless ideas about the beliefs of the community and the historical and social facts. We might include among the features for which the Druze community is famous the jealously guarded secrecy of their doctrines and refusal to reveal them, their belief in reincarnation,[8] their settlement in the mountains, their refusal to be subordinate to authority, their reputation for being fierce warriors and their struggle to survive. In her article "Beating the odds: explaining Druze survival", Linda Abbas Halabi examines many factors of the Druze continuance as one of the Near Eastern minorities, while shedding light on their important social and political roles in most countries where their presence is significant.[9] In addition, they are known for certain historical personalities who have made their mark on the political history of the area, such as the Emir Fakhr al-Dīn, Sultān Basha al-Atrash, the leader Kamāl Jumblatt and his son Walīd, although, for all their importance, they do not embody the whole of Druze history and the community's present reality.

The aim of this book is to contribute to the correction of these simplistic approximations and to lift the cultural veil from the Druze community by taking a contemporary cultural approach that will attempt to be as precise and clear as possible about what is true or simply to help to clarify and separate it from preconceptions and stereotypes. I shall follow this approach by shedding light on the various cultural, social, legal, political and historical aspects of the life of the Lebanese Druze community. The book does not intend to elaborate on Druze doctrine out of respect for the very obligations of that doctrine. Nevertheless, the subject of the book makes it essential to introduce readers to the religious and spiritual heritage of the Druze community, to give them a better understanding of the "spirit" of the community and a better knowledge of how to situate it in the confessional landscape of the Middle East. Neither will there be any question of setting out a detailed history of events and incidents; we will content ourselves with referring to those that are significant for contemporary Lebanon in general, and the Druze community in particular.

Finally, this book intends quite simply to provide the reader with information that will allow him to rediscover contemporary Druze society and to better understand its reality and the truth about it. For the beginner, it will set out a collection of themes in such a way as to provide enough knowledge to construe a form of familiarity with Lebanese Druze society as well as to offer approaches and openings for critical reflection or academic research for those who wish to explore any of these themes more deeply. For those who are already travelling the true way, this book will enrich their search and efforts by offering a fresh look at the Lebanese Druze and a better understanding of their society.

## Notes

1 Such as the dualism of good and evil.

2 Hermeticism is a syncretic, esoteric amalgam of Greek and Egyptian elements whose main symbol is Hermes, the messenger of the gods.

3 Nejla M. Abu-Izzeddin, *The Druzes*, Leiden, 1993, p. 121.

4 Sami Makarem, *Al-'irfān fī maslak al-tawhīd* (*al-duruziyya*), London, Druze Heritage Foundation, 2006.

5 A philosophy founded in the third century AD by Plotinus (d. 270), as an extension and development of the ancient Greek philosophical heritage, particularly the philosophy of Plato.

6 Druze belief.

7 "They ask thee concerning the spirit. Say: 'The spirit [cometh] by command of my Lord; of knowledge is only a little that is communicated to you'" (Q17:85).

8 A distinction must be drawn between the popular belief and the official doctrine.

9 See Appendix 11.

# Chapter 1

# Human Geography

Throughout the proselytization era, between AH 408/1017 AD and AH 434/1043 AD, Druzism slowly evolved from being a religious way into becoming a community with distinctive features and characteristics, originally established in the Lebanese mountains. A short time after their split with Fatimid Isma'ilism, in the early eleventh century, the Druze "Muwahhidun" promoted an ideological faith and kept it shrouded in secrecy in accordance with the practice of *taqiyya*[1] (concealment), thus making possible their survival as a religious minority. Although they were initially a single homogeneous community, their changing circumstances and the rigours of time and place – especially the emergence of states with fixed borders – resulted in their geographical dispersal. Nuances gradually emerged between the Druze communities of Lebanon, Syria and Palestine and increasingly asserted themselves on historical, legal and political levels. Nevertheless, whatever is the national identity of their communities, the Druze always constitute one religious community with respect to their beliefs, customs and pattern of social structure.

Although this book is solely concerned with Lebanon's Druze community, it is useful to open it with a brief presentation of the spiritual and religious heritage of the Druze community at large, thus devoting the first chapter to a study of the human geography of the Druze Muwahhidun worldwide.

It is imperative to start by describing their demographic distribution in order to evaluate the presence of the Druze community in Lebanon and assess its specificity. Chapter 1 will also focus on the Druze in Lebanon in a section dealing with their social and religious infrastructures, commonly shared with their Syrian and Palestinian co-religionists, thus confirming that the identity cohesion of any religious minority and its might are largely determined by these structures.

## Ethnic Origins

During the first half of the eleventh century, the preachers sent from Egypt to spread the message of "Tawhīd" achieved great success in Bilād al-Shām – that is, the area presently including Syria, Lebanon, Palestine and Jordan.

The first Druze communities conglomerated in the mountainous regions stretching alongside the Syrian littoral, and are still firmly established there. The ethnic roots of the Druze community originated from this region and their history is closely linked to it. It should be noted that the adepts of the Druze teachings did not form a single community until they heeded the call of the (Druze) Da'wa and adhered to its doctrine and way of life. Until then, they had formed, either as natives or settlers, an integral part of the population of Bilād al-Shām for several generations. When proselytization opened the door to conversion at the start of the eleventh century, Arab tribes had already infiltrated Syria on a large scale even before the Hijra of the Prophet and the Islamic conquests.

The first Druze communities were therefore established among Arab tribes, or tribes that had been extensively Arabized. Historical records tend to confirm that the Druzes largely belong to the original 12 great Arab tribes and are, specifically, descendants of the Tannūkh tribe, itself a descendant of the large Lakhm tribe, which, in the dawn of Islam, settled the area situated between Aleppo and Hama. According to Druze sources, some Tannūkh clans settled, during the time of the Prophet, in the Gharb area in southern Mount Lebanon, and in the mountains surrounding Beirut. From the Tannūkh tribe emerged the Arslāns and then the Buhturs, two great feudal families who led the Druze community throughout the medieval period.

The Druze also trace their origins to the great Arab tribe of Rabīʿas, from which the Maʿan family emerged. Driven from northern Syria by the Crusaders, the Rabīʿas took refuge in southern Mount Lebanon in the vicinity of the Tannūkhs. There, strong bonds developed between the two tribes. The Maʿans became the leaders of the Druze Muwahhidun in the fourteenth century and their power reached its apogee during the reign of Emir Fakhr al-Dīn II. We do not know how largely the mountainous areas were populated when the Druze feudal families settled there, nor do we know the ethnic origins of their inhabitants. However, it is beyond doubt that the inhabitants of this area were duly Arabized like the rest of the inhabitants of Bilād al-Shām and that they, later on, embraced the Druze faith.

## Current Geographical Distribution

Although the Druze have spread throughout the world, they continue to conglomerate, mainly, in the Middle East – notably in Lebanon and Syria, and to a lesser extent in Palestine and Jordan.

Several historic accounts emphasize the fact that they tended to settle in rugged, hardly accessible mountainous areas where they established homogeneous communities. The choice of many religious minorities to dwell, in their early established days, in mountainous refuges helped to preserve them from outside influences and at the same time avoided persecution by official authorities. Moreover, the mountainous areas parallel to the Syrian coast constituted a real natural barrier to external attacks, whether by the Byzantines or the Crusaders, and the Druze took it upon themselves to be responsible for protecting the western mountain passes from attack. The combined existence of these physical boundaries and independent minority communities of mountain people, among whom the Druze proved to be the most daring and enduring, constituted an impregnable fortress in the defence of the Arab–Islamic empire.

Nowadays, the Druze are spread along the length of the mountain ranges parallel to the eastern Mediterranean coast, stretching from northern Syria to the north of occupied Palestine, passing through

Lebanon. This geographical configuration, which transcends the national frontiers of the states, is known as "Druze Land" and constitutes the historical core of their community. It extends northwards to the vicinity of Jabal al-Summāq, a mountainous chain between Aleppo and Antioch where a number of Druze villages still exist, having withstood Byzantine attacks on Aleppo.

"Druze Land" extends through Syria's central region from the villages of Wādī al-Taym to the foot of Mt Hermon, reaching Palestine, west of Galilee and the area of Safad on the slopes of Mt Carmel, where the Druze formed the vanguard of the Arab forces defending Jerusalem and the Muslim hinterland (the Nation of Islam) *dār al-Islām*. But the "Druze Land" communities with the deepest historical, geographical, political and cultural roots in the area settled in the southern parts of Mount Lebanon – that is, the areas of Shūf, Matn and 'Alay – as well as the Wādī al-Taym region where the two large Druze villages of Hāsbayyā and Rāshayyā are situated. Smaller Druze conglomerations exist around Damascus, particularly in the areas of al-Ghūta and Jaramānā, as well as in the region of Aleppo. It is worth noting that since the 1960s Druze village dwellers were more attracted to urban life, and Damascus and Beirut became, and still are for them, main centres of interest.

At present, the largest Druze community lives in Jabal al-'Arab (traditionally called Jabal al-Durūz) – that is, the area overlooking the plain of Hawrān south of Damascus. There, the Druze population makes up about half of all the Druze community in the Middle East. Druze settlement of this area is more recent than their settlement in the "Druze Land" and effectively started in the aftermath of the Battle of 'Ayn Dāra in 1711 that took place between two opposing Druze factions. The vanquished faction decided to move away from Mount Lebanon and settle in the mountainous region of Hawrān, which was less developed, less populated but still a welcoming place. As the Druze became the majority in this region, it came to be popularly called Jabal al-Durūz (the Mountain of the Druze). It was only after Syria's independence in 1946 that the name was changed to Jabal al-'Arab.

In the wake of the Druze rebellion against the French Mandate (1925–1927), a significant number of Druze left Jabal al-ʿArab to settle in Jordan, primarily in Amman and the town of Zarqāʾ.

Beginning with the nineteenth century, migrant Druze communities were established outside the Middle East, particularly in the Americas, Australia and West Africa. This migration, which began from Syria and Lebanon on an individual basis, turned into a larger movement of groups, fewer in number than their home communities, but still retaining their cohesion. The bulk of the Druze diaspora is currently found in the United States of America, Canada and Australia. Large communities also live in Latin America, especially Venezuela, Brazil, Argentina and Mexico, while smaller numbers reside in Chile and Colombia. Economic development and opportunities for work have also attracted many Druze individuals to emigrate to the Gulf States and Saudi Arabia, as well as West Africa.

## Druze Demography

The lack of recent censuses in most Middle Eastern countries means that a precise figure for the Druze population can only be speculative. In Lebanon, where the composition of the government is based on sectarian proportionality, and consequently on the demographic size of its various communal components, the last official census was held in 1932. The most recent official estimate of the Lebanese population dates back to the mid-1950s. However, the Druze Council for Research and Development conducted, in 1980, its own census of Lebanon's Druze families and villages within the context of a study of their birth and emigration rates.

In Syria, the most recent estimate of the population, conducted on the basis of religious affiliations, was made in 1956, although an official survey carried out in 1960 counted all Christians as one entity and included the other minorities with the Muslim majority. In Jordan, the state does not consider the Druze a separate community; therefore, they are not mentioned in official statistics. However, in occupied Palestine, an official estimate of the Druze population is regularly conducted due to Israel's obsession with monitoring demographic changes within the Arab minority in occupied Palestine.

In conclusion, official Druze population figures are mostly outdated and do not reflect their actual number. Current estimates can only be based on an analysis of reported figures and the use of various old statistical data as samples to be compared with figures derived from a direct field research within the Druze community and attestations from individuals who dwelt in Druze populated areas or visited them. Despite the difficulty of conducting a statistical task through analysis and deduction, and despite the wide differences between analyses and studies, the fact remains that the Druze constitute a religious minority in the countries where they live, regardless of their conglomeration in united, homogeneous communities. In Lebanon, their percentage does not exceed 8 per cent of the global population and ranges in Syria between 3 and 4 per cent. According to the highest estimates, the Druze population of the whole Middle East amounts to less than a million. There are between 400,000 and 500,000 Druze in Syria, of whom more than three-quarters live in the Jabal al-'Arab, and between 280,000 and 350,000 Druze in Lebanon. The 1980 census begun by the Druze Council for Research and Development estimated the figure at about 225,000. There is only a small minority in Jordan, with estimates putting its number between 5,000 and 20,000, while official censuses carried out in occupied Palestine indicate that their number is about 75,000.

## Religious and Social Structures

Belonging to a religious minority reinforces the cohesion and solidarity of its members, strengthens their sense of identity, and creates a need to relate to a single cultural background and a defined religious sect. Therefore, the community of Druze Muwahhidun has built up its own religious and social structures which practically embody its sense of identity as a religious minority. If the religious structures of the Druze Muwahhidun project their attachment to their culture, identity and religious practice or faith, their social structure reflects the homogeneity and cohesion of their community and reveals the nature of the ties of solidarity that exist among them.

## Religious Structures

### Retreat Houses (*khalawāt*)

Although the Druze have some mosques – as will be explained later – it cannot be claimed that they possess special sites that could be considered religious sites dedicated to worship in the way that Christians have churches and Muslims have mosques. The Druze have *khalawāt* – plural of *khulwa* – a Sufi term derived from the Sufi ways (*turuq*). The "khalwa" is not a hermitage where a person withdraws from the outside world to devote himself to prayers and worship, but a retreat home best suited to meditation in the simplest modest surrounding in order to acquire a global knowledge of the rigours of their way of life and its accompanying religious upbringing.

Retreat houses have their particular internal order. They are exclusively for men, each member providing for his own needs. The rules of living in a retreat house are strict and accurate, characterized by absolute seriousness and complete striving for excellence. Any breach of the rules of the retreat house entails eviction from the premises. There is neither boss nor bossed in the retreat houses and it is only the behaviour of those attending the "khalwa" that earns them status and respect.

The educational system of the "khalwa" is based on memorizing the *Books of Wisdom*, learning the principles of pious behaviour, and performing the religious rites and duties. Reading the *Books of Wisdom* – considered as the apogee of the history of *ta'wīl*[2] – is a conduit to the spiritual sphere of the Qur'anic text. In conjunction with the spirit of the Druze religious discipline, the educational system of the "khalwa" follows the precedent set by the puritanical, ascetic, pious people and their conduct. One of the aims of religious teaching is the clarification of the Druze Mawahid duties, and the demonstration of the methodology of following the straight path and the median way. This is based on considering progress as a rational process, as long as "al-Tawhīd" is based upon the contemplation of enlightenment and rationality. Finally, education and religious upbringing is aimed at the Druze Muwahhidūn who choose a life of retreat in the "khalwa" devoted to studying the life accounts of their faithful predecessors in an attempt to learn from them and from the knowledge they acquired.

Every Druze-populated area has its own "khalwa". The most notable "Khalwat" in Lebanon are the Qatālib in the Shūf, and the Bayāda situated on a hill south-west of Hāsbiyyā.

The first "khalwa" in the Bayāda region was established by Sheikh Sayf al-Dīn Shu'ayb in the seventeenth century. Today there are about 50 of them distinguishable by the ways (Turuq) they adopt and the religious programmes and spiritual orientation they propose. The Bayāda "Khalwat" are the best known spiritual Druze centres in the world, and their doors are open to Druze of all nationalities who visit them either for a short stay or to dwell permanently within their compounds without being cut off from their society or becoming hermits. The most distinguished ascetics and esteemed Sheikhs, whether of Lebanese, Syrian or Palestinian origin, seek in the Bayada "khalwa" the seclusion needed to study and worship. There are also other "khalwat" in Jaranāyā, outside Dayr al-Qamar, and in the village of Kfar Hīm in the Shūf. The late Kamāl Jumblatt once described their occupants as: "Very modest people, healthy, concerned with goodness and striving on the way to holiness."[3]

## Assembly Houses (*majālis*)

In addition to the official sites of worship, the Druze Muwahhidūn have dedicated communal sites called *majālis* (assembly houses) for prayer where initiates and veterans gather every Thursday evening for prayer and meditation. There is an assembly house in every Druze village without exception. As their use is not solely restricted to worshipping, and as they are rather very modest buildings devoid of any ornamentation or pictures and the like ... they do not greatly differ from any Druze-owned home.[4]

## Shrines (*maqāmāt, mazārāt*)

These are worship sites distinguished from "majalis" by being set up in a site previously visited by a prophet, or used as a burial site for his remains or the remains of a well-known wise Druze Muwahhid or a great guardian of the faith. The believers visit the shrines to plead for God's mercy or to express their deep faith in the Almighty and their genuine love and allegiance to Him.

Not only Druze zealots visit these shrines. They are frequented by believers from all creeds, religions and denominations. From a spiritual perspective, visiting these shrines is an expression of faith and hope, as well as of respect, reverence and obedience to the divine truth. In the eyes of the Druze, a shrine is a site where he can surrender his self to God, express his love and submission to Him, alongside his faith in Him and respect for His religious creed.

The following list of Druze shrines is based on an unpublished statistical study undertaken by Sheikh Fandī Shujā'a, a Sheikh of the Bayāda khalwat.

### *The Best-Known Shrines in Lebanon*

- The shrine of Emir al-Sayyid 'Abdullāh al-Tannūkhī, in 'Abay.
- The shrine of Sheikh Muhammad Abū Hilāl, in 'Ayn 'Atā.
- The shrine of the preacher 'Ammār at Ibl al-Saqī, near Hāsbayyā.
- The shrine of the prophet Job at the summit of one of the Mountains of Nīhā, in the Shūf.
- The shrine of the lady (*sitt*) Sha'wāna, in western Biqā'.
- The shrine of the prophet Ezekiel, at Blāt, in southern Lebanon.
- The shrine of al-Sharīf at Shamlīkh near Shārūn.

### *Shrines in Syria*

There are numerous shrines in the Jabal al-'Arab, most of them found on the hills and heights and plains. This plenitude of shrines dates back to the massacre in 1730 of 70 Druze pilgrims while on their way to Mecca. This incident aroused the fears of the believers and made them reluctant to take to a pilgrimage route unsafe and exposed to dangers.

Subsequently, the residents of Jabal al-ʿArab and Syria started confining their religious visits to local shrines whenever performing the pilgrimage to Mecca (*hajj*), proved exposed to dangers. Moreover, the fatwa pronounced by Ibn Taymiyya in the fourteenth century condemning heterodox religious minorities – in which were included the Druze – even though based on erroneous and distorted information and unfounded accusations, made them wary of practising the duty of *hajj* and more inclined to conceal their beliefs and revert to the "taqia" practice in self-preservation, especially after this *fatwa* was used by Sunni authorities as justification for their negative treatment of the adepts of the Islamic minorities it referred to. Due to this persecution, the heterodox religious minorities set up numerous shrines in Syria and preserved them to this day. They are as follows.

- The shrine of ʿAmmār Ibn Yāsir and Aways, in northern Syria.
- The shrine of ʿAmmār Ibn Yāsir, in ʿUrayqa.
- The shrine of the prophet Abel, on Mount Qāsyūn, known as the *maqār al-dam*.
- The shrine of Mār ʿAbdā, south of Salkhad.
- The shrine of the prophet Job, in Qanawāt.
- The shrine of ʿAyn al-Zamān, in Sūwayda.
- The shrine of Sheikh al-Balakhī, in Qraya.
- The shrine of al-Mahdī, in Mardak.
- The shrine of Lord Jesus Christ, between Maqhala and Shahbā.
- The shrines of the prophet Khidr, in the villages of Matān, Shaʿaf, Sahwat al-Khudar and Malah.
- The shrine of the prophet Shuʿayb in Qaysamā.
- The shrine of the Angel Gabriel, east of Shahbā.
- The shrine of the prophet John (John the Baptist), in the Umayyad mosque in Damascus.
- The shrine of al-Yaʿatūrī, in the Golan Heights.

### *The Best-Known Shrines in Palestine*

- The shrine of the prophet Shuʿayb, in Upper Tiberias, on the plateau overlooking the plain of Hittīn.

- The shrine of Sheikh 'Alī Fāris al-'Ābid, who spent his life prostrated in prayer at Jawlas.
- The shrine of the prophet Khidr, in southern Galilee.

*The Best-Known Shrines in Baghdad and the Arab Peninsula*

- The shrine of al-Maqdār, at Baqī' al-Qurmud.
- The shrine of Abū Dhar Jundab Ibn Junāda, at Rabdha, in Iraq.
- The shrine of Salmān Bāk, in al-Madā'in, south of Baghdad.

**The Mosques of the Druze**

The Druze built a number of mosques at various stages of their history in order to assert their affiliation to Islam, at the beginning, and later on, in compliance with the demand of Emir al-Sayyid 'Abdallah al-Tannūkhī and, at a later stage, to synchronize their situation with an intolerant Muslim environment. The following list of mosques is also taken from the study made by Sheikh Fandī Shujā'.

- The mosque of Emir Mas'ūd 'Arslān, at 'Aramūn.
- The mosque of Emir 'Umar Ibn Mas'ūd, near 'Ayn 'Aramūn.
- The mosque of Mundhir al-Tannūkhī, at Bāb Idrīs, Beirut.
- The mosque of al-'Amrūsiyya, in Shwayfāt.
- The mosque of Emira Habūs 'Arslān, who is buried near the mosque, in the area of al-Nā'ima.
- The mosque of 'Abay, built by Emir Nasr al-Dīn al-Tannūkhī.
- The mosque of the Emirs of the Ma'n family, at Dayr al-Qamar.
- The mosque of al-Chamoun, built by Sheikh Hussayn Jumblatt, in Sidon.
- The mosque of al-Mukhtāra, which was demolished by Emir Bāshir al-Shihābī.
- The mosque of 'Alay.

**Social Structures**

The Druze community proved its ability to establish its own independently administered social structures, and its capability to oversee the interests of its members. These structures, primarily depending on intra-communal solidarity, confirm the cohesive ties that bind the adepts of any religious minority. According to this logic, the Druze communities in the diaspora, especially in North and South America and Australia, established associations bent on strengthening the bonds and contacts between the Druze communities of these countries and all residents of Arab origin.

In Lebanon, the Druze community founded several institutions under its management, upholding the spirit of social solidarity among its members. These institutions provide a wide range of services related to social welfare and health care, in addition to allotting a special interest to educational concerns.

Since one of the tragedies inflicted by the Lebanese civil war on many families was the loss of their breadwinners, a number of Druze benefactors took it upon themselves to provide their needy co-religionists at all levels with their needs. A school for the martyrs of the civil war children was opened in B'aqlīn, run by a Druze family and including a technical institute. In 'Abay, "Farah Institute" set up an establishment for the wounded and disabled in the war.

If such initiatives illustrate the endeavours deployed to strengthen ties among the members of a religious minority, they also indicate the extraordinary importance given to protecting the history of the Druze, as well as their present and future.

In the same vein, a Druze orphanage was founded in 'Abay around the year 1930 by the late 'Arif al-Nakadī. This orphanage, supported in its humanitarian activities by grants and donations from the Druze at large, is presently caring for about 1,000 orphaned pupils of all ages. It comprises an educational training college pursuing the official curriculum of the Lebanese Ministry of Education, as well as a technical institute that trains graduates in all crafts and fields of activities.

In the educational sphere, the existence of several large schools worthy of commendation testify to the development and expansion of educational zeal. The Druze 'Irfān Institute, for example, comprises a string of five schools, with their administrative centre in Samqāniya, in the Shūf, and several other schools in Sofar, al-Shahhār, Rāshayyā (*dahr al-ahmar*) and Hāsbayyā. Those schools are frequented by around 5,000 pupils, boys and girls, from all religious communities, and are known to provide an excellent standard of education from primary to secondary level. Even though these schools follow the official curricula of the Lebanese Ministry of Education, they also provide religious education for their Druze students. Additionally, the ʻIrfān Institute comprises a religious department that has published numerous works, both secular and religious. The Ishrāq Institute in ʻAlay is based on the same concept as the ʻIrfān schools. There is also a school in Beirut, the Maʻn School, directly affiliated to the Druze *awqāf*, and considered one of the major Druze institutions. The "awqaf" is one of the major institutes of the Druze community. Its role is to manage the community's assets whose proceeds are channelled to charitable purposes and the care of the poor. The Druze community also owns a hostel in Beirut specifically allocated for girls who leave their villages in the Mountain in order to pursue their higher studies in the universities of the capital.

In addition to its great concern with education, the Druze community was also keen on providing healthcare services to its members, courtesy of a major initiative undertaken in this respect by their late Sheikh ʻAql, Muhammad Abu Shaqrā. The community owns and runs a hospital in ʻAyn Wazayn founded in 1978 and opened to the public in 1989. Apart from providing the usual hospital services, it hosts a nursing college and a home for old people. The hospital employs more than 100 doctors on a full or part-time basis, and a staff of about 350. It has a capacity of 100 beds and can treat about 20,000 patients a year. It also hosts about 80 elderly persons in its home caring unit, and is currently preparing a new centre. The hospital is linked, through co-operation agreements, to several major health institutions such as the French Hôtel-Dieu and the American and Lebanese University Hospitals, and is paired with Versailles Hospital in France and the French Broca Hospital for the elderly.

In the same vein, a group of clerics established another hospital in ʻAlay, the Īmān Hospital, to provide for the needs of the inhabitants of ʻAlay and Bʻabda regions. Undoubtedly, social structures, by nature of their cohesion and continuity, ought to be managed with an institutional vision. And the Druze are well known for devoting their efforts to promoting institutional structures, regardless of the size of the institution itself.

## Notes

1 *Taqiyya* is an Islamic religious principle common to Sunnis, Shi'is and other Muslims that allows them to conceal their faith if they are in fear of it, or under threat, or fearful for it, on the basis that giving knowledge to those unworthy of it may be harmful to the one who gives it and may make him doubt what he believes without persuading him spiritually or mystically of the truth of what he has been given. Believers, particularly Shi'is, are permitted to conceal their beliefs when revealing them in a hostile environment would create a risk to their safety and security. See: Sami Makarem, *Al-taqiyya fī al-Islām*, London, Druze Heritage Publications, 2004.

2 Allegorical interpretation.

3 Kamal Joumblatt, *Pour le Liban*, Paris, Stock, 1978, p. 84.

4 The assembly houses will be dealt with in detail in the section on Druze religious structures in Chapter 3.

# Chapter 2

# The History of the Druze, 1017–1943

The Druze, like other religious minorities, suffer from many false and distorted ideas spread about their beliefs, on the one hand, and about their identity and history on the other. Although the Western world portrays the Druze as a hard, rebellious people, their history is only presented through the image of their most prominent personalities, Fakhr al-Dīn II and Kamāl Jumblatt. The reason for the persistence of these pre-conceived ideas about the Druze Muwahhidun can be related to the attitude of the Druze themselves towards the writing of their own history. Because of their nature and geographical proliferation, all their efforts were concentrated on defending their own community, they never had the opportunity, nor perhaps the will, to write their own history. Their efforts were more orientated towards making history than writing it.

At present, the lack of Druze interest in recording their history is decreasing as they are showing a marked preference for historical documentation and expressing a greater interest in registering what they have endured throughout the past centuries, not only for being an essential part of their own identity but also of Lebanon's history.

Some of them started to explore the depths of their history in an effort to expound its true facts and dissipate the distorted images and widespread rumours propagated about the Druze Muwahhidun, thus enabling historians to adopt a more serious, truthful and realistic approach in their assessment of Druze related events.

However, most of the time the persistence of pre-conceived ideas about the Druze indirectly leads to the propagation of a number of contradictions between various historical studies. Whatever the case, a contiguous line connects the history of the Druze community to the history of Lebanon, and in such a way that makes them appear inseparable. A common aspect that historical studies focus on is their policy of constant opposition to any form of foreign domination and their tireless, perpetual search for independence. Confronted with this publicized image of being a rebellious and quarrelsome people, the Druze invoked all concerned parties to admit their historical role as defenders of Islam and Arabism and, on the Lebanese stage, their role as defenders of independence and freedom in the face of oppression and subjugation. Such a constant historical trait defined the outlines of the Druze political vocation and undeniably shaped their role in the evolution of contemporary Lebanon from 1943 onwards.

The aim of this chapter is to highlight the main periods in Druze history starting with their acculturation with the Druze doctrine in Egypt, towards the beginning of the eleventh century, up to the declaration of Lebanon's independence on 22 November 1943.

## The Medieval Period

### Egyptian Origins

The origins of the Druze community date back to eleventh-century Fatimid Egypt – that is, the starting date of the official preaching of the Unitarian call (*al-da'wa al-tawhīdiyya*), in AH 408/1017 AD. Druze doctrines, whose roots sprang from the Isma'ili belief in the expected return of the awaited Mahdi, were associated with the person of the Fatimid Caliph and Imam, al-Hākim bi-Amr Allāh (AH 386–411/996–1021 AD) and his authority. The Fatimid Isma'ili preacher, al-Akhram, organized the first movement proclaiming the divinity of al-Hākim in AH 408/1017 AD, but the official preachers of the "da'wa" in Cairo rejected the idea and al-Akhram was assassinated a few months after the propagation of his movement. In AH 410/1019 AD, a second preacher, Hamza ibn 'Alī, emerged from Khorasan to take over the guidance of the movement and bestowed on the Tawhīd call its final divine theological status.

Assisted by a large coterie of disciples and preachers from Cairo, Hamza promoted a powerful, coherent message and thus became the true founder of the Tawhīd religious way. Mention should be made here of a third person who emerged after Hamza and played an eminent role in the Fatimid state and, upon this basis, attempted to claim for himself the Imamate. This preacher was al-Darazī, a disciple of Hamza who turned into his rival and competitor and began to nurture the ambition of leading the sect of al-Hākim.

Al-Darazī acted independently of his superiors, and doubtless in opposition to them, managing to attract to his side many of Hamza's followers. He was the first person to publicly declare the divinity of Caliph al-Hākim and was thus condemned by both the official body of the Fatimid Call proponents in Cairo and Hamza ibn ʿAlī.

Al-Darazī was killed on New Year's Day of the year AH 410, but the followers of the Call came to be named after him as "Druze". Ironically, although the Druze consider him a schismatic and a renegade character, they were named after the preacher they repudiated – that is, al-Darazī, and the "Tawhīd" Call continues to bear his name to this day.

The official proselytizing body in Cairo persevered in rejecting and refuting the new Tawhīd doctrines. And in the aftermath of the disappearance of Caliph al-Hākim in AH 411/1021 AD, the Cairo authorities embarked on a persecution campaign against his followers, brutally repressing them, especially under the aegis of the new Fatimid Caliph, al-Zāhir. Consequently, the Druze doctrine spread beyond Egypt through the extreme efforts of its preachers who achieved their greatest successes in Bilād al-Shām and Galilee, reaching as far as northern Syria, and spreading as far as the Hijaz, Yemen and India via Iraq and Iran. But the prospects of acceding to the "Tawhīd" Call were abruptly ended in the year AH 434/1043 AD, in a decision that made both conversion and apostasy impossible. The Druze Muwahhidun who, by then, could be regarded as a separate ethnic and political entity, became then a closed community.

### The Druze in Bilād al-Shām

In Syria, several Arab tribes readily adopted the new call, among them the ʿAbdallāhs of the Gharb region, the Sulaymāns of Wādī al-Taym and the Turābs of Galilee. But the Tannūkh tribe was the first to adhere to the call. The Tannūkhs, a branch of the large Arab tribe of Lakhm, included three sub-factions of Arab–Christian families: Bahrā', Taghlib and the Tannūkh. The Tannūkh were settled in northern Syria, western Lebanon and the area surrounding Beirut, since the beginning of the Arab conquest.[1] The said families converted to Islam in AH 165/741 AD then adhered to the Druze doctrine in the early eleventh century. This did not prevent them from continuing to defend their Arab identity and, in particular, proclaim their allegiance to Islam. Throughout the medieval years two major Tannūkh families, the Arslāns and the Buhturs, took turns in leading the Druze community.

The history of the Arslān family begins with the first 'Abbasid caliphs. Having settled in earlier times in northern Syria, the Arslāns migrated, upon the request of the second 'Abbasid Caliph al-Mansūr (AH 137–159/754–775 AD), to the Beirut region in order to defend the coast against the Byzantines. They lost no time in establishing an Emirate stretching from Dāmūr to Sinn al-Fīl, encompassing the town of Beirut and its mountainous surrounding. In the ninth century, led by Emir Nu'mān Arslān, their emirate extended its frontiers as far as Safad in Palestine.

While the Fatimid and 'Abbasid caliphates were embroiled in an unmitigated political and religious struggle for a complete and legitimate control of the Islamic world, the Fatimids were still weighing up the possibility of extending their authority to Iraq and bringing about the fall of the 'Abbasid caliphate, which by then had dwindled into a protectorate of the Seljuk Turks. Bilād al-Shām, at the core of this struggle, was exposed to the pressures of its powerful neighbours and their ambitious schemes, being an unavoidable route to all of them. The Fatimids considered Bilād al-Shām an open gateway to Baghdad. And until the arrival of the Crusader armies in Syria by the end of the eleventh century, the region was controlled by a multitude of authorities – among them local Arab tribes and princes, and Turkish military officers – while the Seljuk princes and the Fatimids were vying for control of Bilād al-Shām. Throughout the turmoil generated by the struggle to control the area, the Tannūkh emirs appear to have decided to remain neutral, although they were de facto subjects of the Seljuk Emirate of Damascus. However, when confrontations with external foes threatened the security and safety of Arab communities in the area, the Tannūkh's traditional policy was always in favour of supporting the government of Damascus. The Emirs of Damascus returned this favour by proclaiming a member of the Tannūkh clan as the Emir of the region.

When the Crusaders conquered the Holy Land and established four Latin kingdoms in the Orient, this Tannūkh policy remained unchanged and they consistently and vigorously supported all struggles against foreign invaders. Led by their Emir ʻAdad al-Dawla, they fought pitched battles against the Franks in support of the Damascus forces.

The Franks made a deep incursion into the Tannūkh Emirate in AH 503/1110 AD and marched on Beirut, which they besieged by land and sea. Despite the fierce resistance of ʻAdad al-Dawla, they overran the city and massacred its inhabitants before advancing eastwards as far as the mountainous region dominated by the Tannūkh clan. Emir ʻAdad al-Dawla was killed in the fighting and the Arslāns were sorely tested. The Emir of Sidon, Majd al-Dawla (from the ʻAbdallah clan), succeeded ʻAdad al-Dawla until he too was killed in a confrontation with the Franks in AH 532/1137 AD. Buhtur, son of ʻAdad al-Dawla and founder of the feudal family of the same name, then assumed the leadership of the Druze community.

In the meantime, Tughtakīn, the Seljuk governor of Damascus, asked the Maʻn clan (from the great Arab tribe of the Rabīʻas) to settle with their families south of Mount Lebanon in order to support the Tannūkhs, who had been greatly weakened by the conflicts. The Maʻns settled in the Shūf region and soon developed family ties with the Tannūkhs through marriages and alliances. Other Druze families, such as the Nakads and the Talhūqs, also settled in the region, joining this major Druze alliance and appointing Buhtur, the governor of Damascus, as Emir of al-Gharb. Buhtur led the confrontation with the Franks, the new masters of Beirut, and defeated them in AH 549/1151 AD at the Battle of ʻAyn al-Tīna, near the River Ghadīr, to the south of old Beirut.

At the end of the thirteenth century, the Kurdish Salāh al-Dīn al-Ayyūbī succeeded in reviving the spirit of *jihād* and organized a huge counter-attack against the Franks in Bilād al-Shām. When he besieged Beirut in AH 583/1187 AD, the young Tannūkh emir Hajjī Ibn Karāma joined him in the hope of regaining the city. After the surrender of Beirut, Saladin confirmed the authority of the Tannūkh clan in the person of emir Hajjī, as well as confirming his title as governor of al-Gharb. Throughout the Ayyubid rule of Syria, the Buhtur clan remained in control, retaining authority over its territories and the entitlement of its members to be called emirs as a means of ensuring their loyalty to the Ayyubids and thus guaranteeing the presence of a Muslim force to protect their flank on the borders of the Latin kingdoms.

Based on this account, the reader might think that relations between the Tannūkh Emirate and the Seljuk Turk rule in Damascus (before it passed to the Ayyubids) were exclusive and privileged at all times. In fact, this was not the case, as internal disturbances and fluctuations in the Seat of power in Damascus imposed on the Tannūkhs times of great difficulty and periods of weakness. The Druze minority, living on the border of a struggle between two worlds, found itself caught between the city of Damascus, governed by the Muslims, and the cities of Beirut, Sidon and Tyre, governed by the Franks, and therefore compelled to take into account the (then) prevailing political balance. The Buhtur clan exercised political caution and did not break its relations with either the Ayyubids or the Franks when, in the second half of the thirteenth century, the Mamluks and the Mughals were engaged in a bitter struggle to control Bilād al-Shām. Indeed, they fought with the Mamluks in the decisive Battle of 'Ayn Jallūt in AH 658/1260 AD, which put an end to the Mughal advance and decisively barred their access to Bilād al-Shām. In recognition of the achievements and victories of the Buhtur Emir Zayn al-Dīn Sālih, who fought alongside the Mamluks and distinguished himself with his courage and audacity, the Mamluk Sultān turned a blind eye to the dichotomy and dilemma that befell the Druze to the extent of rewarding him. As a result, the Tannūkh Emirate, which, alongside the towns of Beirut and Sidon, was attached to the "Wilayet" of Damascus, thrived in the midst of the great Mamluk Empire. The Druze, led by Emir Buhtur, remained loyal to the Mamluks until the end of their reign and took part in battles against Tamburlaine in 1401 AD and in the Mamluk expedition against the Frankish kingdom of Cyprus in 1425 AD.

## The Ottoman Period

### The reign of Emir Fakhr al-Dīn II

By the fourteenth century, originating in Anatolia, the Ottoman Turks emerged as the new rising power in the Orient. They spread their authority, enlarged their sphere of influence and consolidated their power until a confrontation with the Mamluks became inevitable. The Ottomans took on the Mamluks in the year 1516 AD and invaded Bilād al-Shām. The Buhturs, loyal to the Mamluks, lost their privileges in Mount Lebanon and the leadership of the Druze community passed from the Tannūkh clan to the Ma'ns, who lived in the Shūf area. The Ottomans soon clashed with the Ma'ns and history has recorded the ferocious resistance that the Ma'n Emirate put up against the Ottoman Sultanate.

Undeniably the most famous Ma'n ruler was Emir Fakhr al-Dīn II (1590–1635). He was a sophisticated diplomat and a gifted administrator with a liberal and tolerant character. He succeeded in asserting himself as a great leader of the Druze, deploying extraordinary efforts to establish a homogeneous and independent state in the midst of the Ottoman Empire.

First of all, he succeeded in extending his authority beyond Mount Lebanon, although the Shūf region remained his power base. Starting in 1610, he controlled several areas of present-day Syria, Palestine and Jordan. This territorial expansion earned him the title of *sultān al-barr* (Lord of the lands). In his confrontation with Tripoli and Damascus – two cities that stood against him and were subservient to the Ottoman rule – he formed an alliance with the *wālī* (governor) of Aleppo, 'Alī Bāshā Jumblatt, an ancestor of the modern-day Jumblatt family of Lebanon.[2]

Emir Fakhr al-Dīn II showed a keen interest in the economic future of his country and the prosperity of his people, and attempted to carve a Mediterranean niche for Lebanon. During his reign, the ports of Beirut, Sidon and Acre resumed economic ties with the West, and Fakhr al-Dīn himself restored Lebanon's political and military relations with several European states. He spent five years in Tuscany (1613–1618) drawing inspirations from the broad datum of European Renaissance and returned to his country enhanced by several achievements and inventions, especially in the fields of architecture and urbanization, and accompanied by experts and technicians to assist him in modernizing the economic and agricultural sectors of Lebanon. He set up a feudal system in which he was the landlord and the peasants a salaried workforce.

Fakhr al-Dīn's broadmindedness, openness and tolerance played an essential part in the success of his rule. He extended his social policy, unabashedly secular in its orientation, to all his subjects, irrespective of their confession or religion. Under his auspices, and within the prevailing economic prosperity, the Maronites and Druze of Mount Lebanon enjoyed a golden age of mutual tolerance. Also, he did not hesitate in expressing his friendly intentions towards all Eastern Christian communities. The feudal Druze landlords, acting upon his recommendation, and anxious to support his economic policy, encouraged the entry of Christians into their midst in order to promote skilled jobs and trade. They granted them pieces of land to enable them to build churches and monasteries, among them – as an example – the Maronite monastery of Nāʿama, south of Beirut, and the Melkite convent of Dayr al-Mukhallis, in Joon (Shūf district).

Profiting from this alliance, the Maronites consolidated their political and economic position. They settled in most parts of the Druze-inhabited territories in the south and on the Lebanese coast, grew wealthy and prospered, becoming landowners in their own right. Emir Fakhr al-Dīn considered the rule of justice and equality among his subjects as his ideal and aim, proving to be ahead of his time in implementing them, and, according some historians, laying the foundation of the true greatness of Lebanon. Due to his ambitious policy of openness and to economic growth, and the build-up of a homogeneous society, Fakhr al-Dīn's surpassed all his predecessors and all other governors of Bilād al-Shām. As his successes were not devoid of independent aspirations on both political and economic levels, they were soon to arise the suspicions of the Ottomans.

In fact, the Ottomans did not tolerate the independent overtones of Fakhr al-Dīn's policy, and the Ottoman Sultān deployed a large land and sea military contingent against the Ma'nite emir, with the participation of the *wālīs* of some cities. Since Fakhr al-Dīn was unable to confront a force of such technical and military superiority, he decided to abdicate and surrender to the *wālī* of Damascus. He was taken prisoner to Constantinople, where he was condemned to death in 1635.

Fakhr al-Dīn is credited with furthering the vision of the modern state, in the true sense of the word. He was a pioneer in formulating the Lebanese presence, a concept which, after him, disappeared for a long period from the annals of Ottoman history along with any serious attempt at regional autonomy in the area. For the Druze community his passing away ushered the beginning of an era of political decline culminating, later on, in an internal split between Yamanite and Qaysite clans.

## The Political Decline and the Civil Wars of 1840 and 1860

Internecine rivalries and struggles considerably weakened the Druze community and when the last Ma'nite emir died in 1697, power was ceded to the Qaysite Shihāb family. However, the struggle for power persisted until the beginning of the eighteenth century and was resolved, in 1711, by the Qaysites' victory in the Battle of 'Ayn Dāra, which upset the existing balance of the Lebanese feudal system. Following their defeat, many Yamanites left the Shūf district and settled in the Mountains of Hawrān, which, later on, bore the name of the community – that is, *Jabal al-Durūz* (Mountain of the Druze).

As the Shihāb Emir was consolidating his power in Lebanon, the number of local Sheikhs was considerably increasing. The emergence of new clannish rivalries led to the split of the Qaysite clan itself into two opposing factions, the Yazbakis and the Jumblattis, a division that still exists today and forms the ground base of the two main Druze political parties in Lebanon.[3] The Shihāb emirs exploited the internal conflicts within the Druze community to sustain their own power, despite being themselves subjected to continuous pressures from the Ottoman authorities. In 1764, the Shihābs, and all the members of their clan, converted to Christianity and became Maronites, thus paving the way for an imminent civil war.

Emir Bashīr Shihāb II acceded to power in the last quarter of the eighteenth century. His first action was the liquidation of the Nakad Sheikhs clan with the assistance of a number of Qaysite parties, before proceeding to weaken the Yazbaki and Jumblatti parties. In 1825, he inflicted a severe military defeat on Sheikh Bashīr Jumblatt, who was exiled and later on executed by the *wālī* of Acre.

Meanwhile, Bashīr Shihāb II concluded a profitable alliance with the governor of Egypt, Muhammad 'Alī Bāshā, who had snatched Egypt's independence from the Ottoman yoke. By supporting, in 1830, the military campaign of Ibrāhīm Bāshā (the eldest son of Muhammad 'Alī Bāshā) for the occupation of Bilād al-Shām, Bashīr Shihāb succeeded in becoming the sole, unchallenged, ruler of Lebanon.

The Egyptian forces were initially welcomed by the Lebanese, but problems arose when Ibrāhīm Bāshā decided to impose heavy taxes on the Druze, as well as compulsory military service and total disarmament. Revolts broke out against both Ibrāhīm Bāshā and Bashīr II and, along with this dangerous situation, there arose a crisis in Druze–Maronite relations.

Granting lands under the reign of Emir Fakhr al-Dīn II – a practice that extended until after his reign – contributed to deepening the economic and social gap between the Druze and the Maronites, a situation that carried in its roots the seeds of a civil war. Furthermore, the political conflict that erupted in Mount Lebanon by the turn of the nineteenth century took on confessional dimensions following Emir Bashīr II's decision to conscript his Maronite subjects in Ibrāhīm Bāshā's army. Moreover, foreign interference added fuel to the conflict.[4] While the British supported the Ottomans, hoping to increase their influence in Istanbul, the French were trying to gain a foothold in Bilād al-Shām by supporting Muhammad ʿAlī Bāshā. In 1840, while the British were encouraging all Lebanese, including the Maronites, to revolt, Ottoman troops managed to regain control of Syria. Bashīr II was then forced to surrender to the will of the Sultān and the British, and to go into exile.

These actions undertaken by the emir Bashīr Shihāb II, and the Egyptian military occupation of Syria, shook the roots of the feudal structure of Lebanon and at the same time amplified Druze–Maronite animosity. In addition, Bashīr II's efforts to undermine the political power of the Druze community seriously impeded the prospects of a united, independent Lebanon, whose foundations were laid in the reign of the Emir Fakhr al-Dīn II.

Despite the defeat of Bashīr II and his exile, tensions and strife persisted unabated between the Druze and the Maronites and the Ottomans exploited them to further inflame the situation in order to assert their control over Lebanon. In 1841, a ferocious and bloody civil war broke out between the two communities, providing the Ottomans with an opportunity to establish, in 1842, a system of dual rule known as *al-qāʾim maqāmiyatān*, dividing Lebanon into two districts or administrative regions: one Druze, and the other Maronite. However, this badly conceived, inconclusive partition, which left Maronite concentrations in the Druze district and vice versa, led to more violent conflicts and confrontations. Apart from its confessional aspect, those confrontations took on economic and social dimensions, with Maronite farmers trying to achieve their emancipation from the Druze feudal yoke. These disturbances resulted in the disintegration of the large Druze landholdings and dealt a fatal blow to the Lebanese Emirate.

This civil war engendered results of catastrophic dimensions to all Lebanese communities and, in its aftermath, had an enormous impact on the country. Although considerable, internal factors – that is, the confessional and economic rivalries between the Druze and the Maronites – were not enough to justify the severity of the war, nor its scale. The interference of foreign powers, once again, exacerbated the conflicts, with the British supporting the Druze and the French supporting the Maronites. The blazing fires of violence reached their climaxes between 1858 and 1860, mostly affecting the Christian communities. The intervention of French troops in support of the Maronites, who were initially defeated, expedited the collapse of the Druze feudal system and 1860 became the end of Lebanon's first political entity.

The Druze–Maronite confessional conflict only came to an end when, under pressure from the European powers – mainly the French – the Ottoman Empire reunited the two *qā'im maqāms* of Lebanon into one administrative region known as *mutasarrifiyya,* under the rule of a governor who would be, by mutual consent, a non-Lebanese Christian. The new administrative set up, in which the Druze had only a limited number of posts, ensured the political and economic ascendancy of the Maronite elite. The prominent Druze families, while accepting this Christian dominant position, managed to hold their ground and, in spite of this reversal, Mount Lebanon remained calm and the two communities lived in peace for two and a half centuries.

Beginning with 1860, Lebanon witnessed an intellectual renaissance promoted by foreign Christian missions. In particular, the Anglo-Saxon Protestant missions founded the present American University of Beirut in 1864 and the French Jesuits the Université S. Joseph de Beyrouth in 1875. The Druze took an active part in this renaissance, particularly in the fields of literature, languages and the sciences, as well as in the development of the journalistic media.[5]

## The Period of the French Mandate

During the First World War, the Ottoman Empire allied itself with Germany while France and Britain supported the Arab revolt against the Ottoman rule. During this period, Lebanon went through some dark days and was the scene of confrontations between various parties to the world conflict. The Druze suffered the afflictions of this war and a number of them took refuge in Syria, in Jabal al-Durūz. In 1918, Sultān Bāshā al-Atrash, scion of a prominent Jabal al-Durūz family, became the first Druze leader to enter Damascus alongside the Allied troops. At the end of the war, the Druze strongly supported the idea of an Arab government in opposition to the proposal of a British mandate in Damascus and a French one in Beirut. Druze leaders and the intellectual elites expected that Faysal's government would overturn, in their favour, the balance of power in Mount Lebanon. They expressed their desire and willingness to create an independent Lebanese state, which would guarantee them the range of freedoms they long enjoyed in several periods of their past history, especially during the Ottoman rule. But Faysal's Arab government (1919–1920) fell under allied European pressure and came to an end with Faysal's defeat in the Battle of Maysalūn in 1920. Consequently, Syria and Lebanon were subjected to the authority of a French Mandate.

To the Druze Muwahhidun, the mandatory French administration of Mount Lebanon was a new form of Maronite hegemony backed by French power. The mandatory power subdivided Syria along regional and confessional lines into small statelets and in the same vein and logic carved out "Greater Lebanon" by annexing the littoral and the Biqāʿ valley to Mount Lebanon.

Mount Lebanon, the historical homeland of the Druze, became the centre seat of this new state. The Druze elite were convinced that the French had created Greater Lebanon under pressure from the Christians and to their interest, and that this new state, regardless of its size, had been designed to provide a permanent framework for Maronite supremacy. In fact, the Druze lost more of their political autonomy to the benefit of the Maronites, and the only governmental post officially allocated to them was that of *Qā'm maqām* of the Shūf – that is, a minor administrative post.

The policies of the French Mandate provoked general discontent among the majority of Syrians and Lebanese. The partitioning of both countries revealed a lack of prudence and understanding in its execution. Moreover, the administrative measures undertaken by the mandatory authorities denied the local authorities any margin of autonomy in the conduct of their own internal affairs as it resorted to appointing senior French commissioners holding exclusively full authority. An accumulation of a sense of oppression, and a feeling of injustice and humiliation, resulted in the outbreak of the great Druze revolt in Jabal al-Durūz. The spark that inflamed the revolt was delivered by a French forces assault on the house of Sultān Bāshā al-Atrash, where a Lebanese Shi'i, Adham Khanjar – wanted by the French authorities – had taken refuge. The Druze rose in an armed revolt against the mandatory power, which lasted from 1925 to 1927. But their uprising was brutally and fiercely put down by the foreign authorities, and the Druze were compelled to accept remaining under French rule and to rein in their nationalistic fervour.[6]

However, between the two World Wars, and despite all odds, Druze individuals continued to join various nationalistic parties working for Lebanon's independence. The outset of the Second World War opened the way to independence, as the strains of the war began, by 1941, to hamper the authority of the French Mandate in Syria and Lebanon. The Lebanese Constitution, adopted in 1943 by the Lebanese government despite the opposition of the mandatory authorities, recognized the confessional plurality of Lebanon, and consequently allocated the seats of the National Assembly and higher governmental posts between its authority.

On 11 November 1943, the French mandatory authorities decided to arrest the leaders of the emerging Lebanese state: the president of the republic, Bishāra al-Khūrī, the prime minister, Riyād al-Sulh, and several ministers and political leaders, and confined them to the Fort of Rāshiyyā. The Minister of Defence, the Druze Emir Majīd Arslān and a number of other Lebanese leaders escaped the wave of arrests and took refuge in the home of Husayn al-Halabī, in Emir Majīd's constituency of Bshāmūn, where they declared the formation of a provisional Lebanese government. However, British pressures and public demonstrations in Lebanon compelled the French mandatory authorities to release the imprisoned Lebanese leaders, and Lebanon's independence was declared on 22 November 1943. The only martyr to fall in the fight for independence was a Druze called Sa'īd Fakhr al-Dīn, from the town of 'Ayn 'Anūb.

## Notes

1 Louis Cheikho, Bayrūt: tārīkhuhā wa-āthāruhā (Beirut: its history and antiquities), Imprimerie des Pères Jésuites, Beyrouth, 1935 (in Arabic), p. 67.

2 It would be truer to say that the Jumblatt family existed before 'Alī Bāshā Jumblatt arrived in Lebanon.

3 See Chapter 3, on Druze social and communal organization.

4 On this subject, see the text of the preamble to the France–Levant Colloquium held in Lyon, France in May 2002 (Appendix 1).

5 The role of foreign missions in Lebanon, including an analysis of relations between the Druze and the French, is covered in detail in the text of the France–Levant Colloquium, held in Lyon, France, in May 2002 (see Appendix 1).

6 For a fuller analysis of the Druze revolt, see in the text of the preamble to the France–Levant Colloquium, which took place in Lyon, France, in May 2002 (Appendix 1).

# Chapter 3

# Communal and Social Organization

Lebanon is not a secular state; rather, it is a multi-confessional state based upon a confessional political system. This ensures that the Lebanese define themselves, primarily, by their affiliation to a religious community ahead of their affiliation to their country, thus implying that no direct link of citizenship exists between the state and the Lebanese people. Consequently, rights of citizenship are primarily based on the juridical and legal traditions of the various religious confessions of the Lebanese. However, in perpetuation of an Ottoman tradition, the Druze and Muslim communities are considered as part of the state's infrastructure. Therefore, the holders of a number of their religious posts are on the state's payroll, while the Christian communities are not dependent on the state and draw their support from their respective churches.

Before Lebanon's independence, the Druze Lebanese community had no independent organized religious body. The creation of this body was influenced by the legal status of the other Islamic communities and their relations with them.

Following the Lebanese Sunnis being granted the right to form their own council and elect their Grand Mufti, and before the Shiʿis and other Muslim denominations acquired the right to form their own independent organizations, the Druze community managed to ensure the ratification of much legislation overseeing their socio-religious status. Most significant among this was the Law of 13 July 1962, which was the cornerstone of their communal and social organization prior to the promulgation of the new Law of 9 June 2006, the regulations of which were largely inspired by the previous law.

## Communal Organization

As with the rest of the Lebanese religious denominations, the Druze community is officially recognized by the Lebanese state. It is independent in conducting its religious affairs, its religious endowments (*waqf*s) and its welfare institutions. It organizes its own internal affairs and manages its own institutions according to its own religious obligations, confessional prerogatives and communal law, and all relevant rules and laws. Druze affairs are regulated by the laws governing the Druze Community Council (*al-majlis al-madhhabī li-al-tā'ifa al-durūziyya*), the Endowments Council of Trustees (*majlis umanā' al-awqāf al-'āmma*) and the election of the spiritual leader of the community (Sheikh al-'Aql). The laws concerning personal status and the community's judicial system will be dealt with in Chapter 5.

### The New Law Regulating Druze Affairs

#### The Druze Community Council

The 2005 Parliamentary elections held in the aftermath of a major political upheaval caused by the assassination of Prime Minister Rafīq Harīrī, and the compulsory withdrawal of the Syrian army from Lebanon on 26 April 2005, resulted in the "Democratic Reunion" bloc of deputies, led by Walīd Jumblatt, monopolizing Druze representation in the Parliament. The allegiance of the eight elected Druze deputies went to Jumblatt's leadership as all their opposing candidates representing the Arslān faction – headed by Emir Talāl Arslān and former deputy for Rāshiyyā, Faysal al-Dāwūd – lost their bids for election.

The mere fact that all eight elected Druze deputies were affiliated to Jumblatt's bloc (one of them considered as an ally) presented an opportunity to formulate, and subsequently promulgate, a new law organizing the internal affairs of the Druze Muwahhidun community of Lebanon. The relevant law was officially adopted on 9 June 2006 and published in the *Gazette* on 12 June 2006.[1]

The implementation of the new law began on its publication, as it stipulated the abolition of the previous applicable laws and the establishment of a new legal system, partly based on the abolished laws but preserving the unity of the office of Sheikh al-ʿAql. It also specified the mechanism of its implementation – as will be detailed later.

The new law asserted the stipulations of the previous one (Law No. 208 of the year 2000). But whenever the term "Druze community" was used it was replaced by "Druze Muwahhidun community" (Unitarians). The new law retained several of the previous law's texts dealing with the community's independence in running its internal religious affairs and its charity endowments. The sole change was delegating to the community itself the right of legislating its internal administrative systems and running them in accordance with its spiritual rules, religious privileges and all regulations derived from them, on a par with the management of the internal affairs of any other Islamic community regulated by ordinances.

According to the new law, Sheikh al-ʿAql would represent the community in religious matters *vis-à-vis* the public authorities and other religious authorities, and sponsor the community's spiritual and religious affairs and its social interests throughout the Lebanese republic. The law amended the number of the members of the supervisory boards and restricted them to six Sheikhs reputed for their religious knowledge, on condition that one of them came from the retreat houses of al-Bayāda. These were to be appointed by Sheikh al-ʿAql within one month of the assumption of his responsibilities. The law prohibited the appointment of any board member holding family ties with Sheikh al-ʿAql and stipulated that they should be at least 35 years old. They were appointed for a period of three years, open to renewal.

The law also defined the prerogatives of Sheikh al-ʿAql, most significant among them chairing the Druze Community Council, thus restoring the prerogatives curtailed by the previous laws we mentioned herein due to the several citations drawn from their text. Additionally, the law established a permanent administrative body to assist Sheikh al-ʿAql in his official duties.

Concerning the Druze Community Council, the new law reinstated several of its prerogatives cited in the previous law, notably the right to elect Sheikh al-'Aql and supervise the community's religious endowments assets.

The law also reiterated its prohibition of the sale, purchase or mortgaging of any or all of the endowment assets by the council, or the holding of material rights to them, but granted the council the right to exchange or alter the buildings it owned. The law also forbade the council from concluding any contract involving revenues from the endowment assets with any member of the Endowments Committee, or any of its staff members or any person belonging to a body exercising a mandatory authority over it, including the members of the Community Council themselves.

The responsibility of overseeing the affairs of the community was entrusted, by the Law, to the council, alongside the supervision of its schools, universities and associations, and, via the Religious Committee, the overall control of the educational curriculum. The Law granted the council the authority to impose penalties on the community's associations and institutions if it noticed shortcomings in their duties or infringements of laws or regulations.

As under the provisions of the previous law, the council comprised permanent members. They are Sheikh al-'Aql, the current serving government ministers, the current serving and former Members of Parliament, excluding (contrary to the previous Law) the former government ministers. The new addition to the council was the community's judicial body, and two of the sitting members of the Constitutional Council and the High Court.

As for the elected members, the law retained the representation of the same categories mentioned in the previous legislation adding to them one more category – that of chartered accountants.

With regard to the elected members and representatives of the various Druze-inhabited areas in the Communal Council, a new category was added, that of the clerics. Four clerics were assigned to represent the Shūf district, another four the 'Āley district and two for each of the following districts: B'abdā, Hāsbayyā and Rāshayyā. One more member was added to represent Beirut and another the other areas not mentioned in the law. The clerics holding the responsibilities of the khalwāt and the officials of the religious assemblies (*sā'isūn*) constitute their electoral body.

The Communal Council's elected term is six years. At the expiry of this term, if Sheikh al-'Aql declines to call for a new election, then the Communal Council, convenes, de jure, on the first working day following an elapse of 30 days, chaired in this instance by its oldest member.

The Communal Council's elections are held under the supervision of an electoral committee made up of seven members chosen from outside the council, and headed by a retired Druze judge. The Druze Supreme Court of Appeal appoints the committee that becomes the relevant authority for reviewing appeals.

The law added to the required accreditations of any candidate to the office of Sheikh al-'Aql the stipulation that he should have practised his religious duties for a minimum of five years, as per the prevailing tradition. Sheikh al-'Aql cannot be exempted from his responsibilities except upon his own request, or as a consequence of serious matters affecting the dignity and unity of the community or damaging its reputation, or due to health reasons that prevent him from fulfilling his duties, or in case of his reaching the age of 75. Otherwise, his term of office is fixed for 15 years.

At its first meeting, the council elects an administrative council made up of a secretary, a treasurer and the chairmen of the administrative, financial, cultural, social, legal, religious and endowment and diaspora committees. This council is headed by Sheikh al-'Aql.

The law set the number of each committee's members at five for the administrative, financial, cultural and religious committees and three for the legal committee. The endowments and social affairs committees are each composed of nine members all of them selected from the council – including the chairmen of the committees. The law defines the responsibilities and prerogatives of each of these committees. Moreover, an administrative body has been set up for the Community Council and another for the management of the Druze endowments.

The budgets of the council and the office of Sheikh al-'Aql and their administrative bodies are provided for by the state budget of the Lebanese government.

It actually occurred that, within the interim period stipulated by the law – that is, two months from the date of its publishing in the official gazette – and following the reluctance of the (then) deputy Sheikh al-ʿAql, Sheikh Bahjat Ghayth, to hold elections for the Community Council, the Chairman of the Druze community's Supreme Court of Appeal, Sheikh Nuhād Harīz, called for the election to be held and formed a committee to supervise its conduct headed by the retired Judge Sajīʿ al-Aʿwar. On 24 September 2006 the members of the council representing holders of university degrees and free trades were elected in Beirut, alongside the election, in the districts of the area representatives, both secular and religious.

The council held its first meeting on 5 November 2006 and unanimously elected Sheikh Naʿīm Hasan as Sheikh al-ʿAql. Previously, he was a judge in the Druze religious court of Aley. He is a learned and pious man of law, a descendant of a family known for its religious commitment and piety.

The council then elected the members of the board of administration including the chairmen and members of the committees. In the 5th of November 2006 the communal representation of the Druze Muwahhidune was concluded, and the Druze community inaugurated a new era based on a legal foundation and a free election, thus inaugurating a new era of democratic and organizational dealings of its internal affairs in the aftermath of a period of foundering, neglect and chaos.

The passing of the new law, the holding of the election and the setting up of the council's institutions represent an act of abandonment of the old Lebanese formula and the promotion of the Druze community to a new, modern and promising era, which will hopefully deliver benefits to all the members of the community and the country in particular.

### Chronology of the Establishment of the Abolished Community Council

The Druze Community Council was created by the law promulgated on 13 July 1962. Its task was to define and preserve the rights of the

Druze community in Lebanon. It was entrusted with managing the community's secular and financial affairs, representing it in matters related to its social entity, supervising and legalizing the elections of the administration boards of its associations and institutions, and auditing their accounts and budgets. It also intervenes in disputes arising among the executives of these associations and institutions, its resolutions in such cases being final and enforceable. Finally, any purchase or sale of all or part of the endowment assets, and their exchange, mortgage or letting, cannot take place without the consent of the council. Moreover, the acquisition of a firm right or the right of altering a building belonging to the endowments cannot be carried out without its consent. Obviously, the council played a greatly important role in the affairs of the Druze community, particularly on the financial and endowment levels.

The council comprised elected and permanent members representing the community along two different levels: the first comprising university graduates and members of free trades, the second the Druze inhabited Lebanese regions – that is, Beirut, Shūf, Matn, 'Āley, Hāsbayyā and Rāshayyā.

However, this council has been virtually inoperative since the 1970s as a result of internal conflicts, and differences of opinion and interpretations among the various Druze leaders and elites. A number of law proposals were drafted in order to rectify this anomaly and re-activate the Community Council as a reference authority supervising the performance of the Trustees of the Endowments Council, but to no avail until the promulgation of the new law.

## The Council of *Waqf* Trustees under the Previous Law

The Council of the *Waqf* Trustees was established by Law No. 127 of 25 October 1999. While the Community Council controls the management of the Druze community's *waqf* assets and bequeathed possessions, the Council of Trustees is entrusted with the day-to-day management of the *waqf*'s affairs. It lays down the relevant policies dealing with the *waqf*'s assets and the appropriate projects for their development. It proposes beneficial investment plans and feasibility studies concerning the proceeds, costs and profit estimates, and carries out their execution following their approval by the Community Council. It also manages and oversees the services of the *waqf*, invests its resources and appoints regional committees.

The Council of *Waqf* Trustees comprises 25 members appointed by the Community Council. Since the 1970s, and because of the virtual redundancy of the Community Council – whose role is fundamental in the appointment of the members of all Druze foundations and their supervision – the Druze community exceptionally resorted to the assistance of the Lebanese government. Following the promulgation of a special law by the House of Parliament, and in accordance with Decree 1767 issued by the Lebanese government, the members of the Council of *Waqf* Trustees were appointed, on 29 November 1999, by a non-Druze electoral college but with the approval of all the Druze deputies.

Once again, the Trustees Council became paralysed and practically dysfunctional because of the political conflicts and differences within the Druze political hierarchy. Disagreement between the chairman and the director of the council, aggravated by the conflicting interests within the Druze political leadership and external political interference, hindered the work of the council and foiled its activities until the end of its mandate.

Five years after their appointment, the members of the council had not taken up their duties in practice. Moreover, some of their Druze opponents, especially among the clerics, accused the politicians of using the Council of Trustees to lay their hand on the *waqfs*, originally established by a cleric, Sheikh Ahmad Amīn al-Dīn (d. 1224/1809), and before him by Emir al-Sayyid Jamāl al-Dīn ʿAbdallāh al-Tannūkhī, to cater for the needs of the clerics. In turn, the said politicians failed to activate the role of the Community Council as a springboard of all Druze institutions. Consequently, all the community's possessions and bequeathed estates were run, without real consensus, by the (then) deputy Sheikh al-ʿAql, Sheikh Bahjat Ghayth (who was appointed by the late Sheikh al-ʿAql, Muhammad

Abū Shaqrā) on a temporary basis and for a fixed period, until a proper Sheikh al-ʿAql was elected. Sheikh Bahjat Ghayth was assisted by one of the employees of the Druze Community Council, but differences quickly flared up between them and, in turn, with several others enjoying political or religious backing. This situation, unrelated to the civil war and its consequences, reflected the (then) prevailing political climate within the Lebanese Druze community. However, following the promulgation of the new law, the law regulating the Council of *Waqf* Trustees was abrogated and the role of the *waqf*s became dependent on the stipulations of the new law of 9 June 2006 regulating Druze internal affairs.

## Sheikh al-'Aql According to the Old Law

As a result of the Druze community's political division between Yazbaki and Jumblatti factions, the law basically provided for the appointment of two Sheikh al-ʿAqls in Lebanon – one for each of the two factions. Following the death of the Yazbaki Sheikh, Rashīd Hamāda, the Jumblatti Sheikh, Muhammad Abū Shaqrā became, for a long period (and until his death in 1991) the community's sole spiritual leader. The Druze Muwahhidun did not object to this situation as the personality of the Sheikh, his standing and status commanded their respect, in addition to the recognized importance of his role in the contemporary history of the community. Indeed, the Druze resolved, from then on, to have only one spiritual leader. This decision was a positive step towards minimizing their internal political divisions and overcoming them.

After lengthy consultations, Law No. 208 was adopted on 26 May 2000 and amended on 8 June 2000, and promulgated in accordance with the provisions of the Constitutional Council thus annulling the 1962 law, and providing for the election of only one Sheikh al-ʿAql for the Druze community. This law was unanimously accepted to the extent that the Yazbaki and the Jumblatti clans agreed upon a rotation system to ensure the election of a single Sheikh al-ʿAql and sharing the responsibility for his election. According to the new law, as the old one too, Sheikh al-ʿAql enjoys, on a national level, the same respect, rights and privileges enjoyed by the spiritual heads of the other Lebanese religious communities. The candidate to this title should meet certain conditions. Besides being Druze, he must be a Lebanese over the age of 40, and renowned for his piety and uprightness, his commitment to the religious way (Wiseman), the performance of his religious obligations, his exemplary behaviour and conduct, his praiseworthy characteristics, his refined morals and his good social relations, therefore transcending anything detrimental to his religious creed and ethics. He must be a reputed scholar in the spiritual matters, traditions and customs of the Druze. His mandate lasts for 15 years and could legally be extended until he reaches the age of 75.

A council of clerics comprising four Sheikhs assists Sheikh al-ʿAql in his duties, forming a council of five members[2] to oversee the spiritual affairs of the community. On the national level, and in accordance with the previous legal text, the new law granted Sheikh al-ʿAql the same prerogatives of respect, rights and privileges accorded to all the spiritual heads of the other religious communities. He is responsible for everything related to religious affairs, religious rites, holy places and the protection of the Druze clerical status. His prerogatives encompass every area related to the religious affairs of the Druze community. He therefore supervises the management of Druze shrines and holy places,[3] the religious councils, and the study circles and assemblies of religious character. He grants permits for printing and publishing works of religious or doctrinal nature, and prosecutes the offenders in courts. He approves religious education programmes and their implementation before their application. He appoints the persons entitled to practise Druze rites in order to exempt them from military service. He approves the re-registration in the state's Civil Register of any Druze who, having changed his religion, wishes to return to the fold of the community. He approves the composition of delegations assigned religious missions abroad and appoints the representatives of the Druze community in the diaspora. His religious authority applies only to the Lebanese Druze community and has no international dimension, considering that the

Druze communities of the neighbouring countries have their own institutions and Sheikh al-'Aqls (three in Syria and one in Palestine). As for the Druze of the diaspora, they in turn follow the representatives of the Sheikh al-'Aqls of their country of origin.

Sheikh al-'Aql remains, theoretically, an undisputed official authority. Due to residual traces from a Sufi legacy, some Sheikh al-'Aqls are accorded, by their followers and countrymen, a veneration and respect that extends their authority beyond the borders. Such was the case of Emir al-Sayyid 'Abdullāh al-Tannūkhī[4] in the fifteenth century and, more recently, of the late Sheikh Abū Amīn Yūsuf Tarīf, Sheikh al-'Aql of Palestine, and the late Sheikh Abū Hasan 'Ārif Halāwī of Lebanon. The latter enjoyed great moral authority wherever Druze communities resided throughout the world and, to an extent, that made his spiritual authority wider than that of Sheikh al-'Aql of Lebanon. His tomb, in the village of Bārūk (in the Shūf district), has become a pilgrimage destination for the believers. At present, probably only Sheikh Abū Muhammad Jawād Walī al-Dīn, who lives in a kind of hermitage at Ba'aqlīn in the Shūf, enjoys a spiritual authority recognized by the Druze worldwide. He has recently acknowledged the right of a number of Sheikhs known for their piety, godliness and wisdom to wear the round turban, known in the Druze tradition as *tāj al-'arab* (the Arab crown).

This law (no. 208 of 26 May 2000) was also abrogated by the adoption of the new law governing Druze affairs. However, we have referred here to some of its basic provisions which have left – and perhaps continue to leave – their social mark, or which have been retained by the new law.

## The Druze Council for Research and Development

This council was established in 1977 (in the aftermath of the assassination of Kamāl Jumblatt) through a joint initiative undertaken by a number of Druze personalities comprising Walīd Jumblatt, Marwān Hamādah, Halīm Taqī al-Dīn, 'Abbās Halabī, Khālid Sa'b, Nadīm Ma'dād, 'Ādil Hammiya, 'Umar Hamza, 'Adnān 'Arīdī, Akram Hamādah, Khālid Najjār, Sāmī Makāram, 'Abbās Abū Sālih, Walīd Taqī al-Dīn, Anwar al-Khalīl, Makram 'Alam al-Dīn and Majīd Jumblatt. The aim of the council, which brought together personalities of diverse specializations entitled to form a research and working team, was to deal with the difficult situation that prevailed at the start of Walīd Jumblatt's political career, and to confront the smear campaigns to which the Druze community was subjected. The council initiated several projects, among them the census of 1980, and the publication of several books on Druze history, their teachings, customs, traditions, poetry and literature. It also tried to organize the affairs of the Druze of the diaspora through the establishment of a Druze International Council.

### The League of Social Action

The League of Social Action, also known as the League of Druze University graduates, was founded in 1958. It concentrated on providing student grants and loans, and on conducting cultural activities.

### The Druze Heritage Foundation

This institution was founded and funded by Salīm Khayr al-Dīn in London (UK). It is concerned with the revival of the Druze cultural, historic, humanitarian and religious heritage on an academic basis, and has so far produced a number of valuable publications dealing with several aspects of the Druze historic and intellectual heritage.

## Social Organization

Throughout its long history, and to the present day, the Druze social structure revolved around a feudal-type system. Their emancipation from this structure began lately, in the twentieth century. Until then, the Druze relied for their living on agriculture and the largesse of nature, and were uninterested in either commercial or industrial activities. Each village was obedient to the authority of a Sheikh chosen either by the Emir or by the Bey (*bek*), who, in turn, was granted his status by the Ottoman state, backed either by money or merit. The rank and file of the Druze community adhered to an ancient religious system requiring an exclusive obedience to their village Sheikh, an obedience oblivious to any other authority except that of the Emir of the community – that is, the feudal lord. They went to war, submissive to his command as an act, and proof, of their blind obedience. Striking examples of this kind of loyalty were registered in the latest Lebanese civil war. For instance, when Kamāl Jumblatt presented his condolences to the families of men who were killed fighting in the ranks of the Progressive Socialist Party (PSP), the mother of one of the victims assured him that her other three sons were at his service.

As a socio-political sequel of Lebanon's confessional political system, the Druze display to this day an unparalleled obedience to the leader of their community. The Lebanese state encourages this type of clientele-type relationship, since it does not recognize nor define individuals except through their confessional affiliations. The leaders of the religious communities nominate the intermediary or the obligatory channels between any Lebanese citizen and a state institution or procedure. It is therefore in the interest of their community. The authority and respect accorded to the leader of the Druze community emanate from two considerations: a minority complex in the inner minds of some of them, and a residual discipline of a forlorn feudal system. Basically, the Druze leader used to be a military commander, the Emir of the army who would march at the head of his followers to defend their survival or their interests, or to ensure their safety. Second, the leader of the community enjoys a hold on power with all that entails at the level of services or appointments in the state's administrative posts. With only rare exceptions, the government will not accept nominations for any office in the civil service, the judiciary, the army or any other state service, if the candidate's name is not on a list put forward by the leader of the community. In return, the leader retains a monopoly over the provision of public services usually provided by the government, such as the opening of new roads, the appointment of schoolteachers or the transfer of a public servant from one post to another ... In addition to the two factors already mentioned, there is the growing role of the "party" – a veritable electoral apparatus for conducting elections and organizing political demonstrations and events. The steady presence of the party considerably enhances the authority and influence of the leader over the Lebanese Druze community. This dialectical relationship between the government's need for support from the feudal leaders who shortlist the representation of the community, and the feudal leaders' interest in securing their share of power and reaping its benefits explains the insistence of the leaders on participating, in person, in the Lebanese government's depriving others of such an opportunity, except those who owe them absolute loyalty. With this background, we can infer that the social organization of the Druze community in Lebanon is inextricably religious and civil at the same time.

## Religious Organization

Unlike the religious structural organizations of the Muslim and Christian communities, the religious organization of the Druze community is not based on a hierarchy comparable to that of a canon law or Qur'anic shari'a, but on custom and traditions derived from the mystic way commended by their faith. On this basis, the Druze are rated, religiously speaking, between the "wise" (*'uqqāl*) or "spiritual" (*rūhāniyyūn*) – that is, initiated to Druze doctrines – and the "ignorant" (*juhhāl*) or "physical" (*jusmāniyyūn*), who have not yet been initiated to the practice and knowledge of the Druze faith. This stratification also applies to women, whose religious status is equal to that of men. They too attend the religious "Majlis" (council), albeit in a section especially reserved for them separated by a curtain from the men's section. They also have the right to "acquire" their religion – that is, to be initiated and even become women-Sheikhs.

The "wise" persons – that is, those who were initiated or have "acquired" their religion – meet together every Thursday evening at the *majlis,* a locale set for communal prayer. This locale is not exclusively allocated for conducting religious rites and its attendance is not compulsory: a Druze can just as well pray wherever he wishes, as long as his spiritual and religious conduct emanate from a personal endeavour and choice. Each *majlis* has an overseer (*sāyis*) to lead the rite of prayer through three stages. The first stage starts with the reading of preambles, or *muqaddimāt*. This stage is open and any Druze can attend it. The next one is the reading of selected Islamic texts, particularly Sufi texts. This is specifically reserved for certain initiated "wisemen". The third stage comprises a deeper doctrinal study of the doctrine's interpretation. This is attended, exclusively, by the senior "wisemen".

In addition to meetings of the *majlis*, a Druze may devote himself to a spiritual and religious conduct through his temporary isolation in one of the religious retreats or *khalawāt*.[5] It is permitted for the "wisemen" to practise a number of occupations in the educational, agricultural and artisanal fields, and in professions related to medicine and health. However, they are not permitted to receive any payment from the state for their religious role or to take up any public office lest public funds may originate from illicit activities. Their personal dignity and status, their standing and religious faith prevent them from being involved in, or using, any income or procedures suspected of being from a *harām*[6] origin. Nevertheless, Sheikh al-'Aql receives a state salary since his position is part of the state's administrative hierarchy and directly linked to the Prime Minister's office. Under the authority of Sheikh al-'Aql is a complete administrative body made up of civil servants also on the payroll of the state.

The "wisemen" can be distinguished from the other Druze by the white turban, the *laffa*, they wear on their heads, their black gown and their long beards, whereas the women Sheikhs wear a white headcover and a dress known as a *saya*. The "wisemen" who work in private institutions are not compelled to wear religious dress, thus allowing them to wear the garment required by their jobs. The uninitiated can join the ranks of the "wisemen" after successfully passing, after a lengthy period, a very difficult test centred on self-control and repression of physical passions and material desires until reaching a stage of self-torture, though this rarely happens since whatever harms the body is forbidden; the body is, in Druze teachings, the vehicle of the soul. As an example, smoking is considered one of the passions to be controlled and any cigarette smoker looking for initiation should give up this habit. Some wisemen or initiates choose chastity and virginity even after marriage as a form of self-torture. The testing period for new initiates may sometimes last more than a year – until the Sheikhs are certain of their readiness to have access to their doctrinal truths.

The conduct of this path is a free choice taken up on the individual's own initiative; his promotion along the religious hierarchy depends on the personal perseverance and endeavour, as well as the intelligence and personal and social conduct of the initiate, or *juwayyid*. Being the heir of a religious man does not, ipso facto, entitle him to become a religious man. Requesting initiation remains a decision completely based upon the candidate's personal free will. No minimum age condition is set for the initiation, but the candidate must have attained at least the age of reason enabling him to take a decision based on his free will, his full awareness and resolve. However, candidates for the post of Sheikh al-'Aql must be at least 40 years old.

Apart from Sheikh al-'Aql, another seat of spiritual power has emerged currently represented by two Sheikhs known as Sheikh al-bilād. Druze throughout the world consider them as true spiritual leaders, wielding power and authority substantially larger than those of the Sheikh al-'Aql. They are Abū Hasan Ārīf Halāwī, who lived in Bārūk, and Abū Muhammad Jawād Walī al-Dīn, still living in Ba'aqlīn. They are distinguished from other Sheikhs by a particular type of turban, the *laffa mudawwariyya*. After the death of Sheikh Abū Hasan 'Ārif Halāwī, Sheikh Abū Muhammad Jawād Walī al-Dīn granted the right to wear the *laffa mudawwariyya* to two scholarly Sheikhs: Sheikh Abū Sa'īd Amīn Abū Ghinām from 'Armūn, and Sheikh Abū Yūsuf Amīn al-Sāyigh from Shārūn. A fourth Sheikh also wore the *laffa*, Sheikh Abū Sulaymān Hasīb al-Sāyigh from Ma'sariyyatī.

## Civil Organization

In the seventeenth century, the Druze were divided into two parties: the Qaysees, and the Yamanees. In the aftermath of the Battle of 'Ayn

Dāra in 1711, the Yamanees emigrated to Jabal al-Durūz in Syria, while the Qaysees split into two factions: those who supported the Jumblatt family formed the Jumblatti party; and those who supported the al-ʿImād family, led by Yazbak Ibn al-ʿImād, formed the Yazbaki party. Thus, the Jumblatts and the al-ʿImāds of Bārūk pioneered the creation of political parties in the country. Although these political groupings were in fact feudal coalitions, the Lebanese, across their various divisions and confessions, accepted them as their first political structures. Besides the Druze, the two parties included members of all other confessions. And up to the Lebanese civil war, it was not unusual to notice the support of some communities in Mount Lebanon, particularly the Christians, to one or the other of the two parties as a heritage from the days of the Lebanese Emirate. Even today, some Christian families in a number of villages firmly uphold their Yazbaki or Jumblatti political allegiances.

These days, the Arslān family heads the Yazbaki faction and the Jumblatt family the Jumblatti faction. From the day he is born, a Druze inevitably belongs to one or the other of these two factions depending upon his family's allegiance. His loyalty to the leader of the party is absolute and extends to the political leader's family, making the worship of the leader a widespread practice among the Druze. The Druze consider their political allegiance as a second identity and elevate it to the level of their family or village identity. They often treat it as a personal matter without questioning the rationale of belonging to this party or the other. Political competition between Yazbakis and the Jumblattis, a legacy of the feudal traditions, gives the Druze an affiliation reference complementing that of his family or village. However, this sense of allegiance to one of the two traditional parties petered out recently and became marginal, especially among the educated elite.

It is worth noting that the Yazbaki and Jumblatti parties are not based on different, conflicting ideologies. Kamāl Jumblatt attempted to create a political party based on Socialism, but the Druze managed to turn his party into a Jumblatt-ist grouping, giving more importance to the "leader" than to its ideology or political theories. The situation is the same with Emir Talāl Arslān and the Democratic Party he recently founded. Nevertheless, some Druze, moved by liberal and secular ideas, found a niche for themselves in other non-confessional parties such as the Syrian National Party, or the Communist Party. Despite such political differences, the Druze Muwahhidun proved, more than once, their ability to overcome their internal divisions and form a united front whenever the existence of their community was threatened.

In addition to their political allegiance, the Druze social organization revolves around their family and village – two interrelated and complementary affiliations. A Druze belonging to a particular family also belongs to a particular village. As most families are linked to one another by marriage, alliance or allegiance, it is possible for any Druze to trace a family relationship, as distant as it may be, with any other member of his community. Besides, the belief in the eventual reincarnation of every Druze soul in the body of another Druze strengthens the blood ties among the members of the community. Consequently, claims of high profile among Druze families are irrelevant since any member of the community can be reborn into any other family.

With the Druze, as is the case with other religious confessions, the family is not simply an emotional tie. It is, rather, the supporting base of each one of them: through it he becomes known and introduced in his lifetime. No matter what social status an individual may attain by virtue of his education or profession, he remains identified by his kinship and the family name of his birth as "the son of so-and-so", and by the village of his origin, as being from "such-and-such a house". These facts remind us that differences in blood ties and places of origin have a decisive impact in the Druze community. The most prominent families in the highest Druze social and historical ranking are the Nakad, al-ʿImād, Talhūq, ʿAbd al-Malik, Jumblatt and Arslān families. However, other families are beginning to emerge from outside the feudal sources, resulting in the evolvement of a Druze community gradually leaning towards democracy and overlooking its traditional ties to its historical and social hierarchies.

Every Druze has a distinctive place and special role within his family where the wife plays a central part. Besides the responsibility of bringing up the children, she shares with her husband the responsibility of formulating all the important decisions concerning domestic and family issues. However, being brought up in a society where the man plays the role of guide, instructor and conductor, she is called upon to play her part without disputing the idea of a patriarchal hierarchy within the family.

Children represent the future of the community and are treated equal to each other, regardless of gender. Boys and girls enjoy the same educational opportunities, although priority may sometimes be given to boys in families with limited means. The children's attachment to their families, their respect and loyalty to their parents, are matters of fact, and many families are supported by their children, whether they work in Lebanon or abroad. Young people make an important contribution to the dynamism of the Druze community on both the social and cultural levels, as well as in the area of charitable activities. Furthermore, the elderly occupy a prime place in the Druze society. They are treated with respect and care within the household, and by their children and grandchildren.

## Notes

1 Official newspaper, 30, p. 3515, 12 June 2006.

2 Once again, we find the number five, which is so important in Druze symbolism (see Chapter 4 on traditional Druze culture and the meaning of 'Īd al-Adhā for the Druze).

3 See Chapter 1 for the religious and social buildings of the Druze community.

4 For a biographical note, see Chapter 6.

5 See Chapter 1 on the religious buildings of the Druze.

6 The use of any possession illegally acquired and religiously prohibited.

# Chapter 4

# Traditional Culture and the Meaning of the *al-Adhā* Feast

By the end of the nineteenth century, the Druze community had greatly benefited from the intellectual renaissance in Lebanon. Many Druze excelled in several scientific, commercial and literary fields, opening up to the outside world and actively participating in Lebanon's daily life and contemporary concerns. Nevertheless, most of Lebanon's Druze remained attached to their own traditions and customs, a phenomenon particularly noticeable in their rural agglomerations in Mount Lebanon especially within their religious circles. The initiates (*'uqqāl*) – that is, the religious men of the community – remain the true guardians of the Druze heritage and traditions, and hence of the Druze identity per se. Due to their esoteric mystic doctrines and their firm set of values, the Druze preserved many of the customs and patterns of their traditional lifestyle. The religious communities in the villages of the Mountain (not implying they do not exist in the cities too) reflect this cultural aspect more than the urban communities, and provide a model of past Druze society and its traditional values.

## The Seven Pillars

The Druze doctrine, as formulated by Hamza Ibn 'Alī in the eleventh century, exempted its followers from abiding by the bonds of the seven pillars of Islam. At the same time, though, it calls upon them to understand their intrinsic meanings since they define the Druze (Unitarian) Tawhīd faith and its spiritual precepts as well as the relations between the members of the community. Therefore, the pillars constitute the basis of their society and ensure its cohesion.

Hamza ibn 'Alī teaches his followers that the pillars of Islam cannot be correctly and fully observed without following their true meaning (as follows).

- Truthfulness of the tongue, or truthfulness in word and deed and constant faithfulness to truth is the true meaning of prayer.
- Protection of the brethren and their assistance, in their presence or absence, and the ethics of friendship are the meaning of almsgiving.
- Abandonment of the worship of nothingness or falsehood – that is, the renunciation of the pre-monotheistic doctrines that lead the devotee astray from his path – means protecting the heart from polytheism.
- Repudiation of evil spirits and tyrants by avoiding involvement with the followers of other creeds, preventing the Druze from attaining the divine truth.
- Declaring the Oneness of God almighty, that He is the One and Only God worthy of worship, and denying any partner to Him is the meaning of the dual testimony (*shahādatān*).
- Complete satisfaction with God's will is the meaning of satisfaction (*jihād*) and delivery (*wilāya*).
- Complete surrender to the commands of the Almighty, in good and bad times.

## Internal Solidarity

Sheikh Abū Muhammad Jawād Walī al-Dīn, the most eminent Druze Sheikh in Lebanon, compared Druze society to that of bees and depicted several aspects in common among them, mainly in their social organization and hierarchical structure. He also emphasized the part played by each and every member of both "societies" (Druze and bees) in maintaining harmony within their community and, in particular, the respect and reverence the leaders of their communities enjoy. Sheikh Walī al-Dīn also liked to emphasize the fact that a bee does not instigate injury against anyone, but once attacked it relentlessly pursues the aggressor, even at the cost of its own life.

Druze history – interspersed with several military encounters with foreign powers fought for the sake of protecting their territory, liberty and independence – clearly illustrates this phenomenon of systematic response to any external aggression. It is the doctrinal result of the second pillar of the Druze faith, requiring the protection of the brethren, mutual support and solidarity among all the members of the community. This pillar also conveys a clear call for the mobilization and general conscription of the community *vis-à-vis* any threatening danger. It may be claimed that this self-defence instinct is shared by all minorities, as their survival and steadfastness is only possible through the solidarity and cohesion of all their members without exception. This co-operation and mutual support among the Druze is apparent on several levels and extends to various aspects of their social life, traditions and customs. Moreover, many institutions run by the community are based upon this principle and cater for its needs thanks to its remarkable social aims. First among them are hospitals, schools and orphanages.[1] In addition to the social services mentioned, Druze values, traditions and customs focus on the depth of the ties binding the Druze together and recommend solidarity, cohesion, self-preservation, the continuity of the community and the safeguarding of its future.

## Mutual Respect Among Individuals

The Druze Muwahhidun are among the most appreciative and respectful people towards each other and towards anyone considered to be a representative of the body and heart of the community. In their lifetime, they bestow on the family a special status, especially on women and the elderly – that is, all those who embody their life, their continuity, culture and identity. If the family represents the future of the community, the woman is the heart of the family and plays a basic role in raising the children and in running the affairs of the household. She consequently enjoys the respect of her husband and children. Similarly, respect for the elderly is manifested partly by the due respect shown by the children to their parents and partly by the esteem shown to the prominent members of the community, this being a necessary attitude for every Druze. The prominent members of the community are those to whom attaches a significant dignity due to their age, and especially due to spiritual and intellectual prominence that commands the respect of the community. Those characterized by these qualities of personal conduct, humility, faith, piety and godliness are primarily the religious men considered to be the best guardians of the Druze identity. They are prominent not by their religious rank but by their wisdom, knowledge, learning, principles and demeanour.

## Attachment to Traditional Activities and the Roots of the Community

Throughout their history, the Druze relied on very simple means for survival and continuity, preferring craftsmanship and working the land to being involved in commerce or industry. In their mountainous regions they formed agricultural communities and – when needed – warring communities. They devoted their time to land cultivation, cattle raising, bee keeping, sericulture and working in stone quarries to build their homes with their own hands, and to weaving silk for their clothes and so on ... all of them traditional activities still currently practised by the Druze inhabitants of the mountains.

Despite this attachment to the land and simple subsistence activities, the Druze Muwahhidun actively participated in the intellectual and social renaissance of contemporary Lebanon. Thanks to the educational opportunities provided by the foreign missions, schools and institutions in the nineteenth century, an elite group was educated and constituted a class of politicians, intellectuals, artists and writers.[2] Moreover, the Druze, like members of other Lebanese communities, also benefited from emigration and accumulated fortunes that they invested in companies, industrial and commercial ventures, thus participating fully in the economic, industrial and commercial life of Lebanon.[3]

Currently, most of the Druze who remained in their villages still practise crafts and traditional activities linked to their land. The Druze of the Diaspora, who developed commercial activities, and those who belong to the cultural elite, in addition to those who have attained political or intellectual status, remain deeply attached to their roots and land. Their main concern when they emigrate or live abroad, remains building or owning a house in their village, and the amount of money they invest for this purpose reflects the strength of their attachment to their roots and identity, even if they are convinced that they will never be able to return and live in their (original) home. Their presumption remains that if they will not personally live there, it will belong to their children or future generations after them. Even now, a number of villages in Mount Lebanon, dotted with magnificent but empty houses, bear witness to this unwavering attachment to land and roots.

## Community Ceremonies

A number of key events accompany the lifespan of every Druze, from birth to death. The two most important occurrences that regulate the lifetime of the Druze are weddings and deaths. Most social relations among the Druze revolve around these two events and perpetuate themselves through them.

### Weddings

Legal marriage is, by its nature and form, a contract between two willing parties: the husband and his family on the one side, and the wife and her family on the other.[4] The contract is concluded in the presence of witnesses at the bride's family home, or at a community court. In either case, the contract must be registered in court in the presence of a community judge. This contractual aspect of the Druze marriage makes it, from a legal point of view, akin to civil marriage.

However, the marriage ceremonies take different forms according to their location. In a large city like Beirut or New York, a Druze wedding ceremony hardly differs from any other community's ceremony: it has a dinner party a reception, etc. ... But in the villages, weddings retain all the distinctive traditions and customs of the Druze of Mount Lebanon, and follow the same pattern, regardless of a few variations resulting from the social status and financial means of the concerned families.

Generally speaking, a Druze village wedding ceremony proceeds along the following stages: the bride remains in her parents' house, shut in her room, while her parents receive the guests. For his part, the bridegroom celebrates the occasion with his family and friends before accompanying them, in a large delegation, to the bride's family home, laden with gifts and sweets. Upon their arrival, the two families stand in two circles facing one another, exchanging greetings and good wishes. The bridegroom then stands in the midst of the two circles, waiting for the bride's father to arrive with the bride and presents her to him. The couple then take leave of the guests and go to the bridegroom's house. It is customary that the groom's mother does not accompany her son to the bride's family home or even take part in the ceremony. Rather, she stays at home in order to receive the well-wishers who may arrive while her son is away, and to prepare the house and make it suitable to receive the bride.

Wedding traditions in the Druze community may differ slightly from one village to another. For example, the groom's party, before going to the bride's family's home, may organize a *dabka dance* and perform songs especially composed to praise the groom, depicting him as the ultimate bridegroom, the flower of youth and finest of men, continuing with praise for the bride, portraying her as unique in her time ...

## Funerals

A funeral is the utmost expression of the doctrinal and religious symbolism of the Druze Muwahhidun faith. It brands the life of the community with a mark deeper than any other. A funeral does not only involve the family of the deceased, but also the wider family – that is, his whole village. It represents a clear manifestation of the social solidarity among the members of the community. For a Druze, if an absence from a wedding ceremony can be justified, attending every funeral is not just desirable but is regarded as the best expression of his care for the affairs of the community and his sharing in it in hard times.

From a religious perspective, Druze funeral rites greatly resemble the rites observed by all Muslim sects, but still differ from them, on a social level, in a few aspects that make them closer to Christian practices. These similarities and differences substantiate the delineation of Druze individuality.

The prayers recited for the repose of the soul of the departed Druze are verses from the Qur'an following the Sunni tradition, differing only in the arrangement of the verses, their selection and the way of reciting them. Also, the prayer ceremony is longer than the one held by the Sunnis, but the burial procedures bear more resemblance to the Christian practices in Mount Lebanon. The body of the deceased, adorned with his finest clothing and laid in a coffin, is buried in a special chamber or tomb above ground level, although some Druze insist on following the Sunni method of burying their dead in the ground[5] after washing and cleansing the corpse and wrapping it in a long white shroud. At funerals, the religiously initiated Druze men congregate in large groups. Since, in their doctrine, divine rewards are commensurate with hardships, and spiritual and moral rewards are unrelated to material things, they behave with great modesty and asceticism to the extent of refraining even from drinking water throughout the funeral procedures. If they contradict this rule of conduct, they completely lose their divine reward, for their presence at the funeral and their participation in the prayers and all other rites is what brings them closer to God. This conduct emanates from their faith as much as their social solidarity, and their tendency to participate in funerals is greater in the case of simple and modest ones.

The Druze Muwahhidun deal with death in accordance with its spiritual and religious significance. According to their beliefs, death is just a transitory stage towards reincarnation. They believe that the spirit, following the death of its owner, is reincarnated and re-introduced to a new and better life, more pious and closer to God if the deceased person was, in his lifetime, a religious, devoted and wise man. Their belief in this fate means they do not fear death. Even though the passing of a loved one or a relative entails pain and sorrow, the religious men do not recommend shedding tears for them, lest weeping be interpreted as an objection to God's will or a proof of lack of faith and trust in Him. A historical incident exemplifies the degree of firmness Druze piety may reach and the depth of their sincere submission to God, and acceptance of death as Divine Will. In the fifteenth century, 'Abd al-Khāliq, the son of the Emir al-Sayyid 'Abdallāh al-Tannūkhī, was accidentally killed on his wedding day. His father hid the news from his guests and carried on with all his duties as a wedding host without informing them about this dramatic event. Only when they were about to depart did the Emir reveal to his guests the tragic fate of his son in an emotive, soulful speech.

Thus, the Druze express their solidarity and social cohesion by attending their brethren's joyful and sad occasions. As an attestation of the strength of this feeling, they attend most of these occasions and participate in them in great numbers, depending on the importance of the person or the event.

## Religious Life

Typical Druze religious rites are rare, as their doctrine specifically focuses on moral and ethical values and spiritual personal conduct – being a direct consequence of their belief in reincarnation. A steady commitment to high ethical values defines the level of their moral progress or spiritual excellence.

Among the most notable religious practices of the Druze is the congregation of their Sheikhs every Thursday and Sunday evening.[6] During these meetings, the sacred scriptures are read to the benefit of the faithful. The level of these readings and their interpretation progresses throughout the evening to an increasingly advanced state. Therefore, the initiated alone are allowed to remain present throughout the meeting – and then only the more advanced among them. Remnants of Sufi ways are still evident in these gatherings, particularly when the Sheikhs shake their heads in unison with the rhythms of their prayer.

Druze religiosity is, therefore, a matter of personal worship. Each person pursues his initiation into the specifics of the doctrine in his own way, along his own personal tempo, depending on the degree of his openness, the scope of his knowledge and the depth of his piety, and in accordance with the level of his commitment to moral values and his spiritual readiness to live by them. This personal aspect of Druze religiosity is underpinned by the fact that the members of the community are under no obligation to acquaint themselves with the Druze Unitarian doctrine. This knowledge can only be acquired through personal desire and endeavour. Every Druze is free to decide whether or not to attend the prayer meetings in the *majlis* or *khalawāt*. Followers of the faith can only deepen their spiritual knowledge and progress on its path if the more advanced initiates deem them ready and worthy of it. If the non-initiated and the followers of the faith need to prepare themselves for acquiring spiritual knowledge, they do not necessarily have to follow the same pattern. Although the aim of the Druze faith, or Unitarian way, of "knowing God" is one and unique, there are diverse ways of reaching this knowledge. However, the spiritual progress of the Unitarian cannot be achieved unless it is accompanied by ethical and moral attributes. Anything running against ethics and virtue is taboo (*harām*).

God Almighty says in the Qur'an that He is present and close to His subjects, responding to the calls of the supplicant and the imploring of the believers.[7] On this is based the Druze notion of spiritual retreat (al-Khalwa) for worshipping God, showing devotion to Him and trusting in Him, along with forbearance, illumination and seeking the divine path. All these aims spur the believer to surrender his soul, money, children and worldly belongings, in joy and confidence, to the glory of God and closeness to Him. God guides him to the way and draws him to the perpetual light, "the light of heaven and earth".[8] But, deliverance and orientation cannot be dissociated from each other unless the believer hedges them with the praised qualities and sublime ethical standards defined in the eighteenth century by Sheikh al-Fādil:

> The believer must observe God in secret and in public, yielding to Him in all matters, trusting Him with the good and the bad, accepting His punishment, patiently bearing the periods of distress and affliction, praising Him for his grace while mindful of his own sins and shortcomings ... If people are charitable to him, he must remain humble and, if they harm him, he must bear their ill-doing and forgive them.[9]

The description of this way of living is found in Sufi writings. According to the Qur'an, it is the union of light with light, the love dedicated to the beloved, the love reserved to whom we devote sleepless nights for the sake of encountering him.

Those who stay the night vigil rarely sleep. Rather, they join their days and nights in prayer, asking for God's mercy and forgiveness.

Acquiring a spiritual status starts with repentance, and endures with piety, asceticism, poverty and perseverance; it must resolutely lead to an absolute trust in God and a complete submission to Him. This trust in God is a highly important stage in spiritual life and constitutes a very high, and to some extent dangerous degree. According to Sayyid 'Abdallāh al-Tannūkhī, some *'ulamā'*s emphasized the need to love God and exhibit complete confidence in Him, as there is no remission from its contravention, and no escape from death. We may ask God whatever we desire but, on the other hand, we must not be fearful of our inevitable destiny. The highest level of spirituality is, therefore, submission and satisfaction in the delivery. The believers who attain this level live ascetically and austerely and sometimes in poverty in its dual dimensions, material and moral. They emancipate themselves from passions and material desires, disdain worldly glory, wealth and sensory pleasures, only living according to what the right way demands from them, exactly like the early Sufis whom Kamāl Jumblatt describes as follows: "Their clothes are simple and clean. They are aliens to this world even when they are among their peers, neighbours and relatives; they journey in mind and spirit, seeking absolute Truth."[10]

The Druze Muwahhidun doctrines became secret and esoteric as a result of their peculiar nature: they are not open to the rank and file in general, but only to the select who readied and prepared themselves to receive them. That is the reason the *Books of Wisdom* are never printed: to limit their spread and prevent their message from being wrongly interpreted by followers inadequately prepared to understand them. Therefore, the sacred scriptures of the Druze are circulated among them in manuscript forms only. A number of individuals who specialized in copying these texts perform a valuable task in the service of the Druze Unitarian faith, investing in it long hours, great efforts and precious care.

## The Symbolism of Colours and the Number 5

Number 5 frequently occurs in Druze cultural and religious life and is connected with a strong symbolism originally derived from the Druze monotheistic belief in five major cosmic principles emanating from God: the Universal Mind, the Universal Soul, the Word, the antecedent and the subsequent.

The five greatest Druze proselytizers were the only preachers (imams) at the time of the Druze religious advocacy between 1017 to 1043 AD. One of these five great cosmic principles was ascribed to each of these preachers (imams) in sequence of their appearance. Al-Hakīm represented the divine providence at its most radiant and honourable meaning as well as being the source of the doctrine and the virtues. The Druze consider God to be existing and immaculate at the same time, while the advocates of the outworldly (or manifested) – *ahl al-zāhir* – consider God to be only immaculate, and the believers in the inworldly (or hidden) – *ahl al-bātin* – consider Him to be just existing. To the Druze any idea denying either of the two natures of

God is an innovation and a heresy. Hamza ibn 'Alī says, explaining monotheism: "Through monotheism I comprehended all matters. It is through these matters that monotheism is understood. The beginning of religiosity is knowing God, and the perfection of knowing Him is His monotheist system, and His monotheist system is absolving Him from the attributes of the created." That is why the followers of Hamza were called the monotheists, the name dearest to their hearts. They are the followers of monotheism, their religion is the religion of monotheism, their preaching is the preaching of monotheism, and the apogee of monotheism is the infallibility of God, for the Creator is beyond description, perception and definition by names or qualities.

The five colours that make up the current Druze flag are also related to the five imam preachers. Their symbolism is the result of popular beliefs and, in fact, not based on any religious text.

The hierarchical symbolism of the number 5 is as follows:

- The Universal Mind = Hamza = green
- The Universal Soul = al-Tamīmī = red
- The Word = al-Qurayshī = yellow
- The Antecedent = al-Sabīq = blue
- The Subsequent = al-Muqtanā = white

## Eloquence and Decorum (*al-fasāha wa-al-liyāqa*)

The Druze are known for "being extremely courteous, using particular words to express their emotions and convey their thoughts".[11] They value decorum and eloquence as a distinctive form of art, although no religious text commends them or even refers to them, and neither are they part of their folkloric traditions. The Druze take great care in addressing others in courteous and elegant language lest they shock their egos or provoke their sensitivities. Explaining this phenomenon in a simple and elegant way, Kamāl Jumblatt says:

> It must be said that discretion is a characteristic of the Druze Muwahhidun It also is what distinguishes a Druze from any other

person: the Druze does not squander his words. He is always cautious and alert, observing his surroundings in order to assess what can be said, what should be said, and what may or may not be said.[12]

## The *al-Adhā* Festival

The Druze celebrate just one religious festival: the day of *al-Adhā* (although the deeply religious also celebrate the Islamic new year and *'īd al-fitr*).

The Druze celebrate this occasion with prayer, fasting and giving alms throughout the daytime, and studying in the evening. They receive this festival with a full understanding of its meaning, content and purpose. In their view, this event is not simply confined to wearing new clothes and organizing large banquets but is essentially a veritable and truthful pause in the presence of the Supreme One, by which the worshipper expresses his obedience to God and asks for His mercy and Forgiveness.

In the Arab language the word *adhā* means sacrifice – that is, the occasion of offering lambs as sacrifices. The day of *al-Adhā* is the tenth of Dhū al-hijja; it is also called *'īd al-adhā* or *al-'īd al-kabīr* (the Great Festival). At this time, the pilgrims in Mecca sacrifice their animals at Wadi Mina, beginning on the dawn of the tenth day of the month of Dhū al-hijja until dusk of the last days of *tashrīq* (the rising sun) – that is, from the 11th to the 13th of the month of Dhū al-hijja. The said days are called the days of *tashrīq* because sacrifices are offered at the crack of the dawn, and because the meat is cut into pieces and placed in the sun.

The *al-adhā* festival is held as a remembrance of the story of our father Abraham, whose faith was tested by God through a dream in which he saw himself prepared to slaughter his son as a sacrificial offering to Him. Since prophets interpret dreams as signs of a divine revelation or as a direct commendation from God, Abraham and his son willingly responded by obeying God's wish. As they were about to offer this sacrifice, God redeemed Abraham's son with a sacrificial animal, a ram, which took his place. The Qur'anic verses in *Sūrat al-Safāt* report this story in detail and reveal that Abraham intended to sacrifice his son, said to be Ishmael, from whom the Arab Prophet is a descendant.[13] *Al-adhā* is the believers' reminder of the blessings of staying close to God, and of the need of sacrificing to attain this status and gain God's mercy and forgiveness. The believers are urged to draw conclusions from this episode and perform good deeds that will bring them closer to God, such as presenting sacrifices, distributing meat to the poor, giving alimonies, offering charities to the destitute and passers by, and always praising God for his grace and for all He provides to humans as a means of livelihood and self-preservation.

## The Meaning of *'īd al-adhā*

To the Druze the *'īd al-adhā* feast assumes an importance and value similar to the importance of *hajj* (the pilgrimage to Mecca) for the Muslims. Muslims seek to complete their religiosity by observing the seven pillars of Islam[14] once they reach the age of physical and mental maturity, free will, discernment and full ability – the conditions required for progressing along the path of God. The believer loses all the benefits of performing the rite of pilgrimage if he fails to observe the other pillars of his religion, therefore the pilgrim is keen to fulfil the three requirements of *ihrām*.

The *ihrām* requires reaching a state of full devotion to the *hajj* rite, starting with abstaining from practising a number of otherwise allowed practices. Anyone practising *ihrām* should, first of all, purify his intention and elevate it, true pure and sincere, to God Almighty in his endeavour to be united with him. Second, he must obey God's commandments for being truthful, avoid everything prohibited and show this intent by throwing, out of the window, stones symbolizing his will. Finally, the pilgrim takes off the garment of ignorance and disobedience and puts on the robe of humility, submission and obedience, thus allowing his endeavour to worship his Creator on the eve of the festival, devoid of any selfishness. He silences his deep ego, and his loud desires implore God's favour, mercy and forgiveness, seeking, with all the clear conscience and firmness of faith that he has acquired, the renewal of his covenant with God Almighty and his commitment to Him by ascending the levels of faith without recidivism, doubt or hesitation. He must also be inspired by the grace of mercy, forgiveness and pardon to offer his Creator all he owns: his spirit, his body, his material possessions and his children. This alone would prove the pre-eminence of his ethical standards and the meaning of his happiness, and would guarantee his deliverance in this world and the hereafter.

The symbolic meaning of *ihrām* is materialized in the practice of specific behaviours. In Mecca, the pilgrim wears just a white robe, as this is the *ihrām* – a symbol of eliminating human differences and appearing as equals before God. This is the meaning of "taking off the garment of ignorance and disobedience and putting on the robe of humility and obedience". The pilgrims also throw stones at Satan as an indication of their deliverance from sins and material desires. This is the meaning of throwing the stones of one's own will out of the window.

During the pilgrimage to Mecca, as during *'īd al-adhā,* the Muwahhidun (Monotheists), whether Muslims or Druze, look forward to God and direct themselves to obey Him with a sincere intention, covenanting with God and strengthening their will to pursue their striving along the path leading to the Creator. The secret of this monotheistic effort and the inability to limit or weaken it or shed doubt on it, resides in man's perception of it as an ascension of the eternal soul labouring in its striving towards God, in defiance of the ephemeral body, basically not worth considering or preserving. This certainty illuminates the dark and desolate way the believers tread in their quest for a true knowledge of God and for his encounter. It represents the most trustworthy link in the chain of light (that is, the spiritual Miraj road to God and the various cycles preached by any prophet) and doomsday (that is, reaching God in conclusion of the final circle or cycle of human history).

Thus *'īd al-adhā* in its Druze understanding equates to the significance of the pilgrimage to Mecca to Muslims in general. In its turn, Islam kept alive the memory of *al-adhā* and consecrated it as an annual duty or religious obligation. Like all monotheistic concepts that evolved throughout the centuries until the dawn of Islam and then the formulation of the Druze doctrine, the meaning of *al-adhā* also evolved from being an ordinary religious and social ritual to becoming an utter truth. Druze monotheism emphasizes the deep meaning of the duty or obligation a Druze must fulfil throughout his lifetime and his human endeavour whose purpose is to attain the knowledge of God. The Druze eternally committed to the mysticism of his faith by covenant or charter is exonerated from all doubt and absolved from polytheism and oppression.

## *Al-'ushūr*

*Al-'ushūr* are the ten days preceding *al-adhā* – that is, the first ten days of the month of *Dhū al-hijja*. The Druze celebrate these days by holding religious gatherings and evening meetings devoted to preparations for the Great Festival, and this by concentrating on repentance. On this occasion prayers, intercessions, sermons, poems and religious verses are recited, accompanied by the distribution of donations and "zukats" (alms). Throughout Al-ushur many Druze abstain from eating and drinking and rein in their desires and wishes out of respect for, and the sanctification of, these blessed days. Moreover, on this occasion the members of the community remember the Day of the Last Judgement, for, according to Druze teaching, that event will coincide with *'īd al-adhā*. The community's men of religion spend the eve of the festival, until dawn, in contemplations and prayers. The main distinctive mystical conceptions of the festival are: first, obedience and sincere submission to God; second, repentance, forgiveness and sacrifice – that is, relinquishing evil thoughts and desires, and worldly lusts, money and material things in order to come closer to Almighty God and deserve His consent.

To the Druze Muwahhidun the *Al-'ushūr* and *al-adhā* festivals symbolize the spiritual endeavour of several lives brought together in the space of a few days – the ten days that precede al-Adha – with all the exertions resulting from a sincere struggle towards a fixed aim or objective. They also represent the preparatory and introductory stage of the experience of absolute happiness with the encounter of the Creator. In itself, the *al-adhā* festival symbolizes Judgement Day and represents the final objective – reaching God. It is this happiness that constitutes the real festival, a happiness uniquely reached through active endeavour, knowledge and constant striving. The men of religion emphasize these points and consider the festival an annual occasion for renewing their repentance and awareness of the presence of God while awaiting the Day of Judgement. The advent of the festival day brings with it joy, gaiety and good tidings, loudly proclaiming the inevitable judgement in which the believer will find rest and true happiness and reap the best and richest good things, while the disobedient unbeliever will be full of regret, weeping in sorrow over every evil and sin he committed. The Druze greet each other during the festival by saying: "May God consider us as acceptable observers of the feast."

### The Commentary of Emir al-Sayyid Jamāl al-Dīn 'Abdallah al-Tannūkhī

We end this chapter with a commentary from Emir al-Sayyid Jamāl al-Dīn 'Abdallah al-Tannūkhī, explaining the *Books of Wisdom* for the benefit of his contemporary Druze while simultaneously attempting to define the meaning of *al-'ushūr* and the festival of *al-adhā.*

> Here is the festival and its *'ushūr*, time for obedience, blessings and grace.

The tongue is the father of all the great sins and a fracturing tool whose cracks no splint can mend. Thus the worshipper should absolutely guard it from lying. Nothing like honesty embellishes the tongue and the human being ... Honesty should shield him from false promises. Humans are bound by their promises, and breaking them is akin to lying.

The eye was created for the use of the worshipper in contemplating God's wisdom, might and creations, and for his guidance in darkness and his assistance in times of need, and his observance of the wonders of the kingdom of earth and heaven and for taking into account the signs they contain as a means of reaching their creator.

The ear is intended for his use in hearing the wisdom of the Creator, attending to it, listening with awareness to the right and true, for the ear is the funnel through which audible words are absorbed by the heart. So beware of filling it with anything disturbing to your heart as it is subject to ailments similar to the ailments of the eye if not worse ... Be among "those who listen to the Word and follow the best meaning in it" (Q39:18). Guard it from listening to heresies, slanders or obscenities, or from being involved in delusions or evil talk or mendacious accounts about others, for it was created for you to hear the word of God, praise be to Him, and the wisdom of His Messenger and His faithful ones ...

As to the hand, it should be exonerated from dealing with illicit money, or harming any creature, or betraying a trust or a safe-keep, or writing what cannot be orally mentioned – for the pen is the other tongue and should be safeguarded like the tongue ... the hand should not be outstretched to reach anything forbidden, nor fully extended to what is permitted. Do not hinder it from giving or keep it clenched to hold back your generosity. Do not stretch it out to seek anything but God, and use it to help your brethren in need ...

As to the feet, avoid their use for purposes other than intended by God Almighty – ignoring God's blessing by excessively riding instead of walking is tantamount to blasphemy. The least to expect in this instance is the weakening of your strength perhaps permanently. Use your feet to visit the sick, attend funerals and help your brethren in need whenever you are able to do so. In short, your feet should be used to your benefit, not to your disadvantage ... Guard your feet from taking you to a taboo (haram) or to knocking on the doors of the ruler (Sultān), for unnecessarily knocking on the doors of the rulers is a sin. It means showing humility and respect for them whereas God has commanded (you) to shun them. Having recourse to them enhances their mastery and supports their oppressiveness. If resorting to them is an answer to their request, it is a step towards the forbidden ...

The stomach should be kept from indulging on the forbidden or suspected. Only the permissible should be sought after and, if found, seek not to eat it to a full stomach. It is mandatory for Muslims to request only permissible food, worship and learning, while eating forbidden food is like building on manure ... It is also forbidden to eat food from an endowment without the permission of the donor.[15]

The heart, the source of all feelings and senses, has the rightful duty of disavowing any corrupt ideology, malignant intentions or deluding thoughts in order to remain enlightened by faith and monotheistic beliefs. Such a total obedience to faith shall certainly generate benevolence, happiness and "Baraka".

Let us all enter the open doors of repentance. Let us examine ourselves and make these blessed days wholesome leaven for the rest of our life. Let us try to make them days distinctive from our ordinary days, and forgive those who have offended us and bring joy to the heart of a sufferer or the needy by way of a visit, or a present or a gift of money, and refrain from sleeping until we assess our deeds and repent of wicked thoughts and evil deeds ...

When we achieve gradual progress in our knowledge, and commit ourselves to sincerity in pursuance and behaviour, we shall undoubtedly be certain that the essence of the (Adha) festival is to do everything that satisfies our lively conscience and, consequently, pleases our Creator. This is not at all a temporary seasonal happiness, nor a passing enjoyment of the refuse of an ephemeral world, nor the passion of a soul that is leaning away from the Truth.[16]

## Notes

1 See the section on the social structures of the Druze community in Chapter 1.

2 See Chapter 6 on the cultural development of the Druze community.

3 See The diaspora and the cultural development of the Druze community in Chapter 6.

4 See the section on personal status according to statutory law, Chapter 5.

5 Some traditions are not generally followed by Muslims. These traditions go back to the Sufi concept of not attaching any importance to the body after the departure of the spirit, so prayers are recited over the soul of the deceased.

6 In Islam, the new day begins at sunset, so Thursday evening is the beginning of Friday, which is a blessed day. Muslims start this day with prayers and intercessions, and recitation of the Qur'an. As for the Druze, the preaching of their religion began on 1 Muharram AH 406, which was a Friday. The Druze also mark Sunday evening and Monday for political and doctrinal reasons: the preaching of the religion continued thoughout 409 until 1 Muharram 410, which was the end of a Sunday and the beginning of a Monday.

7 See Q2:186: "When my servants ask concerning me, I am indeed close (to them): I listen to the prayer of every suppliant when he calleth on me: let them also with a will, listen to my call, and believe in me; that they may walk in the right way:, and Q11:61: "To the Thamud people (we sent) Sālih, one of their own brethren. He said: 'O my people! Worship Allah: ye have no other god but Him. It is He who hath produced you from the earth and settled you therein: then ask forgiveness of Him, and turn to Him (in repentance): for my Lord is (always) near, ready to answer.'"

8 Q51:17–18 and 24:35.

9 Quoted from 'Ārif Abū Shaqrā, *Thalātha 'ulamā' min shuyūkh Banī Ma'rūf* (Three sages from among the sheikhs of the Bani Ma'rūf).

10 Kamāl Jumblatt's preface to Sāmī Makārim's work *Adwā' 'alā maslak al-tawhīd* (Lights on the Druze spiritual way), Beirut, 1966.

11 Kamāl Jumblat, *Pour le Liban*, Paris, Stock, 1978, p. 84.

12 *Ibid.*, p. 91.

13 The name of Ishmael is not mentioned in the Qur'an nor that of Isaac, but just as in the Torah, what God says is "your first-born son". The name of Ishmael occurs in later Islamic narratives.

14 It is usually said that Islam has five pillars, which are expanded to seven in the texts of jurisprudence. They are: the declaration of faith, prayer, fasting, almsgiving, pilgrimage, *jihād*, and doing what is good and preventing what is evil.

15 Ajjāj Nuwayhad, *Al-Tannūkhī, al-amīr Jamāl al-Dīn 'Abdallah*, Beirut, Dār al-Sahāfa, 1963, pp. 151–157.

16 From an unpublished study by Mu'assasat al-'Irfān al-Tawhīdiyya, *Kayfa nahyā al-'īd wa-'ushūrahā*.

# Chapter 5
# Civil Status Law

Every religious community in Lebanon is independent in the exercise of its own civil status law. The Druze law was published on 24 February 1948 and defines the particulars of its members in matters related to their civil status, which differ from the status of the other communities, including, of course, the Muslim ones.

The Druze civil law covers, among other things, all legislation related to wills and inheritance and is based (and has been since the historical beginning of the Druze community) on Qur'anic texts and the clear and unambiguous meanings of its verses. However, the conception of these Qur'anic regulations was revised as their application evolved in conjunction with the necessities of their time and environment. In all aspects of its application the Druze civil status law draws on studies and interpretations (Ijtihād) based – albeit with mild variations – on other Muslim schools of jurisprudence – the Hanafī, Shāfi'ī, Mālikī, Hanbalī and Ja'farī schools – accredited in Lebanon and the Arab countries. The said studies and interpretations are part and parcel of Druze daily and family life, and have infiltrated their social customs.[1]

Today, the Druze Communal Courts supervise the application of the 1948 law confirming that any matter related to Druze civil status falls within their jurisdiction. All other matters outside this area of law and its application remain under the jurisdiction of the Lebanese civil and criminal courts. This applies to all religious communities in Lebanon.

Alongside examining certain aspects of the civil status law in this chapter, we will briefly elaborate on the judicial structure of the Druze community in Lebanon.

## Druze Civil Status

Paternity and maternity are matters of special and exceptional importance because of their legal basis and social dimensions. The Qur'an refers to parents in 18 verses, mothers in 28 verses and fathers in 112. These verses outline the main legal basis defining the principle of motherhood, and hence the modalities of marital life with all its rights and duties. From this principle stems the structure of the family nucleus according to its genealogical line spanning ancestry and descendants.

Drawing on the teaching of their religion, the Druze were keen to update the legal framework of their civil status law, and to define the rights of the members of the family, their obligations and the cases justifying divorce. At the same time, Druze legislation has maintained the principles of older legal systems and traditions that have become an integral part of their lives and personal and social entity. The shortage of their own legal texts resulted in the Druze drawing from the texts of the Hanafi Islamic school of jurisprudence, thereby resorting in the adoption of their own jurisprudence and civil status law to the interpretation of a number of Qur'anic verses.

As an example, the Druze reject polygamy. This tradition, upheld since the beginning of the eleventh century, is embedded in the civil legal texts of the community's law: "Polygamy is forbidden and a husband has no right to marry two wives. If he does, then the second marriage is considered null." The Druze forbade polygamy in accordance with their conviction that married couples should conduct a life in which individual dignity and confidence in their present and future security should be unconstrained by any restriction or impediment. In addition, they believe that polygamy severs the bonds of love and harmony among children, replacing them with envy and resentment. Children should be the fruit of marriage and its fulfilment, as well as the nucleus of the family and its society.

Druze customs and norms, alongside their legal regulations, were certified and established in clear official texts in the civil status law that was published on 24 February 1948. Here are the main headings of its contents.

| | |
|---|---|
| Provisions for marriage | art. 20–22 |
| The instant and delayed dowry (mahr-) | art. 24–27 |
| Alimony | art. 28–36 |
| Separations (amicable separation or annulment of marriage) | art. 37–49 |
| Preparing and provisions (‘idda) | art. 50–53 |
| Custody | art. 54–66 |
| Spending by parents on children | art. 67–74 |
| Spending by children on parents, and relatives | art. 75–80 |
| The principle of enforced isolation and its consequences | art. 119–125 |
| Missing persons and their representatives | art. 126–136 |
| Kinship | art. 137–144 |
| Wills and inheritance | art. 145–169 |
| *Waqf*s (charitable endowments) | art. 170–171 |

Essentially, the desire to strengthen family ties stands out as the basic principle of the law. Numerous provisions, such as those related to spending and the period of a woman's provision (‘idda) after her divorce, confirm Druze society's awareness of the need to protect the family. What follows is an assessment of the spirit and directives of the Druze civil status law, beginning with marriage and divorce, then wills and inheritance, with reference to both religious teachings and civil law.

## Legislation Concerning Marriage and Divorce, According to Druze Teaching

The Druze Emir al-Sayyid ‘Abdallāh al-Tannūkhī delivered to his Druze contemporaries a cultural message in which he enjoined them to fulfil "the commanded condition of the Imam" – that is, a Druze man should be responsible for a Druze woman; he should consider her his equal and share with her all that he owns.[2] Having lived among the people of his community and known their social status, the Emir al-Sayyid noticed that many of them rejected the Imam's text and avoided abiding by its provision, thus ignoring their wives' rights and treating them as unequal despite the Imam's commandment. Since there were no written texts dealing with the question of relations between a husband and wife and the rights and duties of each of them, the Emir al-Tanūkhī took it upon himself to formulate a legal code enjoining justice and equality. This code, rooted in a religious base, became a divine obligation and one of the pillars of certainty, which is the mutual satisfaction and free consent of the spouses. This condition became a must for reaching agreement, harmony, love, affection, forgiveness and pardon between them. In this respect, the Emir drew on a divine command recorded in the Qur'an: "And among His signs He created for you mates from among yourselves, that ye may dwell in tranquillity with them, and He has put love and mercy between your (hearts). Verily in that are signs for those who reflect" (Q30:21).

## Marriage

God Almighty has set up, through his messengers and prophets, the rules of marriage in order to consecrate this institution – that is the family – as the basis of men's relationship to women. Marriage embodies the commitment of both genders to respect their mutual obligations and intrinsically entails the regulations defining their relationship. Without these regulations, both spouses would lose the security net that protects each one of them from the injustice of the other partner or his transgression, and marriage would cease to be a conduit for co-operation and a means of sharing the burden of marital and social life. The Tannūkhī Emir valued marriage and encouraged it for the sake of progenitors and the preservation of lineal descendants and social life. He did not advocate celibacy, nor abstinence. On the contrary, he used to urge those who frowned on marriage to wed, fearing they might succumb to carnal desires, stressing, at the same time, the need to marry one woman only. Monogamy was widely practised before his time, in accordance with the Qur'anic teaching that considers reaching fairness in the treatment of several spouses unattainable. Historical records confirm the prevalence of this tradition within the Druze society. For example, Sālih ibn Yahyā's *History of Beirut* records[3] that the Tannūkhi emirs used to marry one woman only.

The legislations issued by the Tannūkhī Emir requested the newly wed to meet a number of conditions to make their marriage possible and admissible. Included in these are that the husband should:

- have attained the age of maturity – that is, 15 years, but preferably at least 20
- be able to provide the means for a decent standard of living for his family and, if he happens to be poor, wait patiently until God grants him better means
- be well educated and from a respectable family in order to deserve his future wife
- be older than the girl, even if only by a small margin
- be in good mental and physical health, and unaffected by any illness that might preclude marriage.

As to his spouse, in addition to meeting similar conditions, she should additionally:

- refrain from marriage until past puberty by two years so that her mind and discernment are fully developed and ready for the upkeep of her children and running her household
- be in good health, mentally and physically, and unaffected by any illness preventing marriage.

## Marriage Celebration and Relations between Couples

Marriages were required to be concluded and celebrated in the presence of the families of both partners after ensuring that the aforementioned conditions had been met, especially the age requirement. Marriage could not be concluded without the forthright and unconditional consent of the future bride and groom, away from any pressure or compulsion, and in the aftermath of both families' consent. Marriage was also required to be preceded by an agreement on the value of the bride's dowry (mahr), due both at the time and later. The Tannūkhī Emir advised against excessive amounts of mahr, whether the husband was rich or poor. He also recommended that women about to marry a poor husband should grant him the use of their land, without gratitude or compulsion, provided they pledge not sell any part of it or dispose of it without their prior agreement.

According to the Emir's legislation, in order to ensure a marital life based on understanding, harmony, love and serenity, the bride should possess 78 qualities. By way of examples of these qualities, she should be a believer, chaste, devoid of defects, well mannered, polite and patient. She should neither lie nor swear, and should expect to be scolded and ordered if need be. She should be faithful to her husband and caring, too, treating him kindly and gently, abstaining from deserting him in hard times or leaving him in times of poverty, forgiving him if he slights her and staying patient if he was attracted to another woman.

The Emir's legislation commits the husband to similar virtues. He should treat his wife as his equal both in material and religious matters, making her his equal in spiritual matters. He should grant her his trust and respect, treat her in a noble and dignified way, provide her with garments of similar quality to his own clothes, feed her with the same food that he consumes, and avoid burdening her with more responsibilities than she can bear. He should deliberate with her, take her opinion into consideration, reveal to her his secrets and hide nothing from her. He should forsake any arrogant or conceited behaviour in dealing with her. If his wife is illiterate, he should provide her with literacy tutoring, even if this costs him part of his wealth. With regard to properties or material possessions – considered by Druze teachings as ephemeral matters in this world – the married couple should deal with them on an equal basis: if the wife is rich and the husband poor, she should commit herself to co-operate with him, in good and bad times, in order to secure a quiet and happy life for their family.

## Family Planning

The Tannūkhī Emir legislation advised married couples to settle for two children, or three in conflicting cases, or four in cases of extreme necessity. As for the materially poor husband, one child was deemed enough, although he could be permitted to have a second child as long as there was a lapse four years between the birth of his first and second child, which would allow the mother to devote the same level of care to both children. Druze families, especially in Mount Lebanon, continue to abide by this tradition. It may be considered as a widespread popular cultural practice that became deeply rooted in the Druze community.

## Divorce

In al-Tannūkhī's view, divorce was an utter separation of couples properly joined together according to the legal and social requirements of marriage. The Emir recognized the equal rights of both men and women to file for divorce on the bases of the reasons, circumstances and grounds justifying separation. Divorce was warranted when agreement, harmony and understanding between the spouses became impossible and was replaced by conflicts and disputes. The Emir defined the causes and grounds conducive to divorce on the part of the guilty partner.

As for the woman, the reasons that justify her divorce, entailing the loss of half her dowry (mahr) and possessions, are summed up as: adultery, theft, disobedience to the husband; visiting the neighbours without his permission; robbing household provisions to give them away to the neighbours without her husband's knowledge; disgraceful behaviour and violent temper.

As for the man, the reasons that justify his wife's demand for divorce are summed up as: disgraceful behaviour; violent temper;

avarice; oppressive or unjust treatment; requests to carry out acts beyond his wife's capacity; severe beating of the spouse, injuring her and despising her; treating her with arrogance and superiority, boasting about his background and belongings; suffering from madness, leprosy or sexual impotence.

## Marriage According to the Law: Eligibility for Marriage

In its legal and judicial framework, marriage is a contract. To keep it valid, it must be clear of any error, and its contractual parties must possess the required eligibility for getting married or risk the rejection or annulment of their marriage. According to the Druze Muwahhidun doctrine, marriage is not a matter of simple enjoyment or satisfaction of a desire or lust. It is, rather, one of the rules of this existence designed by God to ensure the preservation of the human species and its continuity. Consequently, it should be assumed that the sanctity of marriage derives from the Sharia Law and any flaws affecting any of its conditions exposes marriage to annulment.

First, future spouses must have reached the age of puberty, legally fixed by the first article of the civil status code at 18 for the man and 17 for the woman. There are, however, exceptions and the said law stipulates that the communal judge may grant an adolescent male the right to marry past the age of 16 (art. 2) and a female past 15 (art. 3), provided they can prove their ability to meet the burdens of marriage and have the permission of their parents to wed. The first paragraph of art. 5 cancels any other exceptions to the age limit: "It is utterly forbidden to marry a boy or girl who has not reached the age of 16 or 15 respectively."

Druze legislation justifies these provisions on the grounds that marriage is a contract requiring consent and acceptance by both parties, and upon it rests the fate of the family, and hence of the nation. The validity of the contract is endorsed by the woman's explicit and free expression of her consent, provided she has reached the age of puberty and is in full command of her mental faculties. In the case that she has not reached the required age, or is not fully capable of discernment and choice, her agreement and consent are of no value.

A further restriction denotes the validity of the marriage contract: a Druze can only marry from within his own community, and since the difference of religious affiliation constitutes a legal inhibition, and since the calls to adhere to the faith were suspended in the eleventh century, any new adherence to the Muwahhidun faith is excluded.

## Wills in the Druze Doctrine

The Tannūkhī Emir defined the will as "bequeathing" everything we command to be done. Everything we leave behind we bequeath in our will, either during our lifetime or after our departure. He left to the Muwahid the complete freedom of bequeathing his belongings to a direct or indirect heir, regardless of his being a foreigner or a member of a different faith.

Every Druze has the freedom to dispose of, as he pleases, his money, property and possessions either by way of selling, donating or any other dealing. However, the Tannūkhī Emir requested every person possessing money, property or any other material belongings to write his will as long as he was in good health and in full possession of all his faculties. It might be thought that giving the testator a free hand in deciding his will contradicts the Sharia religious law. But the opposite is true, as the Druze rely in this legislation on one of God's commands: "It is prescribed, when death approaches any of you, if you leave any goods, that you make a bequest to parents and next of kin, according to reasonable usage; this is due from the God-fearing" (Q2:180). This verse, known as "the will verse" is an established verse that has not been abrogated by the "inheritors verses" (Q4:11–14). In this respect, the Druze are in agreement with most Muslims.[4] But the Emir also stipulated that the testator could not bequeath any of his wealth or fortune without first settling his debts and receiving certification for them. He also urged every testator to cultivate in his brothers the practice of charity, so that it would become a habit and a custom.

Since the Emir always abode by what he commanded or stipulated (thus becoming an example to be followed by his brethren), he bequeathed possessions to inheritors unrelated to him – he left in his will a house, parcels of land and part of the olive harvest (and the oil produced on his property) to a Christian family, the Sarkīs clan. He also bequeathed to others unrelated to him, like Sheikh Zayn al-Dīn Jibrā'īl Ibn Nasr. Moreover, he granted his wife and all who read his will – which he prepared a few months before his death – full freedom to utterly and unconditionally bequeath their belongings to whomever they wished. This provision later became part of the civil law passed in 1948.

The Tannūkhī Emir was particularly keen on bequeathing an amount of money to a number of women, as well as a parcel of land to a woman living in Jaramānā, on the outskirts of Damascus, basing his behaviour on the principle of equality between men and women, considering it unjust for a man to leave a woman, after his death, prey to poverty, hunger or exploitation by her kin or brothers. Therefore, the Emir stressed the testator's duty to fairly distribute his inheritance between his wife and children, and promoted equality in the treatment of sons and daughters. According to the Tannūkhī Emir, the testator should not be entitled to write his will before being assured that his wife and daughters were guaranteed their full rights. He took it upon himself to apply this commitment by bequeathing a large part of his property, houses and money, to his wife 'A'isha – the mother of his son who died in an accident on his wedding day – and granting her complete freedom of disposing of them at her will, with the proviso that she administer them with the assistance of pious and sincere men.

In addition, the Tannūkhī's legislation committed the Druze Communal Judges to compensate the losses of women forced to leave their homes or children by granting them half of their husband's wealth.

Several centuries before the West, the Tannūkhī Emir was the first legislator in history to grant women rights equal to the rights of men, and to recognize their equal social status to men by granting them ownership of half their husband's possessions – not to mention granting them the right to divorce and freely bequeath their possessions, and to independence in overseeing the affairs of their homes and families.

## Wills According to the Law

### Their Validity and Formula

According to the Druze civil status law, "difference of religion or sect does not invalidate a will" (art. 151). On the other hand, the law concerning wills is different from the law of inheritance, both in principle and in consequences: "In the absence of a will, difference of religion or sect precludes inheritance".

A will is valid with regard to all bequests, gifts of alms and bequests to *waqfs*, charitable institutions and educational establishments (art. 150).

Druze legislation does not stipulate any specific form for drawing up the will. It is nevertheless required that it is written down in order to preserve the words and customs inherited from past generations, embodied in the civil status law. Custom states that "the testator should prepare a written will [to be kept] close to his head", while the law states that: "The will should remain with the judge, following the establishment of its validity while the testator keeps a certified copy" (art. 158 ff.).

### In Case of the Death of the Beneficiary Before the Death of the Testator (art. 155 ff.)

If the deceased beneficiary has one or more legal heirs, the will remains valid and the share of the deceased beneficiary is assigned to his heir or heirs. If the deceased beneficiary has no heir, his share of the will is revoked and distributed between the other beneficiaries.

### Types of Will (art. 158 ff.)

Druze civil law allows four kinds of will: the will required during the testator's lifetime – that is, the one registered with the communal judge (art. 158); the unregistered will, which cannot be enforced before the judge confirms its authenticity and the need to act on it (*idem*); the concealed will, which the testator keeps in a sealed envelope stamped in the court with red wax in the presence of a judge and signed alongside the judge by four witnesses; and the will drawn up outside Lebanon (art. 161).

### Their Conditions and Requirements

The testator enjoys complete and absolute liberty in determining to whom he will bequeath, and how, without being constrained by any obligation to leave a minimum share to his presumed heirs or to give priority to one of them over the other (art. 148).

However, this complete freedom of inheriting has another aspect: the right of the testator to completely disinherit one of his heirs, since the freedom of giving entails the freedom of depriving too. To avoid this eventuality, other Lebanese religious communities apply the principles of reserved and specific shares, alloting a part of the legacy to the legitimate heirs [by descent] of the deceased.

The will is made up of three elements: the testator, the beneficiary and the legacy. To each of these elements should be added its relevant private and general requirements, which conform with those of other Muslim communities (although they sometimes differ from them).

## The Rules of Inheritance According to Muslim Legislation

If a Druze Mowahid departs without a will, or if his will is annulled by the communal judge, then the provisions of the Hanafī Islamic school are applied (art. 168). In this case, the possessions and fortune of the deceased are divided as follows: one-eighth to his parents, one-quarter to his spouse, and the rest to his children, bearing in mind that daughters receive only half of the sons' share. However, Article 169 of the Druze civil code omits the Muslim provisions excluding certain heirs from inheriting. The Druze legislation, contrary to those of the other Muslim sects, takes into account the principle of representation. In other terms, if a son dies before his father, his share of the inheritance passes directly to his children. By virtue of this provision, the children do not assume the place of their father, but represent him and act on his behalf *vis-à-vis* their grandfather's legacy. This rule was laid down with the aim of ensuring justice and equality, two principles that are currently being seriously considered by other Muslim sects with a view to being adopted in their legislation. A proposal currently considered purports to amend the Druze civil code in favour of substituting the fairer Ja'farī Hanafi religious jurisprudence (Fiqh) to the Hanafī for cases of inheritance without a will (still under review).

Regardless of all these legislations, the power to issue and ratify judgements concerning death and its relevant consequences, or related to the distribution of an inheritance, is solely confined to the Druze communal judiciary.

## Organization of the Confessional Judiciary

The structure of the Druze judiciary body responsible for all matters pertaining to Lebanon's Druze civil status comprises six primary or communal courts (courts of first instance), and one Supreme Court of Appeal.

### Composition and Powers of the Courts of First Instance (Confessional Judges)

The first instance courts in the Druze judiciary body are as follows.

**The Beirut court:** Its seat is in Beirut and its jurisdiction encompasses the muhāfaza (region) of Beirut, North Lebanon, and the (cazas) of Metn, Kisrawān and Jubail.

**The 'Aley court:** Its seat is in the town of 'Aley and its jurisdiction encompasses the caza (district) of 'Aley only.

**The Ba'aqlīn court:** Its seat is in the town of Ba'aqlīn and its jurisdiction covers the Shūf caza (district).

**The Biqā' court:** Its seat is in the town of Rāshayyā and its jurisdiction covers the muhāfaza (region) of Biqā'.

**The Southern court:** Its seat is in the town of Hāsbayyā and its jurisdiction covers the muhāfaza (region) of the South.

**The Metn court:** Its seat is in the town of al-Qal'a and its jurisdiction covers the caza (district) of B'abda.

Each of these courts is presided over by its own communal judge, and comprises an administrative body including a court clerk, a recorder, an usher and a janitor.

### Composition and Prerogatives of the Supreme Court of Appeal

The Supreme Court of Appeal comprises a president and two counsellors. It sits in Beirut and its jurisdiction covers the whole of Lebanon. It has a secretariat comprising a chief clerk, a recorder, an usher and supporting staff. It also has its own administration headed by the president of the court, who has the role and responsibilities of a general manager, and comprises a head of administration, a finance officer, a recorder, a messenger and a valet.

### Actual Features of the Druze Communal Judiciary

The present Druze communal judiciary contains legislation and codes of the highest degree of precision and clarity. Any would-be candidate for the post of communal judge should hold a university degree in Law equal to the degree required from any other civil judge in Lebanon. It is also favoured that he has a diploma from a judicial institute comparable in its organization, training and preparation to the one attended by the state's judges or that he acquires this diploma from the same judicial institute.

The Druze communal judiciary body is a constituent of the Lebanese judicial system, and is regulated by the civil service act. The age of retirement and the end of service indemnity are defined by Lebanese law and set, for judges, at 68 instead of 64. With regard to its rights and duties, the Druze community's judicial body is similar to the regulations governing the state judicial system. In the same vein, the Druze communal courts apply their own procedural law, which is similar to the civil procedural law applied by the state courts in Lebanon. Furthermore, the salaries of the judges and personnel of the Druze judicial system are provided for by the public purse, and legal expenses are collected to the benefit of the public finance.

The Druze communal judges wear religious robes in court, just as state judges wear judicial robes in court. However, the prerogatives of the communal judges and their authority are limited to Druze civil status matters. As an example, they do not have the right to apply their legal authority over a couple unless both spouses are Druze, and they have no authority at all in cases of mixed marriages. A Druze judge from the courts of justice is delegated to the post of Attorney General at the Supreme Court of Appeal and another is assigned the inspection responsibility of the Druze communal courts.

## Notes

1 See Sheikh Halīm Taqī al-Dīn, *Al-ahwāl al-shakhsiyya 'ind al-Durūz*, Beirut, 1981.

2 The text is found in the manuscript Sharh al-amīr al-Sayyid. See the biographical note about him in Chapter 6.

3 The Druze, unlike Muslims, are not polygamous.

4 See Sheikh Hlīm Taqī al-Dīn and Sheikh Mursal Nasr, *Al-wasiyya wa-al-mīrāth 'ind al-muwahhidīn al-Durūz*, with an introduction by Samī Makārim, 1983.

# Chapter 6

# The Diaspora and Cultural Expansion

## The Diaspora

A precise evaluation of the size of the Druze diaspora is next to impossible because of the lack of official figures in Lebanon. However, the Druze diaspora remains an integral part of the Lebanese and Syrian diaspora as a whole, and part of their geographical configuration. Estimates put the number of Druze émigrés at around 100,000. The largest group, about 30,000 of them, reside in the United States of America; the second largest group is in Canada (20,000–25,000) and the remainder are distributed between Venezuela, Nigeria, Australia, Saudi Arabia and the Gulf States.

Most of the United States Druze are the descendants of early waves of émigrés who arrived there at the start of the twentieth century attracted by the "American dream" and the quality of life. These Druze became integrated in the American society to the extent that they adopted American names such as Roger (for 'Ajāj), Ray (for Rāmiz) and Randy (for Ryād).

The Druze community of the United States of America has always been particularly active. In the mid-twentieth century, the American Druze Society (ADS) was founded, with Los Angeles as its base for those living on the west coast and Washington for those living on the east coast. The society elects its president for two-year terms. Every year, on the occasion of the American Independence Day celebrations (4 July), the ADS organizes a conference that brings together Druze families from all areas, trends and venues to debate cultural, social and doctrinal issues. The conference rarely deals with political subjects.

Every year, the conference is chaired by the president elected by the society's members. In 1982, in the midst of the Lebanese civil war, the Druze of America founded the American Druze Public Affairs Committee (ADPAC), which took upon itself the task of factually informing American politicians and media about world Druze affairs. This committee wielded considerable influence on Washington's policy towards the Druze community in Lebanon, especially during the tragic events of the civil war in Mount Lebanon between 1983 and 1984. In 1982 – to the great pride of the Druze community – the President of the United States of America, Ronald Reagan, appointed Mrs. Roosevelt, born Salwa Shuqayr in 'Arsūn (Lebanon) and wife of Ambassador Roosevelt, as head of Protocol in the State Department.

Dynamism in the United States of America is not solely confined to the members of the Druze community. It is, rather, a general trend shared with the Lebanese Christian and Muslim communities, and is owed to the very nature of their emigration. The freedom the émigrés enjoy in their adopted country encourages every one of them, whether of Arab or Middle Eastern origin, to open up, prove his worth and become innovative and creative in his field, thus promoting the formation of scholars and distinguished specialists in several ranges and fields of activity.

The American Druze adapted with ease to the climate of freedom and democracy in their new society and pursued their activities without fear of repression or suppression. They do not hesitate in expressing themselves freely or expose their identity, even when it comes to debating ideological issues. However, it is worth noting that the situation following 9/11 (the attacks perpetrated on New York and Washington on 11 September 2001) and the setback caused by this tragic upheaval created a wave of racial discrimination against the Arabs, and heaped restrictions on the freedom of expression and action in the United States of America. Nevertheless, the programmes and projects of the ADS continued to be an expression of the successful integration of the Druze émigrés in their new society. The ADS publishes two quarterly magazines – *Our World* and *Our Heritage* – and has also launched a website for information and communication.

In Canada the Druze are almost as numerous as they are in the United States of America. According to data provided by the Canadian Embassy in Lebanon in 2002, there are about 250,000 Lebanese in Canada, about 10 per cent of them Druze. Edmonton boasts the largest Druze concentration, and most of Edmonton's Druze originate from West Biqāʿ and Rāshayyā regions, particularly from the town of Yantā, (Caza of Rāshayyā).

In Canada, Arab emigrants owe their integration in their new society to the efforts deployed by Muhammad Saʿīd Masʿūd, a Druze Lebanese who sponsored, with a number of fellow emigrants, the founding of the Arab–Canadian Friendship Association, of which he became president. This position enabled him to promote the Palestinian cause and explain it to the Canadian people, refuting in the process any Zionist claims. While president of the ACFA, Masʿūd had the opportunity to address the Canadian Foreign Affairs committee and publish the Arab–Canadian Friendship newsletter – distributed free of charge to tens of thousands in Canada, the US, the League of Nations and various world parliaments – in which numerous articles were regularly published in support of the Palestinian cause.

In Venezuela, the Druze community thrived as the result of a wave of migrations from Mount Lebanon and Jabal al-Durūz that began in the early twentieth century. The early émigrés were called "Turcos" – that is, Turks, since, at that time and before the collapse of the Ottoman rule of their countries, they held the Ottoman nationality. In turn, they greatly contributed to the defence of the Arab cause and confronted any misinformation and fact-distorting campaigns.

In Australia, the Druze community is mainly concentrated in the south-west of the country. The Druze first settled in the city of Canberra, then spread out to the cities of Sydney and Adelaide. There is also a sizable Druze community in West Africa, especially Nigeria, where their presence is owed to Muhammad Husayn al-Khalīl. Their emigration to Nigeria goes back to the days of the large waves of Lebanese and Syrian emigration witnessed at the beginning of the twentieth century.

In Saudi Arabia, the Gulf States and Kuwait, Druze presence is relatively recent; it began following these countries' invitation to the Lebanese to work and invest in their economies. This emigration was stepped up in the second half of the twentieth century with the growth of the oil industry in the Gulf States. Among the prominent members of the early wave of emigrants were Fu'ād Hamza, who held the post of foreign minister during the reign of the founder of the Saudi Kingdom, King 'Abd al-'Azīz Āl Sa'ūd, and As'ad al-Faqih, who became Saudi Arabia's first Ambassador to the United States of America and Mexico, and its first representative to the United Nations in New York.

In these host countries, the Druze proved highly active within the frameworks of the Lebanese and Arab immigrants' associations; they have been involved not only in the establishment of their own associations and their integration in the host countries, but have also (during the 1960s) played an important role in founding the "Cultural Federation of the Lebanese Abroad" with its base in Beirut. Anwar Muhammad al-Khalīl chaired the Federation, and Tawfīq 'Assāf presided over its Lebanese branch. Both of them played a significant role in organizing the Lebanese presence abroad, unifying the stances of the immigrants and protecting their interests, while taking full account of the interests of their countries of origin. A number of Druze émigrés established organizations in the diaspora countries to welcome their newly arriving compatriots and facilitate the process of integration in their new societies.

## Cultural Expansion: The Druze Contribution to the Nineteenth-Century Scientific Renaissance

### The Protestant Mission Schools

The political and economic stability enjoyed in Mount Lebanon during the regime of the "Mutasarrifia", at the end of the nineteenth century, enhanced cultural, intellectual and scientific activities.[1] Although the Christians laid down the early foundations of this revival, the Druze also benefited from it, courtesy of the schools established by the Evangelical missions in their areas. Leading Druze personalities, sympathetic to a Great Britain hostile to France, encouraged the Protestant missions to settle in Mount Lebanon and protected their representatives from the pressures exerted on them by the Catholic institutions backed by France. Among their most prominent supporters were the Talhūq clan, who provided for the American University in Ra's Beirut the land on which it built its campus, either on a donation basis or in return for a nominal amount. The eldest and most important of these schools was founded in ʻAbay, in 1843, by American missions. It was followed by the establishment of Evangelical schools at ʻAramūn and Btatir in 1853, and Btakhnay in 1854. As an act of encouragement to the school in Btatir, in its first year, the Sheikhs of the ʻAbd al-Malak clan enrolled approximately 20 of their children in its classes. Additionally, the Sheikhs of the Talhūq clan of the Gharb region enjoined Sulaymān al-Salībī to build a school in ʻAlay, which was subsequently completed in 1855. Similar initiatives were under -taken in several villages of the Gharb region, in ʻAynab, Bshamūn, Ra's al-Matn and Dayr Qūbil.

### The Dāwūdia School

By early 1862, Sheikh Saʻīd Talhūq convinced the Ottoman ruler of the Mutasarrifia in Lebanon of the Druze need for new schools. He proposed establishing an institution to teach Arab culture and foreign languages, its running costs to be covered by the revenues of the Druze *waqfs*. He also proposed turning the cloister of Sheikh Ahmad Amān al-Dīn in ʻAbay into a school. The governor agreed to his suggestions and the first Druze school was founded in 1862. It was named the Dāwūdia School after the name of the governor, Dāwūd Bāshā, who oversaw its establishment and entrusted its administration to the *awqāf*.

### The Influence of Schools

The schools established in the Druze areas contributed to the education of the community's youth. However, the graduates of these schools did not follow the example of their fellow Christians in founding new schools, and seemed content to send their children to the same schools they had attended. This resulted in the formation of an educated elite that played a fundamental part in the Arab renaissance in Lebanon in the fields of languages, literature, science and journalism. Among the first graduates of the College of Medicine in the American University of Beirut, in its first decade, were four Druze doctors: Amīn al-Halabī, As'ad Slīm, Yūsuf Slīm and Dāwūd Slīm. Dr. As'ad Slīm became well known for his extensive scientific research and especially for the publication of his book on sericulture in 1899. His brother, Dāwūd, emigrated to North America where he became well known for his research in electrical sciences.

In the field of sciences, the Druze emir Muhammad Arslān became the president of the Syrian Scientific Association, founded in 1847 and then re-established in 1868. One of its aims was the promotion of arts and sciences. This association, officially recognized by the Ottoman authorities, attracted several intellectuals and writers from a number of Arab countries. Outstanding among them were two Druze: Emir Mustafa Arslān and Sheikh Sa'īd Talhūq.

During this same period, the Druze Muwahhidun founded the Association of Public Schools in order to care for the intellectual and educational concerns of their community. Emir 'Alī Nasr al-Dīn became prominent in the field of journalism. He founded, in 1868, the daily newspaper, *Al-Safā*.

## The Druze and the Arab Awakening

The spread of education by the end of the nineteenth century, as a result of the efforts of the foreign missions and the Ottoman private schools, led to the emergence of reformist and nationalist political movements throughout the Middle East. The cultural background of the students of these schools proved to be permeated with political orientation. The educational programmes adopted by the French mission schools ensured employment and jobs, first and foremost for the Christians, in the administrative bureaucracy of the Mutasarifia governorate. The Druze sent their children either to Protestant schools, or public or private Ottoman Islamic schools. Consequently, the educated Druze elite was not alien to the Lebanese intellectual renaissance. Lebanon experienced a political awakening mainly in connection with the sensitive issue of its role within the Ottoman Empire. This political awakening took two forms: first, the demand for political reforms within the Ottoman Empire; and second, a pan-Arab national awakening calling both for a revival of the Arab cultural heritage and for independence from the Ottoman state. The Druze took a clear stand in favour of the fight for independence.

## The Druze and the Arts

The Druze Muwahhidun harbour a kind of sensitivity towards the various forms of art. Their belief in a single transcendental Divine Truth, Creator of all things, prevented them from drawing figures of living beings or material objects, a concept shared with all Muslims and even some Christians. The Druze, therefore, distanced themselves from graphic art not for lack of interest or due to a prohibition, but simply out of reverence for the One and Only God. Nevertheless, a number of artists acquired a reputation in fine arts and calligraphy, such as Sheikh Nasīb Makārim, who became known as "the calligrapher of kings". It is worth mentioning that the Tannūkhīs were also noted for their Arabic and Qur'anic style of calligraphy.

However, the Druze excelled in the fields of rhetoric, poetry and literature to the extent that their talents became proverbial. Even though poetry and the art of storytelling have retreated in our times with the predominance of the modern ways of media communication, they still retain a great popularity among the Druze Muwahhidun and are still widely practised in villages on various special occasions. The subjects dealt with by these arts of expression are largely and intimately related to Druze historical and cultural heritage. In most cases, they are poems of love and longing, or a commemoration of outstanding events in their history, such as battles that confirm their patriotic feeling. This poetic skill is particularly manifested at specific major events that evolve into a stage contest for rhetoric and eloquence in which the subjects are similar although their presentations may differ according to the nature of the occasion. For instance at weddings, the Druze perform *hidā'*, which consists of two improvised verses of poetry praising the bridal couple; these verses are repeatedly echoed by the celebrants throughout the event. If the occasion is a celebration of a political or military victory, then the *hawraba* prevails. It similarly comprises a few improvised verses praising the glories of the victor. At funerals, the Druze resort to *nadb*, a way of mourning the deceased, and expressing grief for the loss in two or three verses.

The Druze also appreciate music with a fine artistic sense. They are particularly known for playing traditional instruments such as the *nāy,*[2] the *rabāba* and the *mijwiz.*[3] The music they play is mostly folkloric. It may be played by solitary shepherds in the mountains, and may add to the pleasures of family evening gatherings to celebrate engagements and marriages, which usually climax with the famous *dabka,* a dance conducted in a large circle to the beat of the appropriate music.

## Druze Areas of Distinction

The Druze benefited from the intellectual renaissance of the late nineteenth century in Lebanon and the emigration movement, which helped, towards the end of the nineteenth century, the emergence of a cultural elite. This phenomenon continues today and the Druze community continuously breeds artists, authors and intellectuals in every field of knowledge, science, politics and business. It will be difficult within the scope of this book to cover all these activities and giving each subject the attention due to it while restricting mention to a limited number of individuals and topics. Doing so will inevitably lead to arbitrary selection or the overlooking of some names or events. Therefore, the attempt to sketch fields in which the Druze excelled, from the nineteenth century until the present, will undoubtedly be incomplete and limited to a number of selected examples of individuals who were outstandingly innovative in a particular area. The list will be representative but not comprehensive, the aim of the attempt being to highlight the scope of the Druze' intellectual and cultural contribution to their heritage, not to highlight some names at the expense of others, and to elaborate on the various topics previously mentioned.

## Law and Politics

Inasmuch as the Druze proved faithful to their historical heritage, they also distinguished themselves in their contribution to Lebanon's political life. Outstanding in this field were: Nazīra Jumblatt and her son Kamāl, Shakīb and 'Ādil Arslān, 'Alī Nāsir al-Dīn, 'Ajjāj Nuwayhad, Majīd Arslān, Bahīj Taqī al-Dīn, Bashīr al-A'war, Tawfīq 'Assāf, Fu'ād Najjār, Marwān Hamādī and many others. The active role of the Druze and their influence on Lebanon's political life is clearly apparent, and the aforementioned personalities held prominent ministerial and judicial positions. However, the political importance of the Druze is currently due, on the one hand, to the political status allotted to them within the framework of the Lebanese political system and, on the other, to the weight of their representatives.[4] The Druze are also particularly active in the fields of law and justice. Among the numerous Druze individuals who have distinguished themselves in this realm are: Amīn 'Abbās al-Halabī (1900–1948), who was one of the first Druze lawyers in Lebanon; and Shafīq bey al-Halabī (1892–1978), who was president of the state's Consultative Council (Shura Council) and who became the governor of the city of Beirut (mohafez) and mayor of the city. It was he who turned it into a "super" council (Mumtaza).

## Economics

Several Druze emigrated to the United States of America, Canada, Latin America and Australia, and then to Africa, Saudi Arabia, Kuwait and the Gulf States. They invested in Lebanon the fortunes they amassed in their adopted countries, especially in the post-independence period, and founded large commercial ventures. In 1951, the first Druze company under the name of the "Modern Lebanese Share Holding Company for Commerce" was established, as the exclusive agent for Pepsi Cola in Lebanon. It was registered in the Register of Commerce in the name of Mr. Tawfīq ʻAssāf. The Druze became actively involved in the commercial, industrial and touristic sectors in Lebanon, initially conducting their activities in the hospitality, banking and industrial sectors. In this respect should be mentioned the endeavours of Tawfīq ʻAssāf (d. 1996) and his business ventures,[5] Najīb Sālha (d. 1980), who ran the Phoenicia and famous Vendôme hotel chains, the Lico company (the Lebanese Company for Industry and Commerce) and the Eastern Media Company, and Rajā Saʻb, founder of the Summerland Hotel.

The Druze knew how to benefit from Lebanon's economic prosperity just as did its other communities. In this realm, they succeeded in making extensive profits, their share of the economic market of Lebanon exceeding their numbers. However, like all other Lebanese, they succumbed to the burdens of the civil war and its aftermath, and lost much of their previous economic weight.

## Radio, Press and the Media

Many Druze also proved gifted and skilful in writing – as a means of expression and a free platform securing a conduit of communication with the others. They left their special mark on the press sector and contributed to the launching of several daily journals. As an example, the poet, writer and journalist Amīn Taqī al-Dīn (1884–1937) contributed towards editing *Al-zuhūr* magazine (The Flowers), ʻAbdallāh al-Najjār (1898–1976) contributed to the founding in Damascus in 1919 of *Al-qalam* magazine (The Pen) and *Al-majalla* (The Magazine), and Halīm Taqī al-Dīn (1922–1984), a former university professor, once nominated president of the Supreme Court of Appeal before being elected to the membership of the Council of Trustees of the Druze Council for Research and Development, published several articles in various journals during the last ten years of his life. It may be the boldness of these articles that precipitated his assassination. More recently, Marwān Hamāda, deputy and ex-minister, is both a prominent politician and a writer of articles in the Lebanese daily *An-Nahār*.

Beyond journalism and media, several Druze individuals contributed, through their substantial initiatives, in the development of the means of communication and networking. In 1928, Salīm 'Abbās al-Halabī (1902–1966) introduced radio to Lebanese homes through the Westinghouse Radio.[6] During the Lebanese civil war, Ghāzī al-'Arīdī, prior to becoming Minister of Information, was the information minister and Director of *Sawt al-jabal*, the radio station set up by the Progressive Socialist Party.

## Academia

Druze intellectuals and writers have filled the pages of newspapers and magazines, and published a variety of books dealing with internal Druze affairs in an attempt to present the true image of their community, as well as cover general subjects. The Druze historical and doctrinal causes remain the primary issues, and many historical studies shed light on them such as: *The Druze: A New Study of their History, Faith and Society* (in English) by Najlā Abū 'Izz al-Dīn, and *Al-tārīkh al-siyāsī li-al-muwahiddīn al-Durūz* (Political History of the Druze) and *Tārīkh al-imāra al-Shihābiyya* (History of the Shihābī Emirate) by Abbas Abū Sālih, a professor at the Lebanese University of Beirut. Druze authors have also written on Druze doctrinal subjects, among them: *Al-taqammus* (Reincarnation) and *Asl al-Durūz wa-mu'taqadātuhum* (The Origin of the Druze and their Beliefs) by Amīn Talī' (1911–1989), *Maslak al-tawhīd* (The Way of [Druze] monotheism, in Arabic and English), *Al-'irfān fī maslak al-tawhīd* (Mysticism in the Druze Faith),[7] *Al-taqiyya fī al-Islām* (Dissimulation in Islam) and *Lubnan fī mahd al-umarā' al-Tannūkhiyyīn* (Lebanon in the Cradle of the Tannūkhī Emirs) by Sāmī Makarim, a professor at the American University of Beirut, head of its Department of Philosophy and Islamic Studies, and a specialist in Sufism. There is also *Al-taqammus* (Reincarnation) and *Mu'jam a'lām al-Durūz* (Dictionary of Druze Notables), and a book on linguistic studies by Muhammad al-Bāshā[8] (d. 2003), who devoted his activities to explaining the history and doctrines of the Druze.

In a society where religious and civil affairs are closely intertwined, Druze writers dedicated their attention to the inter-relation of these two spheres of interest, as Amīn Talīʿ has done in his *Mashyakhat al-ʿaql wa-al-qadā' al-madhhabī al-Duruzī* (Sheikh al-ʿAql and the Druze Communal Judiciary), or Judge Ahmad Taqī al-Dīn (d. 1935) in his legal work *Sharh qānūn al-makhātīr wa-majālis mashāyikh al-qurā* (Explanation of the Law of Mayoralties and Councils of Village Elders). Halīm Taqī al-Dīn[9] was outstanding in his writings on legal and judicial matters, including *Al-qadā' ʿind al-muwahhidīn al-Durūz, mādiyyan wa-hādiran* (Druze Jurisprudence, Past and Present) and *Al-wasiyya wa-al-mīrāth ʿind al-muwahhidīn al-Durūz* (Druze Wills and Inheritance). His book *Qānūn al-ahwāl al-shakhsiyya ʿind al-muwahhidīn al-Durūz wa-awjiha tabāyunihi maʿa al-sunna wa-al-shīʿa* (Druze Civil Status Law and Aspects of its Differences with Sunni and Shiʿi Law) is an excellent comparative study with the civil status laws of the other Arab Muslim communities. Finally, Sheikh Mursal Nasr, president of the Druze communal courts, dedicated his publication, *Al-muwahhidūn al-durūz fī al-islām* (The Druze Muwahhidun in Islam) to proving, through evidence, the profound affiliation of the Druze to Islam.

### In Support of the Arab Cause

Druze intellectuals publicized in writing their support for the Arab cause and elaborated on its merits, prompted by their awareness of their status as a minority with a role and presence in the Middle East, and their deep sense of Arab identity and solidarity with their Arab brethren. Their sense of Arab nationalism clearly emerged from the end of the nineteenth century in the midst of the intellectual and cultural Arab renaissance that swept Lebanon and had a profound effect on their political orientation and their writings. The political writings of Amīn Taqī al-Dīn infuriated the Ottomans and he only escaped a death sentence by voluntarily opting for exile. Also, a number of Druze participated in King Faysal's Arab independent government, which they strongly supported. Among them was 'Abdallāh al-Najjār (1898–1976), who headed the Department of Translation in the Arab government, and Emir 'Adil Arslān, the assistant military governor. Later on, al-Najjār played a vital role in settling the conflicts that arose between the Druze Muwahhidun and the French mandatory authorities. He never relented in his writing about national issues concerning Syria, Lebanon and the rest of the Middle Eastern countries. Beginning with the mid-twentieth century, Arabs' awareness and enthusiasm for their causes were reflected by the strength of their unconditional support for the Palestinian cause. We already mentioned the efforts of Muhammad Sa'īd Mas'ūd in confronting the Zionist propaganda from as early as 1943 and his struggle to promote the Palestinian cause to the Canadian public.

History recalls several other Druze intellectuals who devoted their full support to the Palestinian cause, among them 'Abdallāh al-Najjār, author of *Atrocities in the Holy Land, Asrār al-mu'āmara al-sahyūniyya* (Secrets of the Zionist Conspiracy) and *Inhitāt al-yahūdiyya al-mu'āsara* (The Decline of Modern Judaism), and 'Ajjāj Nuwayhad (1896–1982), originally from Ra's al-Matn, the translator of Martin Luther's book *The Hypocrisy of the Jews* into Arabic (*Nifāq al-yahūd*), and author of *A'lām Filistīn* (Palestinian Notables) and *Fath al-Quds* (The Conquest of Jerusalem).

## Rapprochement with Islam

Apart from their deep sense of solidarity with the Arab nation and its causes, the Druze sought to achieve Muslim unity and unify the Islamic discourse, while maintaining the best possible relations with the Christians. Halīm Taqī al-Dīn worked for consolidating unity among the various Muslim communities, completing the efforts initiated by Sheikh Muhammad Abū Shaqrā. In 1983, Taqī al-Dīn, alongside the Mufti of the Lebanese Republic, Sheikh Hasan Khālid, and the vice-president of the Shi'i High Council, imam Muhammad Mahdī Shams al-Dīn, took part in defining and publishing the Ten

Islamic Constants, a document affirming Lebanon's Arab identity, independence and final status as the homeland of all Lebanese. In the same year, he participated with Marwān Hamāda, 'Abbās al-Halabī and others in the common Islamic prayers of 'Id al-Fitr that were held at the municipal stadium in Beirut.

In the same vein the great historical role played by Emir Shakīb 'Arslān, and the contents of his writings about the Islamic world and the necessity of a rapprochement among its various communities, should be mentioned. He is still highly regarded by all Arabs and Muslims, especially in the Arab Maghreb countries (North Africa) where he played a prominent role in arousing the awareness of the Muslim world to its cause and in confronting the colonization and Westernization plans for the area. His book *Limādhā ta'akhkhar al-muslimūn wa-taqaddam ghayruhum?* (Why Muslims Regressed while Others Progressed?) remains a cultural and revivalist landmark worldwide in its analysis of the reasons behind the crises of the Islamic world.

## The World of Arts and Literature

Representational arts were totally outside the interests of the Druze Muwahhidun until the end of the nineteenth century, when a number of Druze painters and artists contributed to the wealth of the intellectual, cultural and artistic renaissance in Lebanon. At present, even though the Druze, like other Muslims, generally ignore representational arts, some of them, such as 'Ārif al-Rayyis, Wahīb Btiddinī and Jamīl Malā'ib, have earned an international reputation in these fields. Some creative Druze sculptors such as Salwā Rawda Shuqayr have also proved their worth.

Nevertheless, the Druze Muwahhidun prefer the arts of music and poetry. Aside from the popularity of these, many Druzes excelled in both fields and their fame extended beyond their own community and Lebanon. From Shakīb Arslān – nicknamed "the prince of eloquence" – who was elected president of the Arab Linguistic Academy in Damascus in 1938, to Samīh al-Qāsim, a poet of the

Palestinian resistance, originally from Galilee, the Druze became illustrious in poetry. In the field of music outstanding individuals were noted such as Diana Taqī al-Dīn, an internationally known pianist, Farīd al-Atrash (1916–1974), singer, composer, player of the *'ūd* instrument, film producer and actor, his sister Asmahān (1917–1944), songstress and actress, and Jamāl Abū al-Hasan, famous for his classical and orchestral music.

The distinguished writer Sa'īd Taqī al-Dīn was an outstanding novelist, specializing in writing short stories and essays in a highly personal sarcastic style. He was also a pillar of Lebanon's theatrical life. A collection of his works was published in 1969. The writer and poet Nadia Hamadī Tuwaynī also acquired a wide reputation throughout Lebanon, the Middle East and worldwide beyond the frontiers of the French-speaking countries.

## Social Solidarity

We previously explained how Druze doctrines and their Civil Status law emphasize the privileged place of the woman as the core of the family, granting her ample freedom and a wide margin for expressing herself. This aspect of Druze doctrine prompted a number of writers to devote several studies and researches to this issue, among them the unpublished manuscript of Amīn Talī', *Dirāsa hawla la-mar'a al-duruziyya* (A Study on Druze Women). Therefore, it was not surprising to see a number of Druze women involved in social and humanitarian activities, prompted by an awareness of their freedom and equality. An outstanding example is Nazīra Zayn al-Dīn (d. 1976), who founded the first Arab Women's Federation and later became a member of the International Federation. She was also the first woman to call for the rights of women, especially their right to decline wearing the veil (the *niqāb* –the full veil that does not just cover the head alone). Her books *Al-sufūr wa-al-hijāb* (Unveiling and Veiling) and *Al-fatāt wa-al-Sheikh* (The Girl and the Sheikh) played a significant part in preparing hearts and minds for the emancipation of women from many social chains. Najlā'

Sa'b (d. 1971), who participated in the establishment of the 'Abay Orphanage Home and became (for a while) president of the Arab Women's Federation founded by Nazīra Zayn al-Dīn, made a major contribution to the Lebanese fight for independence. When the French mandatory authorities decided to imprison the leaders of the independence movement in 1943, Najlā' Sa'b organized and led, at the head of a movement of women for independence, a women's demonstration lasting for more than 20 days and knocked on the doors of all the Western embassies in Lebanon to present the case for independence. Zāhiyya Salmān also rose to prominence as a result of her work for mothers' and children's care and, today, Anisā Najjār continues to carry the torch in the Mountain, struggling for the welfare and wellbeing of women, while Khūlā Arslān devotes her time to the support of the Druze Orphanage Home.

The activities of these women and their involvement in public life does not exhaust the topic of the role of Druze women. We must not forget that, as mothers, wives, sisters and daughters, Druze women demonstrated their epic achievements throughout the years of the civil war in bearing hardships and pain, suffering the disasters of losing their loved ones and relatives, and supporting the exertions of defending their Mountain and their community.

## Historical Personalities

We cannot conclude this chapter without a brief account of the achievements of a number of prominent and impossible-to-ignore lay and religious Druze community personalities.

### Al-Sayyid Jamāl al-Dīn 'Abdallah al-Tannūkhī (AH 820–884/1417–1476 AD)[10]

Al-Sayyid al-Tannūkhī was known for his compassion and wisdom, and was considered an authority for people of all regions, venues and communities who needed guidance and advice. He had numerous mosques built and restored. He commended reading the Qur'an constantly and correctly, avoiding every forbidden act, practising and encouraging the permissible. He commended the promotion of virtues, the prevention of vices, and abiding by virtuous manners and praiseworthy behaviour. He devoted a day each week to teaching his students, training and preparing them to become preachers in their own villages. The overwhelming kindness that emanated from his gentle nature touched everyone he came into contact with and extended to all religious communities, for he believed that all human beings were the children of God. Although his success, knowledge and good reputation aroused jealousy and rage among mobsters, he never contemplated confronting those who envied him nor opposing them, but rather chose to tour Bilād al-Shām in order to spread his wisdom and familiarize himself with lawyers and scholars. He continued his journeys for 12 years, during which time he gained the respect and appreciation of all who knew him or heard about him. The Emir founded a library filled with valuable documents, containing 340 manuscripts. He also wrote several works, the most famous of which is a book entitled *Sharh al-Sayyid* (The Commentary of al-Sayyid), comprising 14 volumes. Additionally, he wrote an exegesis entitled *Kashf al-haqā'iq* (The Uncovering of Truths).

### Zayn al-Dīn 'Abd al-Ghaffār Taqī al-Dīn (AH 900–965/1495–1558 AD)

The experience, competence and religious zeal of Zayn al-Dīn 'Abd al-Ghaffār Taqī al-Dīn, in addition to his extensive knowledge and wisdom, rank him immediately after Emir al-Sayyid 'Abdallah al-Tannūkhī as a prominent authority. It is known that he explained in a brilliant thesis the theory of the physical and intellectual existence of mankind on this planet according to Druze monotheistic doctrine. Some Druzes consider his theory superior to the theories of Darwin, Lamarck and Spencer. Taqī al-Dīn wrote *Al-nuqat wa-al-dawā'ir* (Points and Circles) and *Mukhtasar al-bayān fī mijrā al-zamān* (A Short Explanation of the Trend of Time), and commented on various Qur'anic verses, especially in his book *Sharh al-shahādatayn* (Explanation of the Two Certificates).

### Sheikh Muhammad Abī Hilāl, Known as 'al-Sheikh al-Fādil' (The Virtuous Sheikh) (d. AH 1050/1640 AD)[11]

He was known as al-Sheikh al-Fādil (the virtuous Sheikh) because of his praiseworthy virtues, his benevolent way of treating others, his advice, sermons, generosity and his loving character. His transcendental zeal and higher level of spiritual knowledge led him to pursue a life of asceticism, piety, chastity and isolation in the mountains, removing himself from the world in order to devote himself solely to the worship of God. Following that period of isolation, al-Sheikh al-Fādil went down either to Beirut or one of the coastal cities of Lebanon, or to Damascus seeking knowledge of jurisprudence, and to improve the recitation of the Qur'an (Tajweed) and the grammar and the study of "hadith". One of his basic aims was the protection of the Noble Book of God from non-believers, making it accessible to the deserving according to their level of discernment and capacity. He adhered to the interpretation of al-Sayyid Emir Jamāl al-Dīn al-Tannūkhī, observing its limitations, exhorting obedience to its directives and emulation of its approach. He urged contentment and subsistence, and warned against indulging and squandering, highly appreciated sublimity and altruism among brethren, friends and relatives, following the example of the ascetics who embarked on their way to the hereafter exclusively wearing blue garments, for wearing black contradicts Islamic ways, while white does not tolerate dirt. He commented on a number of judgements, such as the case of under-age marriage, the man who charges a woman with sin, and the woman who repudiates her family and runs off with an outsider. He advised against announcing his obituary or being buried in a marked grave. He specified the money to be allocated to alms as well as that to be personally owned, and the respect of women.

His best-known works are *Sharh al-khusal wa l-ghurur al-khums al-hisān* (Explanation of Qualities and the Five Distinguished Attributes).

### Fakhr al-Dīn II (AH 998–1044/1590–1635 AD)[12]

Ahmad Amān al-Dīn (d. AH 1224/1809 AD) was well known for his role in reconciling Emir Bashīr Shihāb II and Sheikh Bashīr Jumblatt.

He was much respected by Emir Bashīr, who nicknamed him "the gentle Sheikh". However, a conflict set them apart and intensified with time as Emir Bashīr was scornful of the Druze Sheikhs in general. Following the death of shayhk Ahmad, Emir Bashīr looked for a new Sheikh al-ʿAql who might support him and chose Sheikh Abū Husayn Shiblī. When the latter realized the Emir's motives, he found excuses to decline the office. According to some sources, he even gave up his position as Sheikh al-ʿAql and withdrew into the retreat of Bayyāda, leaving all his property in trust to the Druze community.

### Hubūs Arslān (AH 1182–1239/1768–1824 AD)

This virtuous woman assumed the responsibility of ruling following the death of her husband, Emir ʿAbbās Ibn Fakhr al-Dīn. She governed the regions of the Beirut plain and the Gharb region in a wise and brave way that impressed her rivals. She knew how to confront and contest them, and to deal with everything related to governing and administrating. Civil and criminal courts were under her direct authority. When Emir Bashīr Shihāb II was imprisoned with Sheikh Bashīr Jumblatt and his brother, Hubūs supplied the emir with large sums of money and took care of his family. She then went to Acre to persuade its governor, Ahmad bāshā al-Jazzār, to release the three prisoners in return for the payment of a sizable ransom. This offer allowed Emir Bashīr to return to power, but was soon afterwards ousted again by al-Jazzār and replaced by the two Shihābī emirs Hasan and Sulaymān. Hubūs Arslān accompanied Bashīr Shihāb and Bashīr Jumblatt to Jabal al-Durūz and spared none of her wealth in helping them. It is said that there she confronted the Bedouin who raided the Druze villages and defeated them. When Bashīr Shihāb and Bashīr Jumblatt returned to power, Hubūs continued with her policy of maintaining close relations with them, especially in public affairs. But when Emir Bashīr used the support of Muhammad ʿAlī Bāshā to overthrow Sheikh Bashīr Jumblatt, Hubūs Arslān stood against him and supported the latter. As she witnessed the continuous conspiracies against Sheikh Jumblatt and realized her fate would eventually be similar to his, she decided instead to take refuge in Bshamūn in the year 1823. The Shihābī emir persisted in humiliating her, ousted her from power and installed her son, emir Ahmad Arslān, in her place. He also tried to seize whatever was left of her dwindling fortune depleted by her previous generous payments. Some sources claim that Emira Hubūs died in 1824 succumbing to the suffering and humiliations to which she was subjected by Emir Bashīr, although she had spared no effort in helping him when he was desperately in need of help.

### Khattār al-'Imād (Second Half of the Nineteenth Century)

The fame of Khattār al-ʿImād is due to the heroism and courage he demonstrated when a young man in the ranks of the Ottoman army in its conflict with Ibrāhīm Bāshā. Al-ʿImād went to Egypt where he stayed until 1840. Upon his return to Lebanon, Ibrāhīm Bāshā was in the process of retreating with his army after a crushing defeat, while his father, Muhammad ʿAlī Bāshā, was awaiting him in order to honour him with the finest medals and pompous titles. Muhammad ʿAlī Bāshā occupied Bayt al-Dīn and chose it as his residence. There he established his new government, delegating a high level of authority to Khattār al-ʿImād. This made him very influential and gave him the last word in all matters brought to the attention of the new authority in Bayt al-Dīn.

In a report to his government dated 28 December 1873, the French consul in Beirut quotes him as saying: "Never forget that our sole enemy is the Turkish rule. We have reached the situation we are in because of the Turks. The Christians are our adversaries, but not our enemies. Seek a rapprochement with them, unite with them and never trust a word from any Turk."

### Shakīb Arslān (AH 1286–1365/1869–1946 AD)

We have previously mentioned how Emir Shakīb Arslān spearheaded the early activists working for Muslim and Arab unity, blatantly opposing foreign interference in the Middle East. Emir Shakib was a thinker, writer and activist at the same time. He ultimately became involved in all Arab–Islamic movements and struggles. He studied Turkish, *fiqh* and *tawhīd* with the prominent masters of his time. In

1890, he travelled to Egypt where he met Sheikh Muhammad 'Abduh and the political leader Sa'd Zaghlūl.

Emir Shakib excelled in his outstanding literary style, rhetoric, eloquence and poetic gifts, which earned him the epithet of "prince of eloquence". He was elected as president of the Arab Academy of Science in Damascus in 1938. He has left tens of books and printed works, along with numerous manuscripts, letters and newspaper articles. Among his famous writings are: *Al-mas'ala al-sūriyya* (The Syrian Question), *Limādhā ta'akhkhar al muslimūn wa-taqaddama ghayruhum?* (Why Muslims Regressed and Others Progressed?), *Tārīkh al-futūhāt al-'arabiyya fī Faransā wa-Suwīsrā wa-Ītāliyā wa-al-Jazā'ir* (History of Arab Conquests in France, Switzerland, Italy and Algeria), *Shawqī aw sadāqat arba'īn sana* (Shawki, or 40 Years of Friendship), *Ta'līq 'alā Muqaddimat Ibn Khaldūn* (Commentary on Ibn Khaldūn's "Introduction"), *Hāsir al-'ālam al-islāmī* (The Present Situation of the Islamic world), *Al-wihda al-'arabiyya* (Arab Unity), and *Sīra dhātiyya* (Autobiography). He also left a number of manuscripts, among them: *Tārīkh al-Jazā'ir* (The History of Algeria), *Tārīkh Lubnān* (The History of Lebanon), *Al-fawda al-islāmiyya* (Islamic Chaos) and *Al-nizā' bayna al-'ilm wa-al-dīn* (The Conflict between Science and Religion).

### 'Ādil Arslān (AH 1305–1373/1887–1954 AD)

Emir 'Ādil Arslān was a member of the Qahtani Association created following the collapse of the Arab Forum in 1909, and then a member of the Covenant Association. In 1919, he went to Damascus where King Faysal appointed him as an assistant to the military governor. But he resigned later in order to be appointed political adviser to the Arab Emirate. In 1920, General Allenby, then in Palestine, advised King Faysal to assent to the wish of General Gouraud, commander of the French forces in the Middle East to see the French army enter Damascus, though not as conquerors. Faysal's refusal led to the Battle of Maysalūn which ended in the defeat of the new Arab Emirate and forced Emir 'Ādil Arslān to leave and travel to Europe.

Following his return to Transjordan, Emir ʻAbdallāh, the brother of Faysal and future king of Transjordan, appointed him as head of his government and later on became his personal adviser. But it wasn't long before Emir ʻĀdil had disagreed with the Hashemite king and was forced into voluntary exile in Hijaz, where he joined the great Syrian revolution and was put in command of the Golan front. He was condemned to death three times. When the revolution ended he returned to Europe, where he devoted his time to the support of Arab causes. In 1936, following the formation of a national government in Syria, Emir ʻĀdil returned to Damascus and was appointed ambassador to Ankara. However, the speedy collapse of the national government in Damascus led to his arrest by the French and his exile to Tadmur, in Syria.

Emir ʻĀdil held several posts during his political career. He was twice Minister of Public Education, once Minister of Foreign Affairs and also deputy for the Golan region in the Syrian Parliament. He was twice charged with forming a Syrian government but declined on both occasions. He was twice the Syrian delegate at the international conference on Palestine that was held in London and was then appointed president of the Syrian delegation to the United Nations. He resigned from this post in protest against Arab government policies towards the Palestinian problem and only returned to his native country, Lebanon, when he retired from his political activities. Emir ʻĀdil wrote several books, including his personal memoirs, which were published in three volumes as *Mudhakkarāt al-amīr*[13] *ʻĀdil Arslān*. He also wrote a fourth supplementary volume about 1948 and the loss of Palestine, plus his memoirs about Husnī al-Zaʻīm.

### ʻĀrif Nakad (AH 1304–1395/1887–1975 AD)

ʻĀrif Nakad was a patriot and a man distinguished for his knowledge and creativity. He studied Islamic jurisprudence under the Sheikhs Ahmad ʻAbbās al-Azharī and Hasan al-Mudawwar, and also qualified in law. He was appointed Director of Supplies during the First World War. However, for political reasons, he was subsequently removed from his post by the French in the aftermath of their occupation of Lebanon. In the meeting of 'Aynab,[14] he urged the Druze to adopt a united stance towards the King–Crane commission[15] in support of a declaration of Lebanon's independence within the Arab government of Faysal. He was elected as a member of the Arab Academy of Science in Damascus and then as associate member of the Academy of Science in Iraq. Among his publications are *Al-'adāla fī al-Islām* (Justice in Islam) and *Al-mas'ala al-sharqiyya* (The Eastern Question). Among his unpublished works are *Hayāt Muhammad* (The Life of Muhammad), *Al-harakāt al-lubnaniyya al-thalāth fī 1841 wa-1845 wa-1860* (The Three Lebanese Movements in 1841, 1845 and 1860) and *Al-wilāyāt al-muttahida al-ūrūbbiyya* (The United States of Europe). In the social field, 'Ārif Nakad founded the Druze orphanage in 'Abay, and the Tannūkhī School for girls, also in 'Abay. He renovated the Dawūdī School and provided extensive service to several causes such as the Druze endowments (*waqfs*).

### Sultān Bāshā al-Atrash (AH 1308–1402/1891–1982 AD)

Sultān al-Atrash was the leader, and hero, of the Great Syrian revolt against the French in 1925–1927. He was the first supporter of the struggle for a united Arab Syria when the French Mandate subdivided the country into sectarian provinces. He opposed the French policy in Lebanon and Syria, and called for greater Druze autonomy and the withdrawal of French troops. Naturally, the mandatory authorities ignored his demands. Druze resistance and rebellion slowly began to gain momentum; they reached their breaking point following the arrest of the Lebanese Shi'i Adham Khanjar. He had taken refuge at the home of Sultān Bāshā al-Atrash. This incident became the spark that set the fire of the great revolt in Jabal al-Durūz, as the whole Jabal (mountain) erupted in support of its emir, who considered the arrest of his guest a breach of Arab and Druze rules of hospitality. Sultān Bāshā al-Atrash personally participated in the battles he led to bring about the withdrawal of foreign forces from Syria and its liberation from France, exhibiting a bravery that became legendary. It was he who refused the establishment of a Druze state in favour of a united, independent Arab state of Syria.

### Emir Majīd Arslān (AH 1326–1403/1908–1983 AD)

Emir Majīd Arslān began his political career at the age of 18 and had to amend his birth certificate to be accepted as a candidate for elections. He was elected deputy for Jabal Lubnān in 1931 and held this position until his passing in 1983. He held a number of ministerial posts and his name remains particularly associated with the Ministry of Defence. When the mandatory authorities showed their intention of excluding Druze representation in government – appointed by the French High Commissioner – Emir Majīd declared his opposition to such a government. When the French authorities arrested the Lebanese president, the prime minister and a number of other ministers and politicians in 1943, Majīd Arslān withdrew (with a number of ministers, deputies and supporters) to his stronghold of Bshamūn. They declared the continuity of the legality as opposed to the mandatory authorities,[16] a move that made him the first hero of independence and one of its great symbols. In 1948, he actively and effectively participated in the Palestinian war against the Zionist forces, notably at the Battle of al-Mālikiya. During the armed upheaval of 1958, and despite his opposition to the politics of Kamāl Jumblatt, Arslān opted for the strengthening of the bonds of Druze unity. His son, Talāl, has followed him as leader of the Arslān clan.

### Muhammad Abū Shaqrā (AH 1328–1411/1910–1991 AD)

Muhammad Abū Shaqrā was elected Sheikh al-'Aql of the Druze community in 1949. He was a gifted and charismatic personality and played an outstanding role in the Druze modern history in a dangerous and complex period. His main concern was the unity of the Druze community. He eschewed the splits-and-rivalries game of all parties and clans, which earned him the respect of even those who did not share his views. He proved outstanding on two main levels: first, his revival of the Druze religious discourse; and second, his vital role as a man of institutions, especially by his call for unity between the Druze and the Muslims. He also worked for the peaceful co-existence of various Lebanese communities, especially the Druze and the Christians in Mount Lebanon. It was during his term of office as Sheikh al-ʿAql that the Druze communal courts and the Druze Communal Council – which elected him as its president – were established. He initiated, with a number of Druze personalities, the building of the Druze Community Home (*dār al-tāʾifa*) in Beirut, as well as the health institution in ʿAyn Wazayn, which combined a hospital, a caring centre for the elderly, a nursing institute and a medical college affiliated with the Lebanese University.

### Tawfīq ʿAssāf (AH 1333–1416/1915–1996 AD)

Tawfīq ʿAssāf was a prominent businessman and renowned politician. He emigrated to Venezuela, where he spent 13 years before returning to Lebanon in 1951 to set up a branch of the International Pepsi Cola company. This was the first Lebanese limited company set up by a Druze. In 1956, he founded the Bank of Beirut and Arab Countries (BBAC), and contributed to the economic revival of Lebanon at that time. He also founded several companies in various sectors such as the plastics industry, insurance, real estate, media and other fields of activity. In the political sphere, he was elected deputy for ʿAlay and became the founder of the Ministry of Industry and Oil. ʿAssāf contributed to the drafting of the Tāʾif agreement, being the only Druze representative at this historic conference.

### Kamāl Jumblatt (AH 1336–1397/1917–1977 AD)[17]

Kamāl Jumblatt was a popular leader and both a Lebanese and Arab political figure in the full meaning of the word. This veteran, skilful ideologist and politician was considered by many as the utmost intellectual, politician, and man of knowledge and culture throughout the whole Arab East. Kamāl Jumblatt developed his own philosophy and shaped it around a selected synthesis of thought combining Indian and Greek philosophies, and the Arab Islamic–Druze heritage.

He was deeply acquainted with modern Western culture, a fact that was reflected by his general culture, as well as his piercing intellect, his extensive general knowledge, his urbanity and his humility.

From 1943 to 1956, Jumblatt was elected deputy representing the Shūf region in the Lebanese Parliament, but failed to be re-elected in 1957 as the result of a political conspiracy. In 1949, he founded and presided over the Progressive Socialist Party (PSP), and created in 1951 the Socialist National Front, which peacefully brought down the rule of President Bishāra al-Khūrī in 1952. Jumblatt spent his political career fighting corruption and the perversion of Lebanese politics, both inside the country and beyond it. He ceaselessly called for Arab co-operation, and opposed and resisted Western alliances that prevented the Arabs from communicating with the outside world. He presided over a number of organizations committed to the Palestinian cause. This strong commitment to the Palestinian cause could have been one of the reasons for his assassination.

Kamāl Jumblatt also practised natural and herbal medicine, deeply probing the mechanism of the human body's functions. He prescribed extensive health advice based on natural remedies and the use of wheat herbs in treating many illnesses. The committee for the commemoration of Kamāl Jumblatt's legacy published an index of his writings, which shows the greatness of his contribution in writing introductions, newspaper articles (both in Arabic and French) scholarly works, speeches delivered on national, Arab and international occasions, and his interjections and statements in the Lebanese Parliament and at general political and public events. He also treated topics related to the Progressive Socialist Party, the Socialist National Front and other Lebanese and Arab political parties. Kamāl Jumblatt published some of his works in Arabic and French, including *Gandhi wa-al-ʿālam al-jadīd* (*Gandhi et le nouveau monde*), *Lubnān wa-harb al-taswiyya* (*Le Liban et la guerre du compromis*), *Al-dīmūqrāṭiyya al-jadīda* (*La nouvelle démocratie*), *Farah*, *A-masīhiyya al-ishtirākiyya* (*Le christianisme socialiste*) and *Min ajl Lubnān* (*Pour le Liban*). He also translated a number of works, including *Nashīd al-nūr* (*L'hymne de la lumière*) and

*Al-hayāt wa-al-nūr* (*La vie et la lumière*) by Krishnamurti, and *An nakūn aw lā nakūn* (*Etre ou ne pas être*) by Von Robensky. Walīd Jumblatt is the current president of the PSP and is rightly regarded as a national leader, worthy of being described as "his father's [Kamāl's] son".

## Notes

1 Cf. Chapter 2.

2 Nāy is a musical instrument resembling the flute.

3 The *rabāba* is a stringed instrument with a single string and the *mijwiz* is a wind instrument made of two holed reeds.

4 See the summaries of the autobiographies of Kamāl Jumblatt and Majīd Arslān in the section on prominent Druze historical personalities (pages 110–113).

5 See the note on his life in the section on prominent Druze historical personalities.

6 *Lubnān*: *Al-qarn fī suwar* (*1900–2000*), by Fāris Sāsīn and Nawwāf Sallām (Beirut: Dār al-Nahār, 1999) refers to this initiative as one of the turning points in the modern history of Lebanon and illustrates it with a photograph taken from an advertisement that appeared on the day Westinghouse Radio company was launched.

7 See Appendix 3 concerning the book *Al-'irfān fī maslak al-tawhīd* (*al-Duruziyya*), London: Mu'assasat al-Turāth al-Duruziyya, 2006.

8 See Appendix 8, "Muhammad Khalīl Bāshā, *al-mushi" bi-nūrihi*".

9 See Appendix 2, a personal testimony on Sheikh Halīm Taqī al-Dīn: a man of knowledge, piety and compassionate action.

10 See Appendix 9 for more details.

11 Ajjāj Nuwayhad, *Al-Tannūkhī*, Beirut: Dār al-Sahāfa, 1963.

12 The part played by this emir in the development of Lebanese thought has already been described in Chapter 2. See pages 21–23.

13 Mudhakkarāt are the "memoirs" of 'Ādil Arslān.

14 'Aynab is a village in southern Lebanon.

15 King-Crane commission was a US body investigating the disposition of non-Turkish areas within the former Ottoman Empire.

16 Lebanon was by a decision of the League of Nations under French Mandate after the collapse of the Ottoman Empire.

17 See Appendix 4 for a personal view of Jumblatt.

# Chapter 7

# The Political Role of the Druze from Independence to the Present Time

The Druze and their leaders have been highly involved in, and deeply committed to, Lebanon's political life ever since its independence in 1943. This involvement remained within the context of the international situation and the events witnessed by the Middle East over that period. Because of its sectarian political system and the influence of a number of foreign powers on some of its religious communities (the French influence on the Maronites, for example), the precarious political relations between Lebanon's Muslim and Christian components reflected the implications of all Islamic–Christian conflicts in Europe and Asia. From 1943, Lebanon's history seemed far from being immune to the ongoing conflicts between the various Arab states or regional axes. Consequently, several international events had a resounding and deep impact on Lebanon.

In 1943, the Franco–British conflict over the Middle East set Lebanon on the road to independence. In 1948, the establishment of the State of Israel caused a dangerous upheaval in the political landscape of the Middle East and its deepest effects were felt in Lebanon. As a small, newly independent country with a fragile political system, Lebanon found itself in the midst of a regional and international political storm, instigated by the Palestinian disaster and the urgency of opening its border to thousands of refugees who fled their country in the face of Zionist terrorism. This displacement upset the already delicate demographic and political balance of the country. In 1956, Lebanon joined the axis comprising Saudi Arabia, Iraq and Jordan in opposition to the axis led by Gamal Abdel Nasser's Egypt. This alignment sparked an uprising in 1958 against the rule of the (then) president, Camille Chamoun. The Arab defeat in the 1967 June War and the Israeli occupation of Arab territories[1] encouraged the emergence of a guerrilla movement – the Palestinian Fidāyyīn, which used Lebanese territory as a springboard for its attacks on Israel. In 1970, Hāfiz al-Asad's coup in Syria shuffled the cards anew in the area, particularly regarding the Arab–Israeli balance of power. Lebanon found itself enclosed between Syria and Israel in an extremely complicated and dangerous situation that made it impossible to restore a balance of authority between its various communities or delineate the basis of a genuine power-sharing scheme that would bring about accord and stability. In 1975, the Lebanese system imploded and was ripped apart, dragging the country and its communities into a destructive civil war that lasted 15 years. In accordance with its historical heritage, the Druze community tried, in the midst of this painful schism, to play a role conducive to safeguarding Lebanon's sovereignty and independence on the one hand, and preserving Arab interests on the other.

## 1943: Political Performance

As early as the seventeenth century, thinkers were working at the idea of an independent Lebanon. However, by the year 1943 the Druze were exhausted and politically weak. The conflicts of 1841 and 1860 had undermined their position *vis-à-vis* the gains achieved by the Maronites with France's support. The European mandatory powers were intent on undermining the political power of Islam in the Middle East, to the benefit of the non-Islamic communities. While Iraq, Jordan and Palestine were subjected to a British Mandate, the destinies of Syria and Lebanon were entrusted to a French Mandate. That same year – 1920 – the French High Commissioner, at his Qasr al-Sunūbar (Beirut) residence, announced in the presence of prominent attendants from all Lebanese religious communities the creation of the state of Greater Lebanon. The French gave preferential treatment to the Christian communities, particularly the Maronites, and granted them privileges in the new state's administrative apparatus to the detriment of the remaining communities. The Druze Muwahhidun were not the only party to experience deprivation of strength as they became, like all Muslim sects, the victims of a French policy consecrated by the 1926 Constitution and enforced throughout the period of the Mandate until Lebanon's independence from France in 1943.

The 1926 Constitution stipulated the election of a (Maronite) president of the republic for a non-renewable term of six years. Between the First and Second World Wars, Lebanese political life was dominated by a political feud between two protagonists who were descendants of two traditionally established Maronite families: Emile Eddé, representing the National bloc; and Bishāra al-Khūrī, representing the Constitutional bloc. While the former adopted a pro-French policy, the latter pursued a policy closer to the British who, consequently, supported the idea of an independent Lebanon.

This political division in Lebanon became an extension of old feudal disagreements within the Druze community and of the legacy of the historical splits between the Qaysee and Yamanee clans, and the Yazbakees and Jumblattees. In fact, this division was more of a rivalry between two parties than a sectarian split, as each party had supporters belonging to all the Lebanese communities. Nazīra Jumblatt, the mother of Kamāl Jumblatt, allied herself with Emile Eddé with the hope of resuscitating the idea of the defunct smaller Lebanon, while Majīd Arslān stood by Bishāra al-Khūrī's bloc. In 1936, Emile Eddé was elected president of the republic.

The Second World War indirectly prepared the way for Lebanon's independence. The German occupation of France divided the country between the partisans of the Vichy government and the supporters of the Free French movement led by General Charles de Gaulle. This situation resulted in France losing the initiative of its foreign policy, especially in the Orient. Even its mandatory army was split along the lines of the French internal division. The mandatory authority was drawn into a deep crisis, its prestige diminished and its control over its territory curtailed. This development helped Britain's foreign designs. Benefiting from this shift in the balance of power, its local allies in Lebanon elected Bishara al-Khūrī of the Constitutional bloc to be president of the republic in 1942. Soon his new government, presided over by his friend Riyād al-Sulh, declared Lebanon's independence and full sovereignty, with the support of the British to the detriment of the French.

The new Lebanese constitution reflected the recognition and respect of the pluralistic communal map of the country. It was based on an agreed National Charter trading the Christians' renunciation of the French Mandate for the Muslims' repudiation of their call for Syrian or Arab unity. Although the National Charter was based on a balance of two negatives, Lebanon's sovereignty could not be theoretically ensured without the consent of its dual communities. The journalist Georges Naccache expressed his doubts on the stability of such a balance in an article in his newspaper L'Orient, in which he considered that "two negations do not make a nation".

Nevertheless, this National Charter secured the sovereignty of Lebanon and remained uncontested until the year 1975.

The new constitution stipulated in its article 95 that seats in government and Parliament be distributed along confessional lines in accordance with the demographic weight of each community. Since then, the Lebanese customarily abode by the allocation of the presidency of the republic to a Maronite, the premiership of the government to a Sunni and the speakership of the Parliament to a Shi'i. This implied omitting the Druze from constitutional arrangements, despite their well-known and recognized historical role in promoting the idea of a Lebanese national entity and achieving Lebanon's independence. In the view of Kamāl Jumblatt, the newly independent Greater Lebanon should have reinstated the Emirate (imāra) rather than being a continuation of the 1864 protocols, which brought about the official abolition of feudalism. Jumblatt was disappointed by the new constitution, which gave Lebanon a sectarian representation retaining priority to the Christians. When the French realized that some aspects of the new constitution were detrimental to their interests, they refused to recognize Lebanon's independence. On 11 November 1943, the French High Commission resorted to the arrest of Bishāra al-Khūrī along with his prime minister Riyād al-Sulh and a number of ministers, deputies and officials, and jailed them in the fort at Rāshayyā. He suspended the new constitution and appointed Emile Eddé head of state. Following this dangerous coup d'etat, a violent wave of popular discontent and protests spread through Lebanon. Demonstrations broke out and violent clashes erupted in all the towns and cities – particularly in Beirut – while members of the government who had escaped arrest took refuge in Bshamun, where they declared a provisional government under the leadership of Majīd Arslān. Faced with the broad and deep opposition and protests, the French were forced to give in to the demands of the supporters of Lebanese independence. They released the members of the government and recognized the independence of Lebanon on 22 November 1943.

## The Druze in Lebanon's Political Life (1943–1975)

The political role of the Druze community cannot be appraised independently of the role assumed by its most prominent leader, and martyr, Kamāl Jumblatt. He was a leader of exceptional calibre on political, intellectual and cultural levels. His leadership made it possible for the Druze community to regain its distinctive role in Lebanese affairs in both Arab and international circles. This does not obliterate the part played by other Druze political and spiritual leaders in dealing with the sensitive and critical events of this period, nor the role undertaken by Druze civil society, which showed outstanding vitality and activity during this period.

The creation of the State of Israel in 1948 carried the seeds of the storm that swept the Middle East and eventually fomented dangerous events in Lebanon. Kamāl Jumblatt initially seemed to accept the United Nations resolutions for the partition of Palestine into two independent states – one Jewish and the other Arab. He saw the partition as a temporary or transitional solution that would allow the Palestinians to benefit from the establishment of their state as a base for prolonging the struggle against the Zionist occupation of their land and its liberation by their own means. He also considered that the partition resolution would at least halt the flow of displaced Palestinians seeking asylum outside their occupied land, especially in Lebanon. The refugee issue became a worrying humanitarian concern as a result of the miserable, homeless existence they encountered in the camps in which they were assembled – a situation that still exists today.

Jumblatt was influenced by socialist and leftist currents while studying in France. This led him to found the Progressive Socialist Party (PSP) in 1949, which he based on a more humane socialist philosophy than orthodox Marxism and on principles more likely to be implemented within an Arab or Lebanese social context. Jumblatt envisaged a popular emancipation from the bonds of confessional policies and their schisms, and from the ties of clannishness, along with the family and feudal legacies in favour of the wider scope of the human being and his causes. He hoped to rally support for this cause from all communities and areas in Lebanon.

The PSP played an outstanding role in Lebanon's political life and, along with other parties such as the Syrian National Party and the Communist Party, drew on the overwhelming liberal attitude within the Druze community to initiate a cultural and political movement harmonious with internationalist and nationalist ideologies.

By the late 1940s Lebanon was witnessing an intensification of the internal political feuds and conflicts among its religious communities and main political families. Bishāra al-Khūrī resorted to rigging the Parliamentary elections of May 1947 in order to secure a Parliamentary majority loyal to him, thus allowing him to amend the constitution and renew his mandate in 1948, contravening constitutional principles and Lebanese political traditions.

Opposition to his second term gained momentum and was supported by prominent personalities from various political trends, confessional backgrounds and geographical areas. They were led by Kamāl Jumblatt, Pierre Emile Eddé, Camille Chamoun and Ghassān Tuwaynī. This "white revolution" led to the resignation of Bishāra al-Khūrī from the presidency before the end of his extended period of office, and to new Parliamentary elections in 1952 and the election of Camille Chamoun as president of the republic.

Kamāl Jumblatt was the leader of the National Socialist Front, which was formed to spearhead the political struggle against the regime of Bishāra al-Khūrī until it toppled him. Majīd Arslān became the main ally of the new president Camille Chamoun.

Despite the economic prosperity, stability and progress enjoyed by the Lebanese on all levels during Chamoun's regime, a large segment of the Lebanese population resented his harsh treatment of the rest of the country's political leaders. As a result, Kamāl Jumblatt, who supported him to begin with, decided before any of the other political leaders to break off his alliance with him. But what actually precipitated the eruption of the armed conflict in the country was Camille Chamoun's foreign policy, and particularly his siding with the Baghdad Pact sponsored by the United States of America and comprising Iraq, Iran and Turkey, with the avowed aim of confronting Nasser, considered a hero of Arab nationalism and a friend of the Soviet Union in the Middle East. Seeking to prevent Soviet infiltration in the region, Western and American alliances conducted diplomacy with a hostile policy towards Arab nationalism and the economic development championed by Nasser. This resulted in a deep split within the Lebanese political class over the kind of attitude to adopt towards Nasserist Egypt and its pan-Arab policy. With the rise of American influence at the expense of the Franco–British influence in the aftermath of the tripartite attack on Egypt in 1956, Camille Chamoun considered that siding with the USA was more beneficial to Lebanon, while Kamāl Jumblatt remained faithful to his commitment to Arab nationalism, especially in an atmosphere of broad Islamic support for Nasser. In the 1957 elections, President Camille Chamoun attempted, in his turn, to amend the constitution and extend his mandate. He was met with a wide opposition that soon turned into an armed resistance, unlike the "white revolt" of 1952. An armed rebellion broke out in 1958 fomented by Lebanon's Arab nationalists, supported by Nasser. The Druze community energetically and effectively participated in the rebellion, faithful as usual to its tradition of protecting Lebanon's Arab identity. Despite an American intervention, which materialized as a troop-landing operation on the Lebanese coast, Camille Chamoun's presidential mandate expired by the end of its constitutional term and the Lebanese Parliament elected, in September 1958, the commander of the army, Fu'ād Shihāb, as its new president.

President Shihāb endeavoured to modernize the state's bureaucratic institutions while emphasizing the need to build up Lebanon and develop it to ensure its prosperity. Under his regime, the state's administrative, judicial and security branches underwent extensive reforms as he restructured its various institutions while carefully respecting a genuine separation of powers. Shihāb attempted to gain the loyalty of Lebanon's various religious communities by holding a delicate balance among them and ensuring their mutual agreement in accordance with respecting the National Charter on the one hand, and relying, on the other, on the two pillars of Lebanese politics – the Maronite Phalangist Pierre al-Jumayyil, and the Socialist Druze Kamāl Jumblatt – as the cornerstone of his governments. Jumblatt enthusiastically supported "Shihābism", and acquired a distinguished Arab and international standing as a result of his siding with Nasser and the Soviets and his leadership of the 1958 rebellion. All these factors promoted him to the rank of a national and Islamic leader, rather than merely a Druze leader.

In 1964 Charles Helou succeeded Shihāb as president of the republic, vowing to continue his political path. In spite of his competence and intellectual capacities, he was politically weaker and his term of office witnessed the security forces assuming control over Lebanon's internal affairs. These forces interfered in their course, a development that proved detrimental if not catastrophic to Shihāb's achievements and conducive to their winding up.

In 1967, Lebanon was, once again, subjected to insurmountable pressures resulting from the deterioration of the regional and international situation in the aftermath of Egypt's disastrous defeat in the Six Day War of June 1967 and the Israeli occupation of the Sinai Peninsula, the Gaza Strip, the West Bank and the Golan Heights. In the wake of this defeat, Nasser resigned from the presidency; he later revoked his resignation in compliance with the wishes expressed by the masses in huge spontaneous demonstrations that erupted across the whole of the Arab world, including Lebanon. The swift Israeli advance in Sinai and the Golan together with the easy defeat of the Arab armies became the two factors that upset the stability of the Middle East in the post-war period. One of the main related issues of the June defeat was the emergence of armed Palestinian resistance in the wake of the Palestinians' decision to take over responsibility for regaining their usurped rights. Lebanon became an essential base for the fidā'iyyīn movement and the Lebanese territory the springboard of their military operations. The surging flow of refugees descending on Lebanon from the newly occupied Palestinian territories, the increase of their numbers coupled with the rise in their armed presence on Lebanon's soil, became another source of division within Lebanon's political circles to be added to all the other burning issues. These developments fuelled the flames of Lebanon's crisis.

While the Palestinians found support in Lebanon within the political left and most of the Druze and Muslim communities, they encountered hostility from the Christian communities and a faction of the Druze community too, particularly regarding their armed presence. Clashes erupted between the Palestinian fidā'iyyīn on one side, and the Lebanese army and Maronite parties on the other. The unceasing and dangerous escalation of the crisis raised the issue that the armed Palestinian presence and its spread beyond the camps was an infringement of Lebanese national sovereignty and encroached on the morale of both the army and the security forces. With time, the crisis evolved into an open conflict considered to be the beginning of the catastrophe that later befell Lebanon. The Cairo Accord of 1969 was devised to provide a solution to this problem.[2]

However, this was not the end of the matter and it became clear, later, that this accord – vigorously opposed by Raymond Eddé – was a grave error regarding Lebanon, its security and stability, as it turned the Palestinian Liberation Organization (PLO) into a state within a state. From that point onwards, Lebanon was unable to control or monitor the operations of the fidā'iyyīn initiated from within its borders. The armed Palestinian presence became a precarious issue dangerously exposing Lebanon to Israeli retaliation and forcing the country to deal with a confrontation way beyond its power and ability.

Following the signing of the Cairo Accord, a new Lebanese government was formed and Kamāl Jumblatt was asked to take over the responsibilities of the Ministry of Internal Affairs, since he was, at the time, the only person capable of enforcing internal security and able to persuade the fidā'iyyīn to refrain from destabilizing Lebanon. Given his alliance with them and his Arab and international connections, he successfully shouldered the responsibility of protecting both Lebanon and the Palestinian resistance movements.

At the end of President Helou's term of office, Sulaymān Franjiyya, a native of the northern village of Zaghartā, was elected president of the republic in 1970, thus becoming the first Maronite president from outside Mount Lebanon. President Franjiyya belonged more to the ranks of the feudal lords, noble knights and factional leaders than the ranks of a president steering a country along the path of modernism. In actual fact, he won the presidential vote against the Shihābī candidate by a margin of one vote only (50 votes to 49), a score that reflected the depth of the country's division at that time. He won the support of Kamāl Jumblatt through promises of achieving reforms, which were then utterly ignored throughout his term in office.

The year Sulaymān Franjiyya was elected president bore witness to a fundamental political change in Syria, brought about by the coming to power of Hāfiz al-Asad. He was the promoter of Syria's influence in Lebanon and considered it a means of defending Lebanon's Arab identity *vis-à-vis* Israel's intervention in Lebanese affairs and of countering the relations entertained by some Christian politicians with the Zionist entity. Initially, the Syrians urged the Lebanese political protagonists to initiate a national dialogue committee with the aim of alleviating inter-communal tensions and upholding the National Charter. The Druze were represented on this committee by Kamāl Jumblatt and Majīd Arslān. At the time, the Maronites controlled the state apparatus and their positions were enhanced by their control of the army and their political parties' deployment of armed militias. The Muslims felt marginalized and excluded from active participation in government, and saw in the Palestinian presence a means of redressing the balance of power within the state.

## The Druze Community During the Lebanese War (1975–1989)

Tension in Lebanon reached its climax when, on 13 April 1975, the spark of civil war was kindled by a clash between Palestinian and Phalangist groups, which left 30 Palestinians dead. This became known as the 'Ayn Rummāna bus incident. Although the country was caught up in repeated interspersed clashes, no one imagined the conflict would last for the next 15 years. During the war, two fronts were formed: the first one comprised a coalition of rightist parties, antagonistic to the Palestinian presence in Lebanon, with a Maronite majority; the second was leftist, rallying the Muslim communities (both Sunni and Shi'i), the Druze community and the Palestinian forces, which constituted the front's armed wing, along with the armed militia of the Shi'i Amal movement. However, the Christians, who held the reins of government and a predominant military position and who were prepared for confrontation, prevailed on two basic levels: in politics, and in field manoeuvres.

On a political level, Kamāl Jumblatt remained the representative of roughly half of the Lebanese population. Apart from leading the Druze, he was the leader of the majority of Muslims and had a strong alliance with the Palestinians and, through them, with the Arab states and the Eastern bloc, not to mention the backing of the progressive and leftist Christians and others who gathered around him. This distinctive political situation accentuated by the civil war marginalized, to a large extent, the other leaders of the Druze community throughout the war. The Druze rank and file responded to the sense of threat to their community and identity by congregating, initially, around one leader, Kamāl Jumblatt, and after his assassination around his son, Walīd.

As the conflict broadened and its threats escalated, Kamāl Jumblatt felt the need to salvage the state of co-existence between the Druze and Christian communities in the mountain regions. Recent and distant history reminded everyone of the massacres that took place between the two communities in the nineteenth century, as well as of a precious legacy of peaceful co-existence. This co-existence demanded their concerted efforts to preserve it and safeguard it. Jumblatt considered that the Maronite preponderance in the ruling hierarchy of Lebanon should not justify a civil war that might eventually spread to the Mountain. For a period of time he pursued his efforts to preserve peace in the region. However, he was compelled to seek President Hāfiz al-Asad's intervention in consolidating the Leftist–Palestinian alliance against the Christians. Thus, events offered the Syrians an opportunity to re-establish their hegemony over Lebanon. In fact, the Syrians became indirectly involved in the conflict through the pro-Syrian Palestinian forces of al-Sā'iqa, which fought alongside the Leftist–Palestinian coalition. In the meantime, a segment of the Christian camp found, in Israel, a trusted ally. Later, a number of developments compelled Kamāl Jumblatt to modify his political stance.

A disagreement erupted in Jumblatt's relations with the Syrians when he appealed to them to refrain from interfering in Lebanon's internal affairs and desist from supporting Eliyās Sarkīs, the Shihābite candidate to the presidential elections of 1976. That said, he felt compelled to involve the Druze Muwahhidun in the conflict to avoid being accused of trying to spare his own community the rigours of a conflict in which he was both leader and instigator at the expense of the remaining Muslim communities. The breaking point between Kamāl Jumblatt and Damascus occurred when Syria opted for a direct military intervention in Lebanon on the side of the Maronites. The reasons for this Syrian decision became the subject of several analyses and speculations. Yet it is difficult to determine whether it was in response to a call for help from one or another Lebanese faction involved in the conflict or an action undertaken by Syria itself in order to protect its own interests in Lebanon and the region. Whatever the case, Hāfiz al-Asad was perfectly aware that the protraction of the civil war could culminate in the break up and partition of Lebanon, as well as in a greater Israeli interference in Lebanese affairs.

The Palestinians and the Lebanese national movement led by Kamāl Jumblatt opposed Syria's military intervention and the deployment of Syrian troops in Lebanon in June 1976. The Druze attempted to block this intervention on the ground, while Kamāl Jumblatt made an appeal to the entire Arab world imploring them to stop Syria's intervention in Lebanon's affairs. His appeal was not met with any firm Arab response while Syria remained adamant in its interventionist policy. Two Arab summits – one in Riyadh and another one in Cairo – attempted to bring an end to the war in Lebanon, but Kamāl Jumblatt rejected their resolutions, assuming that Syria would not abide by any of them or stop its manoeuvres in Lebanon. Because of his violent opposition to Syria's military intervention, he was advised by several people to leave Lebanon, which he categorically refused, maintaining that his anti-Syrian stance did not mean a rejection of an Arab presence in Lebanon, whether Syrian or Palestinian, but rather the rejection of foreign tutelage over Lebanon. After the Lebanese war was over, President al-Asad admitted that Kamāl Jumblatt, with his deep knowledge of Lebanon's internal politics, knew, unlike the Syrians, that Israel was manipulating the Christians and pressing them to adopt an antagonistic attitude towards the Syrian presence in Lebanon.

Kamāl Jumblatt was assassinated on 16 March 1977, undoubtedly because of his fervent advocacy of Lebanese sovereignty. His son, Walīd Jumblatt, succeeded him in the leadership of the Druze community and the PSP. He was invested as leader by the Sheikh al-ʿAql Muhammad Abū Shaqrā during the funeral ceremony held for his father in accordance with old feudal traditions. Not long afterwards, the growing feeling of the Lebanese indicated that they were gradually losing control over their own country. This feeling began to gain momentum in conjunction with the continuous build-up of Palestinian control over several regions. The Palestinian armed presence was no longer a cause of grief just to the Christians, but to the Muslim communities too. Several armed clashes flared up between the Shiʿis and the Palestinians, mainly in southern Lebanon and Beirut's southern suburb.

In 1982, the Israelis embarked on a direct intervention in Lebanon, following the proliferation of Palestinian presence in Lebanon and its growing power, which was considered a serious threat that warranted the destruction of the Palestine Liberation Organization (PLO) base in Lebanon. The Israelis invaded south Lebanon in a matter of a few days and reached the outskirts of Beirut – on which they imposed a rigorous siege – by advancing through the Shūf region.

The Druze were accused of not offering any resistance to the Israeli advance in their areas. That said, they were practically unable to do so, given their lack of even the minimum capabilities required to oppose the advance of one of the most effective armies in the world without instigating a massacre and maybe the annihilation of their small community. Israeli forces surrounded Walīd Jumblatt at his residence in Mukhtāra village and prevented him from returning to his home in Beirut. A political communiqué issued from his residence by three Druze personalities – Halīm Taqī al-Dīn, Marwān Hamādī and ʻAbbas al-Halabī – demanded that he be given freedom of movement and that the Israeli forces withdraw from the mountains. Walīd Jumblatt was only able to leave Mukhtāra after an arrangement was reached through the American ambassador in Beirut, Robert Dillon.

In contrast, the Maronites, under the leadership of Pierre al-Jumayyil and his son Bashīr, participated in the siege of Beirut with the avowed intention of driving the Palestinians out of the town. Confronted with this military pressure, and hoping to protect civilians and save the country from imploding, several Lebanese leaders tried to persuade the Palestinians to withdraw from Lebanon. Yasser Arafat finally gave in, and he and his forces left for Tunisia. The Israeli army withdrew from Beirut, but set up bases over a wide area of southern Lebanon.

These events caused friction between the Maronites and the Druze in Mount Lebanon, following the decision of the Israeli army of occupation to allow the Maronites to retain their armed militias and set up checkpoints between, and even within, Druze villages. The Maronites aspired to control the central area of Mount Lebanon, even if this meant driving the Druze out of it, while the Druze consider this area as their historical homeland. Many popular initiatives were undertaken in the hope of preventing the outbreak of an armed confrontation between the two sides, among them an initiative sponsored by the Permanent Bureau of Druze Institutions comprising representatives of all the community's institutions. The Bureau drew up a contingency plan, and started by organizing a march in Beirut in which hundreds participated. The march, which began at the Druze Community Centre in Verdun Street and ended at the prime minister's residence at Sanā'i', called for the dispatch of Lebanese army units to the tense mountain areas in order to diffuse the prevailing tension and alleviate the strain of the inhabitants through a show of military presence in the region.

However, as soon as Israel withdrew from Mount Lebanon, the Druze rose up and, in September 1983, a second civil war, which came to be known as the "mountain war", broke out. This war had a disastrous and devastating effect on Druze–Maronite co-existence, much cherished by Kamāl Jumblatt and patiently weaved, thread by thread, by both communities over long centuries despite casual disagreements and conflicts. In a single day, nearly 70 Christian villages fell into the hands of Druze gunmen; the inhabitants were either killed or forced to flee in an exodus that left the Mountain area utterly void of its Christian population and created what became known as the issue of the displaced mountain people. Two attempts, undertaken in Lausanne and Geneva (Switzerland) with the aim of launching a national dialogue to put an end to the Lebanese war, did not produce any plans for agreements or solutions.

In the meantime, the situation continued to deteriorate – especially within the Christian camp, which witnessed disputes and armed confrontations among various groups and tendencies, exhausting all of them – until the Tā'if Accord of 1989 became a decisive landmark between two eras. The Ta'if Accord put an end to fighting and armed conflicts, and laid down the foundations of an era of national peace and concord. Under Syrian and Saudi tutorship, and with the firm support of the USA, the Vatican and the Arab League, Lebanese delegates formulated and completed, in Tā'if, a new national agreement aimed at rebalancing the constitution by allocating all religious communities a share in the process of governing Lebanon. The Tā'if Accord represented a momentous step forward, as the call for a wider participation and a more equitable and realistic balance of power were at the roots of the Muslim grievances that fomented the civil war as the result of their feelings of being marginalized and excluded from power.

Walīd Jumblatt did not attend the Tā'if conference as he was not, yet, an elected Member of Parliament. However, the Bayt al-Dīn forum, set up in 1988, nominated a Druze delegate to attend at Tā'if to present the Druze position. This forum was headed by Sheikh al-'Aql Muhammad Abū Shaqrā, and included Walīd Jumblatt, Talāl Arslān, Tawfīq 'Assāf and a large number of prominent Druze. The Druze were represented at Tā'if by Tawfīq 'Assāf, the only Druze Member of Parliament at that time, accompanied by his son-in-law, 'Abbās al-Halabī, in his capacity as member of the forum's general secretariat, and his personal adviser. The delegates agreed at Tā'if on a new Parliament elected on a national, rather than sectarian, basis. The Druze did not achieve gains in the structure of the Lebanese political system, apart from the proposition to set up a Senate to be headed by a Druze.

Nevertheless, Tawfīq 'Assāf's active participation in the Tā'if conference constituted a major contribution to Lebanon's national accord and the safeguarding of the welfare of all Lebanese. This was achieved by his insistence on reinstating equilibrium in the internal balance of power, promoting equality in its distribution, abolishing sectarian policies, his endeavour to ensure a wider all-Lebanese participation in administrative and military decision making, and finally the adoption of the principle of a balanced development in Lebanon.

## The Post-Civil War Period

Throughout the civil war, the Druze proved their mettle in their defence of Lebanon's Arab identity, its independence and sovereignty. Many of them became martyrs, wounded, or disabled and displaced, their towns and villages destroyed and ruined. After the cessation of hostilities, all of Lebanon's communities began to draw on the lessons of the war and re-assess the end result of their behaviour during the war.

The Christians emerged in tatters as the Lebanese army, under the command of General Michel Aoun, became engaged in fierce battles with Lebanese forces under the leadership of Dr. Samīr Ja'ja'. This internecine war shattered Christian unity, and inflicted human and material losses greater than anything they had endured during the previous years of the civil war. Pope John Paul II responded to a plea from the Catholic Church of Lebanon and extended preferential treatment to the Christians of Lebanon by summoning a special synod to be held for the sake of Lebanon. Such synods are usually held to discuss a whole continent or a major issue. Calling for a synod to be held for a small country such as Lebanon – which the Pope described as "a country with a message" – proved to be, in the prevailing circumstances, more than exceptional.

Preparations for the synod started in 1991 and culminated in a meeting of Lebanon's Catholic bishops at the Vatican between November and December 1995. The synod aimed to allow the Christians, and particularly the Catholics, to renew their discourse and draw from the lessons of the war, review their thoughts and actions, and reflect on what they had done during the course of these events.

With regard to Lebanon's particularity, Pope John Paul II also extended an invitation to its Druze and Muslim communities, as well as the non-Catholic Christian communities, to participate in this synod and delegate representatives. At this point, several consultations took place between both political and religious Muslim and Druze leaders to define the appropriate stance towards an invitation primarily intended for Christians and the nature of their representation in it. They welcomed the Pope's invitation and announced their acceptance of it, substantiating the common co-existence and destiny binding together all Lebanese, despite their sectarian or political differences. At the synod, Muhammad al-Sammāk represented the Grand Mufti of the Republic, while Sa'ūd al-Mawlā represented the president of the Supreme Shi'i Council and 'Abbās al-Halabī the Druze community, in agreement with its two prominent leaders Walīd Jumblatt and Talāl

Arslān.[3] They attended the Synod as observers but also participated in its deliberations.[4]

In 1999, on the occasion of the visit of the Maronite Patriarch (Cardinal Mar Nasrallāh Butrus Sfeir) to the Shūf, a large national reconciliation took place at Mukhtāra between the Druze and the Maronites. Walīd Jumblatt declared in a historic speech that the page relating to the painful and bloody events of 1860 and 1983 had been turned, never to be repeated. Conflicts and disturbances between the two communities, and between Muslims and Christians in Lebanon, were rejected out of hand. It became evident that the eras of peace that embodied the notion of shared co-existence among all Lebanese communities were wider and more important than the eras of war and conflict. Within the context of this national reconciliation, the Maronite Patriarch acknowledged that Kamāl Jumblatt, the man of principles and convictions, was assassinated because of his resolve, faith and commitment to both his own and his community's integrity. This reconciliation confirmed that only a genuine national unity could provide the salvation of Lebanon and open the door to its transition to the future.

## The Current Political Situation

During the civil war, Kamāl Jumblatt, alongside other prominent leaders of the Druze community, embodied the hopes of the Druze Muwahhiddun and their ambitions. The tragic circumstances of his death, and the Druze instinct of self-preservation and self-defence, led to a rallying around his son Walīd who, as a result of the political legacy of his father, found himself at the head of a national movement that did not recognize sectarian differences. The "mountain war" presented Walīd Jumblatt with an opportunity to prove his capability of defending his community on the one hand, and establishing himself as a military and political leader on the other. Moreover, the erosion of the authority and influence of Sheikh al-'Aql in the aftermath of the death of Sheikh Muhammad Abū Shaqrā, the dwindling political presence of the Arslānī leadership, and the ability of the PSP to transform itself into an armed militia fighting on all fronts and in all battles against the Christian forces contributed to bestowing on Walīd Jumblatt considerable political status.

Despite their small numbers, the Druze played a vital political role in Lebanon and the Middle East. However, the conclusion of the war altered the equation and stripped this role of much of its lustre. With the rise of fundamentalism and the lack of an Arab leader of Nasser's stature, the Arab nationalist movement foundered. Moreover, the implementation of the Lebanese constitution, as defined by the national charter of 1943 and re-affirmed by the Tā'if Accord in 1989, granted a number of religious communities a larger role in Lebanon's affairs to the detriment of the remaining communities. This was aggravated by the (then) prevailing practice of overriding the principle of the separation of powers. The National Charter of 1943 was concluded between the Maronites and the Sunnis, while the accord of 1989 encompassed all the communities of Lebanon but soon developed into a tripartite understanding between Sunnis, Shi'is and Maronites. The concentration of authority and major key posts in the hands of the three mentioned communities (the presidency of the republic with the Maronites, the head of government with the Sunnis, and the head of Parliament with the Shi'is), resulted in the marginalization of the minority communities such as the Druze, Greek Orthodox and Armenians. They became excluded from the rule and administration of the new Lebanon. Similarly, the regional development plans drawn up by successive governments favoured the capital, Beirut, and some regions in the south at the expense of other Lebanese regions, especially the Mountain, still suffering from a stifling economic crisis and lack of growth.

The conclusion of the civil war and the implementation of the Tā'if agreement turned Walīd Jumblatt into a local Lebanese leader despite inheriting his father's prominent international and Arab leadership role. In the circumstances, the Druze were compelled to fall back from the internal Lebanese political scene, as the new constitution allowed them only limited participation. The apparent discrepancy between their historical legacy and their current political reality gave rise to a strong sense of disappointment and oppression.

A further factor in the Druze loss of influence derives from their failure to generate a new political elite, as the weight of the feudal legacy and the clan system have, so far, kept the Jumblatt family at the forefront of the community, unexposed to any challenge or questioning, or even a review of their authority and power. Walīd Jumblatt lost none of his community's affection and loyalty, neither towards him nor his status as its leader. In this context, the Druze community seems to lack a sense of critical approach. However, it should be noted that Walīd Jumblatt's strength and political gravitas, which led the Druze community to rally around him, are not just the result of feudal traditions and historical circumstances; they are also due to his political dexterity, skill and personal qualities. Given that Kamāl Jumblatt assumed both international and Arab status, his son Walīd deserves the title of a skilled Lebanese leader and politician, an expert in internal Lebanese politics. He stands out today as the Druze community's exclusive leader, with an almost absolute claim to their political representation.

The political trends that sidelined Jumblatt's leadership within the community lost their glow and influence during the civil war when the Druze faced a major ordeal that threatened their future existence and prompted them to unite their ranks transcending all clan or partisan differences in order to stand as one entity behind Kamāl Jumblatt. The second Druze political mainstream, represented by the Yazbaki clan, was greatly weakened. The protraction of the civil war consolidated Walīd Jumblatt's inherited leadership of the Druze community from his father Kamāl. But when political manoeuvring replaced war games, and the external threats regressed, internal opposition to the House of Jumblatt re-emerged. Although the Yazbakī party remains weak and represents only a minority within the Druze community, it has found a flagbearer in the person of Emir Talāl Arslān, son of Majīd Arslān. The Parliamentary elections of the year 2000 substantially summed up the current political situation within the Druze community: of eight elected Druze deputies, five were loyal to Walīd Jumblatt, with only one representing the Yazbaki faction – that is, Emir Talāl Arslān in person. The other two deputies were independents representing regions where the Jumblatti–Yazbaki divide is rather irrelevant.

Nevertheless, the original political issue differentiating between Jumblattis and Yazbakis has all but vanished these days. While Kamāl Jumblatt represented the Arab nationalist trend in Lebanon, Emir Majīd Arslān was more associated with traditional Lebanese politics and the Maronite school of governing. These ideologies have now disappeared and will remain non-existent as long as Walīd Jumblatt and Talāl Arslān remain subjected to a Lebanese political system controlled by Syria. The split between a Yazbaki and a Jumblatti trend is purely an issue of personal and individual interest bearing no relation to political theories.

Currently, it seems as though the political weight of the most prominent Druze leader, Walid Jumblatt, epitomizes the political weight of the Druze community. The Druze emerged from the civil war severely weakened, despite their military victory in the Mountain. Their large casualty rate and the massive exodus of Christians from the Shūf and 'Alay regions constrained the dynamism of both areas, alongside their economic, cultural and social activities. The Druze became unable to assume any serious role on political, social, economic or demographic levels in Lebanon. Only the presence of Walīd Jumblatt is compensating for this general weakness through the political and social mobilization that he generates.

### The Post-2000 era

On 25 May 2000, Lebanon inaugurated a new era with the liberation of its southern region from Israeli occupation. This was largely achieved thanks to the popular support the Lebanese national resistance enjoyed from all political venues, in addition to the Army's backing. This great national achievement, which did not oblige Lebanon to sign a peace treaty with the Israeli aggressors in return for its land, prompted a transfer from a state of war to a state of peace and prosperity. The liberation of the South led to calls for implementing the National Charter clauses providing for a gradual withdrawal of Syrian troops from Lebanon. Considering that Syria maintained that its military presence in Lebanon constituted a strategic counterbalance to the Israeli occupation of the South, the liberation of this region deprived the Syrians of their justification for keeping their military presence in Lebanon. In September 2000, the Maronite bishops issued a statement openly and plainly requesting the Syrians to withdraw from Lebanon and leave the Lebanese to run their own affairs with complete independence. Walīd Jumblatt supported this demand in a speech he delivered in Parliament; it differed from the Maronite bishops' call by suggesting a repositioning of the Syrian Army in accordance with the Tā'if Accord.

This development generated a tumultuous period in the relationship of a number of Lebanese leaders with Syria, especially in the aftermath of the extension of President Emile Lahhūd's term of office in September 2004, until eventually a great rift occurred leading to the assassination of (former prime minister) Rafīq Harīrī on 14 February 2005. At that point, raised voices called for the immediate withdrawal of the Syrian army, with all Lebanese, Muslims and Christians united in this demand. The assassination of a moderate, open-minded Muslim personality with a broad popular following within all the religious communities, and who had nurtured personal relations with a large number of highly placed and influential international leaders, caused a wave of fierce anger on the day of his funeral and those that followed it. It is still felt today.

Although this open crisis was ignited by the assassination of Prime Minister Rafīq Harīrī, the adoption of resolution 1559 by the Security Council and the mandatory extension of General Emile Lahhūd's term of presidency – resulting in the removal of Rafik al-Hariri from the post of prime minister – were two of its direct causes.

Resolution 1559 demanded the withdrawal of Syrian forces from Lebanon and the disarming of armed militias on Lebanese territory. The Lebanese were divided about this resolution, although they were united in condemning the crime of the assassination.

Prior to this, on 1 October 2004, the Druze minister and elected Member of Parliament Marwān Hamāda was the target of an assassination attempt which almost cost him his life. His accompanying guard, Ghazi Bū Kurūm (from Mazraat el-Shūf) was killed.

As a result of these events, and for the first time since the civil war, a cross-community Lebanese national front was formed. This brought together Walīd Jumblatt with a group of Maronites and other Christian personalities belonging to the political opposition gathering known as "qarnat shahwān", the Lebanese forces, the "Free Lebanon" movement led by General Michel Aoun, and the "Future" movement led by Rafīq Harīrī's son Sa'd al-Dīn, as well as a number of independent Shi'i personalities. The discourse of this National Front accused Syria of turning Lebanon into a police state, and considered the Syrian presence as a blatant encroachment on Lebanese sovereignty and independence. It eventually ended up demanding the immediate withdrawal of Syrian forces and security agencies from all Lebanese territory.

The assassination of Rafīq Harīrī resulted in the death of ten other Lebanese and caused injury to hundreds more. Accusing fingers were pointed at Syria, claiming that it was behind the operation. Syria was known for its political scheming and extensive knowledge of the Lebanese situation. Questions were raised concerning its role in the assassination plot, which was likened to a suicide operation led by a team from within the Syrian regime.

Hundreds of thousands of people, most of them Shi'is, took part in a demonstration on 8 March 2005 in Riyād al-Sulh Square in central Beirut, sponsored by Hizbullah, to thank Syria for the part it played in Lebanon and its support of the resistance. Just days later, on 14 March, another demonstration – the largest ever in the history of popular gatherings in Lebanon – took place in Riyād al-Sulh Square and Martyrs Square, renamed Freedom Square. The masses, comprising members of all Lebanese communities, particularly the Sunnis, Christians and Druze and some Shi'is, called for freedom, independence, free decision making and the withdrawal of the Syrian army. They didn't have long to wait: as a result of popular and international pressures in the wake of resolution 1559, particularly from the US president George Bush, who pressed (in daily appearances) for Syrian withdrawal, it took place on 26 April 2005.

In the aftermath of the Syrian withdrawal from Lebanon, and for the first time since 1975, Parliamentary elections were held without the presence of any foreign troops on Lebanese soil. They were based upon the electoral law passed in 2000, as it proved inappropriate to pass a new election law in the short period that separated the Syrian withdrawal from the date of the elections.

All observers, including some foreign teams, bore witness to the freedom and fairness of the electoral procedure, its integrity and the proper conduct of its process. Despite some logistical loopholes and administrative shortcomings, the elections produced a Parliamentary majority comprising representatives from the "Future movement" led by Sa'd al-Dīn al-Harīrī, the Democratic Alliance led by Walīd Jumblatt and their allies from the Lebanese forces, the Phalangists and the qarnat shahwān gathering. The elections also resulted in the Hizbullah and Amal movements overrunning the Shi'i political arena and monopolizing the representation of areas where the Shi'i voters formed a majority, particularly the regions of the Biqā' and the South.

Although the "Future movement" and its allies benefited from the compassion shown by the Lebanese towards the tragic assassination of Rafīq Harīrī, the elections were also a referendum favouring Lebanon's independence and sovereignty, and its liberation from Syrian military and intelligence presence.

A new Lebanese government was subsequently formed under the premiership of Fu'ād al-Sinyūra, who gathered the highest support in the binding Parliamentary consultations for the nomination of a prime minister. This result reflected the popular support of the Parliamentary representation.

On a different front, international pressure escalated demanding an international tribunal to try the criminals who carried out the assassination of Rafīq Harīrī. However, Syrian influence over the Lebanese political and security situation did not abate and the assassinations continued – including the gifted journalist Samīr Qasīr; George Hāwī, the leading Communist nationalist who changed his stance to oppose the Syrians; Basil Falīhān, the promising minister who was accompanying Rafīq Harīrī in his car when he was assassinated; Jubrān al-Twaynī, the young politician who embodied the hope of the *An-Nahār* newspaper; Pierre Amīn al-Jumayyal, a prominent potential leader in the Christian camp; Walīd ʿĪdū, the courageous deputy and former judge, with his son; and finally Antoine Ghanem, the Phalangist deputy, member of the Democratic bloc and others. This list does not include assassination attempts perpetrated against other personalities such as May Shidyāq, the Minister of Defence Elias al-Murr and, before them, Marwān Hamāda.

The most striking development on the Druze stage was the sweeping electoral gains achieved by Walīd Jumblatt, which made him, with the Progressive Socialist Party, the exclusive representative of the Druze community. He took over seven of the eight Parliamentary seats allocated to the Druze in Lebanon, the eighth being held by his ally Anwar al-Khalīl from Hāsbayyā. The 2005 elections confirmed the political ascendance of Jumblatt, a phenomenon first witnessed in the 2000 elections.

All Druze representatives belonged to the Democratic Encounter bloc – apart from Anwar al-Khalīl, who belonged to the "Liberation and Development" bloc led by the speaker of the House of Representatives, Nabīh Birrī (an ally of Jumblatt). This facilitated the promulgation of a new law regulating the Druze communal affairs,[5] eventually leading to the creation of the Communal Council and the election of a new Sheikh al-ʿAql. This development put an end to an era of loss and bewilderment experienced by the Druze community over many years due to the lack of institutions representing their civil society.

Today, after passing the test of adopting a new law, conducting elections and achieving a wise selection, the Druze are looking forward to a new era in their history based on the institutionalization of the bodies entrusted with the management of their affairs – like the rest of the Lebanese religious communities, especially the Islamic ones. This era will lay the ground for more consultations and dialogues regarding the management of their spiritual and secular affairs. It is Walīd Jumblatt's initiative that facilitated the creation of the institution that forms the very basis of any institutional activity within the Druze community, particularly in the field of religious endowments (*waqf*) which raised – and still does – many debates involving several parties as a result of the widely waged charges of chaos and corruption.

The Druze Muwahhidun hope that this development will initiate a new era in which the dispersed portfolios of the Druze endowments will be retrieved, clearly identified and wisely invested to assist the social classes in benefiting from them – according to the stipulations of the donor, on the one hand, and the needs of the functioning institutions for the necessary financial and material aids, on the other, to continue supporting and providing their services.

## Future Horizons

Other communities in Lebanon did not benefit from the lessons of the civil war nor its outcome, even though it incurred a heavy cost on them – due mainly to Syria's inclination to maintain a balance among the main players on the Lebanese political scene by reining in their leaders and defining, or even marginalizing, their roles. In theory, this should have led to the establishment of a strong state in Lebanon, but the reality clearly shows the ascendancy of the sectarian leader over the state's institutions. The late imam Muhammad Mahdī Shams al-Dīn described this unhealthy state of affairs by pointing out that "a situation where the state is stronger than its society leads to tyranny, and a situation where society is stronger than the state leads to chaos".

The lack of a sense of institutionalism, and the desire of all Druze leaders to control the political process of decision making and exclusively benefit from the state's privileges and services, ruled out the possibility of generating a new political class among themselves. Moreover, the absence of a Druze Communal Council,[6] the conflict regarding the personality of the previous acting Sheikh al-ʿAql, the sterile activities of the secretarial council of the *waqf* in the previous period, and the exodus of the young and competent led to a regression in the Druze presence. The inertia of its intellectual elite, along with the lack of will and the inability of its political activists to take the initiative in resolving these problems, obstructed all attempts to rekindle hope within the Druze community.

The political weakening of the Druze did not result in a lack of concern in Lebanese internal affairs. They aspire, first and foremost, to live under a political system that safeguards their freedom and their particularity within the context of safeguarding the freedom of all other communities and their particularities. Consequently, the required majority in Lebanon is a qualitative majority, not a majority monopolizing power by virtue of its numerical or demographic status. The Druze favour the advanced political principle of a consensual democracy that embraces the political scene, and the sphere of group presence on a basis of ethical, social and cultural values.

This commitment to consensual democracy explains the active role played by the Druze in promoting a Christian–Islamic dialogue, both in Lebanon and on the wider Arab level. Current Christian–Muslim relations are not at their best in Lebanon. In fact, they are passing through a serious crisis due, first, to internal problems; second, to mixing religion with politics; and third, to the impact on Lebanon of Christian–Muslim conflicts throughout the world. In order to preserve clarity and transparency in dealing with this issue, and to maintain in a productive and effective dialogue, it is imperative, from the onset, to draw a distinction between the sectarian and the religious. Although religion, or religiosity, is not in itself a source of division and conflict, the exploitation of religion in politics engenders inter-communal conflicts. Politicians use sectarianism as a means of safeguarding their personal interests in the internal political struggle waged under the pretence of acting to protect the rights of their community. Thus, the problem of Lebanese politics is not begotten by the system as stipulated in the constitution, but by the process of governing, and the practice of political nepotism and corruption. The Druze are among the furthest Lebanese denominations from this state of affairs and the least concerned with it. They are, consequently, struggling for a fairer power participation that would grant all competent individuals an opportunity to prove themselves and exercise their competence, regardless of the sect to which they belong.

The Christians made an attempt at self-criticism and re-assessment of their experience in the civil war. Muslims and Druze are also invited to undertake a similar criticism and to visualize their future. It is possible that the current Sunni–Shii conflict in Lebanon, fuelled by similar events in the region (especially in Iraq), along with the aggressive role assumed by Iran (benefiting some Shi'i groupings in Lebanon and elsewhere), will prompt the hoped-for process of re-assessment in order to avoid these groupings sliding into armed confrontations and re-enactments of the past tragedies of some political conflicts wrapped in religious interpretation (Ijtihad). It is also for the Druze to determine the causes behind their becoming a marginalized minority after being the rulers of Lebanon in the seventeenth century. This assessment must be carried out in the light of their historical message guided by what this message might evolve into in the future, taking into account the nature of the current situation in Lebanon and the Middle East. Today, a ray of hope looms on the horizon as a result of the election of a new and promising Communal Council.

## Notes

1 That is, the West Bank, Gaza and the Golan Heights, which are still under occupation, and the Egyptian territory of Sinai, which was liberated.

2 The Cairo Accord is a protocol between the Lebanese government and the Palestinians allowing the latter to bear arms in areas defined by the Accord, which President Nasser oversaw personally shortly before his death.

3 See Appendices 12 and 13.

4 Cf. in Appendix 6, the text of ʻAbbās Halabī's address delivered at the Synod.

5 See Chapter 3.

6 The Druze Communal Council was re-elected on 24 September 2006 after the Council of Representatives passed a law to regulate it, which was promulgated on 9 June 2006. Sheikh Naʻīm Hasan was elected Sheikh al-ʻAql. The committee that oversaw the first election of the council was headed by his Worship the retired judge Sheikh Shajīʻ al-Aʻwar.

# Chapter 8

# The Druze Message: Plurality and Unity

To date, no academic assessment has been made of the meaning of the message of the Druze Muwahhidun to this world. All who have written about the Druze have dealt with various aspects of their history, doctrine or the sociological aspects of their community. Only Kamāl Jumblatt attempted, in his writings and various interviews, to offer a deep analysis of all aspects of the life of the Druze, their current status and their future. Accordingly, this chapter will rely, basically, on Jumblatt's thoughts and observations, particularly those collected by Bernadette Shink in her work,[1] and in which Jumblatt examined in depth the historical status of the Druze and the role they have played in the Middle East.

Nowadays, it might not be adequate to remain confined to this analysis as it needs updating. This chapter attempts to foresee the Druze future and to visualize the proper dimensions of their mission in today's world.

Like all other Arabs and Muslims, the Druze are today confronted with a profound crisis. They are compelled to live in a hostile international environment which, however, *is* showing greater concern to safeguarding "the rights of minorities". In fact, under the close scrutiny of the media and human rights organizations, it has become difficult, if not impossible, to persecute any minority in the world. Any incident, no matter how trivial, evolves promptly into an international issue. One of the complexities of the crisis currently experienced by the Arab and Muslim world is due to the continually dwindling number of Christians in Lebanon and the Middle East as a whole. Although this is partially due to economic factors, the main reason remains the absence of democracy and the lack of safety and security. Minorities generally feel steadily threatened in their identity and existence – especially the Christian minorities, whose presence has always represented an element of stability and security for the rest of the minorities and has conferred on the Middle East an exceptional particularity. The weakening of the Christian presence in the Arab East poses a challenge to Arabism as a cultural order capable of assimilating diverse ethnic minorities such as Kurds and Berbers, and religious minorities such as the Druze and the Alawites. Arabism is also reeling under the threat of Islamic extremism defined as "fundamentalism". Fundamentalist movements are characterized by their tendency to eliminate the "others" and promote self-seclusion, thus precluding the possible survival not only of the Druze Muwahhidun but also of all ethnic and religious minorities, and probably raising the spectre of suppressing moderate Muslims. This prevailing situation raises the need to re-define the role of these minorities and their status. For example, the strength of the Druze is based on their dual sense of belonging to an impressive history, which allows them, on the one hand, to adhere to their distinctiveness and feel proud of their Druzism, and, on the other, to value their commitment to a much broader area and culture and, therefore, to emphasize their desire to remain an integral part of their Arab and Muslim environment.

Inasmuch as the Druze Muwahhidun firmly uphold their cultural and religious identity, along with their doctrinal and confessional distinctiveness, they firmly resist any separatist or partitionist propositions and refuse to be classified in a marginal, distorted political or social slot. The Druze reject any claim that could imply tainting them politically with isolationism or separatism, or religiously with heresy or atheism.

In order to preserve their distinctive status, the Druze have always advocated Lebanese unity and promoted it as a conceptual ideal. They steadily contributed to Arab causes from a Lebanese patriotic, nationalist and religious perspective mindful of Arab and Muslim interests. With this discipline, they have preserved their cultural and confessional distinctiveness, and consolidated their roots in a country in which they feel proud of having been among its founders and builders. The Druze assert that their commitment to their distinctive religious identity in no way contradicts the higher interests of their country nor the wider and greater interests of the Arab and Muslim worlds. On the contrary, the awareness of their distinctiveness is accompanied by a stronger historic and patriotic awareness that has always prompted them, as Lebanese, Arabs and Muslims, to engage in an effective and dynamic role in the Middle East.

It must be emphasized that the Druze Muwahhidun, despite being a minority, have never experienced a minority complex – unlike other religious minorities, especially the Christians.

## The Historical Message of the Druze

An analysis of the historical role of the Druze in the Middle East shows that four factors governed their message – all being integral to the nature of their community and confession.

- On a national level, the Druze constitute – as described by Kamāl Jumblatt – a "fighting minority" involved in the events experienced throughout the political history of Lebanon, including the contemporary history of *bilād al-Shām* and the Middle East.
- On an ethnic level, the Druze are Arab by origin and roots[2] as a result of the proliferation of the Tawhīd (Unitarian) doctrine during the Fatimid period among the Arab or Arabized tribes of *bilād al-Shām* – already completely Arabized.
- On a religious level, the Druze consider their doctrinal discourse as the enshrinement of all religions' messages and schools of thought, making it the sole true path to mystical knowledge. By defining themselves as Muwahhidūn (Unitarian) they convey a conclusive perspective as to the nature of their beliefs.
- Also on a religious level, the Druze persevere in encompassing themselves with their Muslim brothers despite the lack of depth of this corollary and its lack of consensus among them. This perspective is still met with many objections by a number of Druze and is only grudgingly accepted by the Muslims. Indeed, many Islamic religious authorities refuse to recognize the Druze as Muslims.

An approach in depth to these four factors may provide a better understanding of the ideological and political attitudes adopted by the

Druze, especially the impact of several decisive historical developments on their current political situation.

## "Fighting Minority" and the Guarantee of Unity

Throughout their history, the Druze have projected the image of a powerful and dynamic factor on both the local Lebanese level – being the founders of Lebanon's history – and on the regional Middle Eastern level. The survival of the Druze community – demographically, religiously, socially, culturally, politically and even militarily at times – is not due to any numerical superiority but rather to their geographical location, determination and steadfastness, and to the existence of a "fighting aristocracy" which has proved, time and again, its highly elaborate political and leadership skills. This enabled the Druze to compensate for their minority status and to carve a habitat for their community within the ethnic, religious and political fabric of the Middle East. A look at their history shows that they never yielded or surrendered without resistance, and never segregated themselves within the confines of an inferiority complex or became a religiously or socially isolated community. These facts enhanced their current personal awareness of their cultural, religious and political heritage.

Kamāl Jumblatt's description of the Druze as a "fighting minority" fits them perfectly as a description of a society with self-pride and self-reliance, scornful of humiliation and submission, dynamic and well organized. Despite their inner differences and divisions, the Druze have always stood firm, in commitment and unity, against all dangers threatening their country or their very existence. Their solidarity reflects a social bond that evolved from a sense of common awareness and discipline that negates all attempts to confine it to a confessional or communal motivation. The Druze hold the conviction that any weakness in any link in the chain that unites them undermines the whole chain. Their belief in reincarnation – according to which a Druze is reborn within the community – enhances this sense of minority bond, and ensures a continued concern for the survival of the community, the guarding of its past, present and future, through time.

The Druze retain a strong instinct of self-defence, an instinct that prompted them to react speedily to the repeated acts of persecution to which they were subjected throughout their history. In this context, they appear, ideologically, more united in times of confrontation than any other political or demographic entity. By comparison, the Christians of Lebanon can rely on the support and assistance of the Vatican and the West, the Sunnis can depend on the Islamic world and its billion Sunnis, or at least on the support of Egypt and Saudi Arabia, just as the Shi'is can rely on Iran. By contrast, the Druze Muwahhidun have no party but themselves to rely on for ensuring their survival – that is, their community and their own steadfastness and wit in manoeuvring local and regional politics. In addition to their fighting spirit and military prowess, they master enough political acumen, far-sightedness and proficiency in dealing with difficulties. Throughout their long history of fighting for survival and continuity, the Druze have become used to being rather wary of their political environment and sensitive to what is happening in their surroundings, generally adapting to their environment, carefully weighing their options, words, actions and diplomatic relations. It is worth remembering that the historical weight and credibility of the Druze Muwahhidun was achieved at a high cost and with great bloodshed. Their reputation as a "fighting minority" was the outcome of many battles and at the cost of many martyrs –among them notables, sheikhs, and poor and simple Druze – who all fell defending their identity, their homes and their land. They never wavered for a moment in fighting for their values. Sheikh Abū Hasan 'Ārif Halāwī[3] frequently said that the Druze always enjoyed divine support and protection in their defensive fights as they never transgressed or assaulted others. Such qualities secured a political and moral presence for the Druze since their community was first established in the eleventh century AD until it occupied its current distinct and important status in the history of Lebanon and the Middle East.

## Contribution to Lebanese Unity

It must be remembered, from the start, that "The Arab Emirate was established in Lebanon by the Muslims and, mainly, the Druze". The establishment of the Emirate by the Druze Emirs at the beginning of the seventeenth century became the founding stone for Lebanese unity. The Emirate practically laid down a comprehensive social and economic structure within a political and constitutional context, which impressed upon the Lebanese the necessity for a common, if not unified, evolution. The Lebanese conglomerated into a single people, living within the framework of a united state. Through the new framework that was then formalized, the Emirate laid down the very basis for the modern state of Lebanon. The great Druze families, led by the Ma'n family, governed this entity for more than two centuries and "assumed the political burdens of the Emirate's institution", granting it a specific and distinct political, social and cultural undertone. The Ottomans officially recognized this emirate with its "Druze–Fatimid undertone" and even called Mount Lebanon "Djebel Druze" (the "Druze Mountain") – not to be confused with the more recent "Djebel Druze" in Syria. On a political level, the Druze Emirate has adopted since its establishment liberal and rational approaches while taking advantage of the political realities of its era and area; it has also consecrated the notion of a confessionally pluralistic Lebanon. This endeavour promoted a "spirit of secularism" based on tolerance towards divergent thoughts and beliefs, consequently legalizing the freedom to practise different religious rites. This political choice, initiated by the Druze Emirs, laid down the foundations of Lebanese unity, bypassing confessional and religious constraints, stressing, in particular, the peaceful and cultural co-existence among the various Lebanese communities, be it Christian or Muslim.

Emir Fakhr al-Dīn II based the foreign policy of the Lebanese Emirate on the probability of the evolution of an entity relishing a degree of independence from the Sublime Porte, safeguarding the continuity of this independence, and substantiating the notion of "an active state involved in all the affairs of the Middle East". In this context, "true Lebanese unity" was the result of an effective and independent Emirate, engaged in an active foreign policy on the one hand, and based on the steadfastness of the Druze Muwahhidun and their secularity on the other. It was imperative for this nascent unity to realize the notion of a common nation based on inter-communal co-operation and complementarity, and proceed to achieve Lebanon's independence and sovereignty. This could only be achieved within the framework of a "liberal mentality", rejecting, first of all, nationalistic chauvinism, then firmly confronting the external enemy – a duty for which Lebanon had to be ever prepared. By establishing the Arab Emirate and embodying its unity, the Druze Muwahhidun secured Mount Lebanon's independence for two centuries and earned the title of "architects of modern Lebanon" as they laid down the political and social frameworks without which Lebanese unity could never have been achieved.

This narrative portrays in an idealistic way the part played by the Druze Muwahhidun in establishing the Arab Emirate in a coherent geographical and political entity, and their contribution to the creation of the sovereign and independent modern Lebanese state. By assuming this responsibility, the Druze Muwahhidun asserted their status as an integral component of the Lebanese people and an essential constituent of Lebanon's history. In summing up the importance of this role Kamāl Jumblatt noted that:

> What became known after 1917 as Greater Lebanon was based upon the Druze political notion of a pluralistic Lebanon ruled by the Druze and Muslims – that is, upon the notion of self-governing which recreated the history of the small Arab Emirate. The only difference between them was the political regime adopted for Greater Lebanon and the creation of a confessional system based more on religious than secular lines, thus unjustifiably paving the way for a Maronite hegemony. It was disastrous.[4]

Although the Druze Muwahhidun designed the politico-ideological infrastructure upon which modern Lebanon was based, their continuous control over it slipped completely from their hands at a later stage. Despite being victorious in their military campaigns, they failed to exploit their victories politically. This happened in 1860 and is still happening today. The structure they erected and its values were squandered by those who inherited power, and the Druze were neither able to oppose nor prevent it from happening. Today they are still experiencing this weakness and the gradual erosion of their influence in Mount Lebanon. Within this context, history is prodding us to rethink the meaning of present-day Lebanon, and is offering us lessons implying that Lebanon cannot be ruled by a single community at the expense of others. We must remember that the only side that has benefited, and that should profit from the outcome of all conflicts in Lebanon, past and present, is the fatherland, and not this side or this sect – although, most regrettably, the opposite seems to be true today.

## Contribution to the History of the Middle East

The Druze Muwahhidun participated in the Arab struggle for freedom and independence, which entitled them to become a constituent of Arab strength and an integral part of the Arab–Muslim history of the Middle East. Just as Mount Lebanon, or "Djebel Druze", took up the position of the Arab Emirate while remaining the centre of its political power – due to the skills of their rulers and their steadfastness *vis-à-vis* the other regions – in the same way Lebanon became, under the rule of the Druze emirs, a dynamic centre at the heart of the Middle East. The Druze Muwahhidun waged a long sequence of national wars of liberation purporting to restore Arab–Islamic rights and interests. They exercised an influence that enabled them to become vigorously, and effectively, involved in Middle Eastern affairs, and play a pivotal role as a "fighting minority" untainted by any isolationist tendencies. The full and steady support for Arab–Muslim causes has, without exception, been the hallmark of all Druze leaders – a characteristic that largely contributed to the development of Druze personal awareness and national consciousness.

At the time of the Crusader war,[5] (from the end of the eleventh until the thirteenth centuries) the Arab rulers of Damascus called upon the support of the Druze and their help to repel the Frankish attacks and to protect the Syrian coast from their raids. As a result of their location between the Frankish Latin states and the Arab kingdoms, the Druze chose to side solidly with the Muslims and to protect Arab interests, especially when Saladin launched his counter-attack to regain Jerusalem and the occupied land, and raised a call to *jihād*. Beginning in the thirteenth century, the Druze constantly supported resistance to various foreign forces attempting to extend their influence over Bilād al-Shām. They took part in the fighting against the Mongols, the forces of Tamerlane, the Ottoman central government and the intervention of the major Western powers. The nationalist wars of the Druze Muwahhidun continued into the early twentieth century with their involvement in the Arab revolt of al-Sharīf Husayn and King Faysal against the Ottoman Empire. From 1925 to 1927, the Druze rose in revolt against the French occupation of Syria and, despite their ultimate military defeat, contributed to the progress of Syria and Lebanon towards independence. During the second half of the twentieth century, the Palestinian Druze refused to desert their lands and villages after the establishment of the State of Israel, remaining faithful to their culture, heritage and affiliation. From 1929, they joined the Arab resistance against the British Mandate and Zionist immigration, and from 1936 to 1948 they confronted Israeli political and military colonization, and supported all Palestinian uprisings. They maintain, up to the present time, the closest relations with the leaders of the Palestinian and Lebanese resistance movements, for which they have paid a high price. In this context the name of the Druze Samīr al-Quntār should be mentioned. He was known as the "veteran of the Arab prisoners" because of his participation in a military operation against Zionist forces in occupied Palestine for which he was held prisoner in Israel for more than 25 years.

The Druze "feel the pulse of Arab nationalism" and spare no military effort in asserting their support for all Arab causes. It is worth noting that the struggle for independence undertaken by Lebanon's Emirate may have contributed, indirectly, to the Arab awakening in the nineteenth century, and became, in a way, the starting point for the subsequent Arab Renaissance. Arab national awareness and Renaissance resemble, practically, the main traits of the political heritage aspired for by Druze hopes and demands since the beginning of the twentieth century, mainly the shaping and construction of a

Middle East independent of the Ottoman Empire. Throughout their history, the Druze remained among the most committed communities to the genuine Arab heritage, whether through their culture, their thinking, their political leanings, their customs and traditions or their classical language. Emir Fakhr al-Dīn II, one of the cultural pillars of the Arab renaissance, embodied the model to follow.

At present, the Druze consider themselves the architects and spearhead of the Arab cause to the extent of assuming that, in this respect, they have played a role greater than that of the Sunni Muslims. In fact, the Sunni Arabs proved less enthusiastic than the Druze to rebel against the Ottoman Empire. This reluctance was gradually overcome by the early twentieth century following the Hashemite opposition to Ottoman rule and its adoption of the Arab nationalist movement. This led to a partial Sunni Arab participation in King Faysal's movement, while many remained committed to the Ottoman Caliphate in Istanbul. Then, with the rise of Nasser in the second half of the twentieth century, the great majority of Sunnis joined the ranks of the Arab nationalists.

## Arab Origins

By virtue of "blood ties, mentality and struggle" the Druze Muwahhidun are pure Arabs and belong to Arab culture, on the level of genealogy, mentality and loyalty. In an early historical study, Philip Hitti attempted to cast some doubts over the ethnic origins of the Druze, claiming they had descended from a mixture of Persian, Iraqi and Arab peoples.[6] By contrast, Druze authors, writers, intellectuals, historians and leaders assert the pure Arabism of the Druze, even if it may have been surrounded by historical ambiguity. This ambiguity is negated by the Druze doctrinal outlook, since the doctrine of reincarnation, as they defined it, and the religious rule forbidding marriage outside the community, have transformed the Druze into a closed circle. According to historical studies, the Druze descend from the 12 great Arab tribes who settled Bilād al-Shām even before the Islamic conquest. Consequently, they were able to preserve their ethnic roots and relations by restricting marriage to their own community and by virtue of their belief in reincarnation. Druze writers put forward other arguments in support of this theory, equally justified from a doctrinal point of view. Most quoted among them is their usage of a pure and correct Arabic idiom that is rarely used by other Arabs.

But in practice, these presumed ambiguities, together with their refutations, have gradually faded in the face of their open-mindedness. Their repudiation of any regional or local isolationism, and their involvement in wider Middle Eastern affairs, have made the pure Arabic language they practise less substantial in this argument. Similarly, many of them have married, and still marry, from without their community.

Moreover, historically speaking, the Arab Caliphs and the governors of Damascus had hitherto urged the Tannūkh and Lakhm al-Dīn families – from whom many major Druze families descend – to settle Mount Lebanon and the coast in order to resist foreign incursions, namely by Byzantine and Frankish forces. Here may reside the original underlying motive for all the wars waged by the Druze in the name of the Arab cause, a motive that remained valid in the twentieth century. This has had a deep impact on the individual and collective consciousness of the Druze. Being an "Arab" in the eyes of the Druze does not just mean belonging to a deep-rooted origin and speaking classical Arabic; it also means possessing a firm and unwavering loyalty to Arab interests. In this context, the Emirate founded by the Druze emirs in Mount Lebanon was the expression of Lebanese unity achieved through Arab ruling families. Its long survival was proof of its normal integration within the Arab political and cultural fold of the Middle East.

## The Druze Way: The Sum of All Religious Teachings and Guarantee of Plurality and Difference

Due to their cultural roots and spiritual core, the Druze consider their religious faith as "a way of wisdom and Unitarianism" and a converging spot for all creeds and religious beliefs. While affirming this aspect, they endeavour to highlight the common themes among all religions. In their view, they are the true Unitarians and believers in the oneness of all religions, according to the revealed word of God in Q2:115: "God owns the East and the West; wherever you go, God is there; God is great and knowing."

There is no doubt, from a historical and theological point of view, that the genesis of the Druze faith rests within the womb of Islam. Its cultural structure includes several elements derived from Islamic mysticism, Qur'anic thought and the teachings of the Hanīfis (that is, ascetism, abstinence and true and authentic monotheism known since the time of Abraham). It is also true that Druzism encompasses many elements derived from esoteric mysticism, neo-platonism and the Persian religion. The Druze faith, by virtue of its various elements and their reconciliation, proved to be the synthesis of several spiritual and intellectual currents.

The inter-relationships and contact opportunities afforded to all religious communities by the state of co-existence in Lebanon project a lucid image of the cultural, intellectual and religious exchanges that were taking place in Bilād al-Shām throughout history. The legacy of the various communities and sects also stimulates the mind to ponder the realities of the great cultures and civilizations of the Middle East and their historical record of co-existence, contiguity, inter-communion and succession in Lebanon and the Middle East. This supports the notion that the Druze doctrine includes residues of a past that is still alive in the minds and consciousness of its followers. The Druze faith distinguishes itself from other religious creeds in being the meeting platform of all ancient religious, cultural and spiritual beliefs, of their interaction and embodiment in a synthesis representing a new peak that, in turn, produced a new and unique doctrinal system. This system, in a way, "resembles ancient Greece, small and humanitarian at the same time, or the public squares in her ancient cities" that were meeting forums for dialogues, discussions and rich cultural and intellectual exchanges.

Among the major elements that define the essence and nature of the Druze faith, a prominent consideration is accorded to "asceticism, the vision of substantial reality, and the belief that nothing can obstruct the search for the Absolute". Accordingly, the Druze faith cannot be defined as a religion of canon (Shari'a) and laws, like Islam or Judaism, but as a religion of "spiritual piety". Defining Druzism as a religion with no dogmatic rituals emancipates it from restrictions or obligations and from any contradiction with other monotheistic religions and makes it a meeting ground for all religions and philosophical teachings. It preaches an esoteric mysticism with no limits in time or space. Consequently, the Druze cannot be accused of confessionalism or sectarianism as long as they represent a social and political entity more than a religious sect closed on itself. Their solidarity and commitment emanates from their nationalist feelings more than a sense of belonging, exclusively, to a particular religion. As a meeting platform for all religions, Druzism affirms the common origin of all of them. Although all religions vary in structures and rites, they all base their message on the theory that man is called upon to liberate himself through his search for the Absolute Truth that transcends the barriers and bonds of matter, all of them endeavouring to attain wisdom. Only through religious asceticism and abstinence can one answer the great questions about Existence, its raison d'être and meaning, about the origin of life and the concepts of birth, life and death. By holding to a firm pattern of ethical values, the Druze advocate transcending all religious divisions in order to reach a deeper humane truth – the essence of true spirituality. Religions, in their view, are tributaries flowing into one single river.

## The Druze as Members of Islam

Although the Druze faith is, undoubtedly, the meeting platform of all religions, it was conceived in the womb of Islam and was inspired, spiritually and actually, by Islamic teachings. The Druze categorically refuse to abandon the origin of their creed and faith, and acknowledge the close tie that binds their doctrines to the mainstream of Shi'i Ismā'īlī Fatimid thought, which conveys legitimacy to their Islamic affiliation, despite the schism that occurred between the Druze and the Fatimid caliphate in the eleventh century. The Druze consider themselves the true and legitimate heirs of Islam and the guardians of the spirit of the religion of Abraham, the true root of Islam and the teaching of the Prophet Muhammad (PBUH). Therefore, they insist that they fully and completely embody the truth of Islam, its core and spirit. Thus, they take pride in considering themselves as belonging to the "early true Muslims" by virtue of their faith in, and understanding of, monotheism, and their respect for the Qur'anic revelation, the main source of their spirituality.

## Notes

1 Bernadette Schink, *Kamal Gunbulat. Das arabisch-islamische Erbe und die Rolle der Drusen in seiner Konzeption der libanesischen Geschichte* (Kamal Joumblatt. The Arab Muslim Legacy and the Role of the Druze in their Understanding of Lebanese History), Berlin, 1994. Quotations in this chapter for which no reference is given are translated from the Arabic edition (Beirut: Dār al-Nahār, 2000).

2 Cf. Chapter 1.

3 See Appendix 7 (pages 213–215).

4 Kamal Joumblatt, *Pour le Liban*, Paris, Stock, 1978, p. 28.

5 This term continues to be used to make use of the ambiguities it conveys. A better term would be "the Frankish wars".

6 Philip Khuri Hitti, *The Origins of the Druze People and Religion: With Extracts from their Sacred Writings*, New York, 1928.

# Summary and Conclusion

The rule of Emir Fakhr al-Dīn II embodied the ideal solution to the "Lebanese Issue". He knew, wisely, how to promote equality among all Lebanese and how to grant them equal rights and responsibilities. He united their ranks without discrimination on confessional, clan or any other grounds. On the contrary, he seemed contemporaneous in his political practices and scorned the exploitation of religious divisions between Christians and Muslims. He applied a fair system of equality in the Middle East long before it was adopted in the West. Then emerged the idea of establishing a united Arab state that would encompass all Bilād al-Shām. This idea gained the support and enthusiastic commitment of the Druze. Although the Druze were aware that they would constitute a small minority in such a state, they spared no effort in promoting this dream, giving their patriotic and nationalist commitments priority over their minority or confessional feelings. To this day, the Druze remain the Middle Eastern community that is least concerned about its minority status and its demographic weakness. Throughout their history, they have never raised a claim for a kind of "Druze nationalism" aimed at transforming their "distinctness" into a political entity, even when opportunities favoured such a scheme during the rule of the Tannūkhi and Ma'anī emirs.

Under the French Mandate, the Druze community of "Djebel al-Durūz" in Syria showed an unparalleled commitment to Arab nationalism even at the expense of its own interests. The Druze revolt against the French authorities in 1925 may be construed as an Arab revolt "par excellence" judging by its development, details and motives. Sultān Bāshā al-Atrash showed unparalleled solidarity with the other Syrian regions in rejecting the proposed French administrative partition of Syria although it meant laying down the foundations for an independent Druze state. His revolt against the French assumed an overwhelming Arab nationalist aspect, not confessional, regional or religious. Even at the height of his victories, Sultān Bāshā al-Atrash refused to abandon his Arab nationalistic principles in return for privileges offered to the Druze by the French mandatory authorities. In recent times, Kamāl Jumblatt, in turn, struggled to preserve Lebanon's Arab identity advocating at the same time, at least initially, stronger relations with Syria, thus ensuring support and protection for the Palestinian resistance movement in Lebanon during the civil war.

However, the current situation reveals, on the one hand, a dramatic gap between the historical legacy of the Druze and particularly the pivotal role they played in the making of modern Lebanon, and on the other, the reduced, almost marginal, role left to them in present day Lebanon.

It is unconceivable to belittle the change and transformation that Lebanon has experienced since the nineteenth century in the context of declining role and status of the Druze Muwahhidun. On the one hand, the impact of the European and mandatory policies and, on the other, the uneven implementation of the 1943 "National Pact", and subsequently the 1990 Ta'if Accord, reveal that Lebanon's internal situation still buckles under the consequences of the transformations currently taking place in the Middle East and the Arab world in general. The Druze, aware of the significance of this situation, have endured its results and consequences, including the loss of their distinctive role as a by-product of the rising influence of the other Lebanese communities on the cultural, financial, economic, and especially demographic, levels. The demographic factor has played a critical role within the context of Lebanon's internal balance by drastically reducing the minorities' margin of manoeuvring – including that of the Druze.

Although they constitute a religious and confessional minority, the Druze do not harbour a minority complex either on the Lebanese or the Arab level, and have always considered themselves an integral, inseparable, component of the Arab Muslim majority. Their importance in Middle East history emanates from a differentiation between their religious and their national identity. This differentiation is clearly apparent in their ethical behaviour, their religious creed and their political practice. Although their political conduct appears to be always guided by values and ethics shaped by their religious customs, it would not have succeeded in asserting itself had it not been for the transcendence of the Druze faith over Druze politics.

The Lebanese politico-sectarian system is definitely incompatible with the Druze political, social and cultural heritage. Nevertheless, the Druze transact realistically with this system in order to safeguard their basic rights. This rational option, which has become a kind of political conduct, is a provisional solution, for history has shown that the Druze are more at ease and at harmony under a secular,[1] nationalist, non-sectarian system. Only a nationalist, secular system can keep in check any sense of minority complex and encourage a more efficient role on the national and Arab levels, allowing the Druze to fulfil the historical vocation they have held since the days of their ancestors.

Consequently, it is clear that the Druze Muwahhidun endeavour to remain faithful to their historical political aim of safeguarding Lebanon's Arab identity and its independence. At the same time, they persevere in remaining the flag bearers for the "Lebanese idea", which they have promoted and upheld since the seventeenth century, refusing to create a geographical entity of their own or to acquiesce to the partitioning of Lebanon. Today, more than ever before, they express their desire to participate fully in the management of their country, to live under a fairer and more equitable distribution of powers between the various communities of Lebanon to ensure greater transparency in the government and the administration. They think only of the Lebanese entity within its current borders, sovereignty and independence. They reject any foreign interference in its internal affairs and are determined to stand against any Israeli aggression.

The Druze share the values, visions and orientations of the Muslim majority in the region. This ensures their sincere, unequivocal, historic affiliation to the Arab nationalist mainstream in the past, present and definitely in the future.

## The Political and Demographic Fabric

Despite the harsh and difficult political circumstances currently sweeping the Arab world, it is unwise to overlook the weight of the Druze communities in the Middle East or belittle their role, as they constitute a strong, reliable and closely knit network. Wherever they are, the Druze demonstrate their patriotic and nationalist feelings through their commitment to their land and their historical legacy. Outside Lebanon, where they play an influential part in political life, the Druze are established in the Israeli occupied Syrian Golan Heights and in occupied Palestine where they form an active and homogeneous community, and in "Djebel al-Durūz", where they have a strong demographic presence. Within the context of the regional balance of influence, this demographic proliferation across several vital Middle Eastern areas represents an important factor for Arab interests and a valuable assistance in the confrontation of Israel's influence and its expansion.

## The Druze Muwahhidun and Syria

The Druze of Lebanon firmly believe in the necessity of maintaining a distinctive relationship with Syria. They actually have a long history of close relations with Syria. In their view, it is their country of haven par excellence and an unwavering ally. They established close and distinct political and cultural relations with Syria during the years of the Mount Lebanon emirate, founded in the seventeenth century by Emir Fakhr al-Dīn. During the Druze internal Qaysi–Yamani conflict, Syria became a haven for the latter when they were defeated in the Lebanese contest, just as it was a haven for the Druze Muwahhidun who were expelled from Lebanon by either the Ottoman or the French mandatory authorities. In 1925, the Druze "Djebels" (Mountains) of Syria and Lebanon earned the appellation of "the heart of the revolution against the Mandate", which was known both as the Greater Syrian Revolt and the Jabal al-Durūz Revolt. Syria's Jabal al-Durūz provided fighters who joined the ranks of their brethren in Lebanon during the 1958 revolt. During the Lebanese civil war (1975–1990), the Syrians tried to protect Lebanon from partition and to preserve its Arab identity, and supported the Druze and other Lebanese communities in their patriotic struggle. The Druze Muwahhidun remained appreciative of this support, of the role played by the Syrians during the war in Mount Lebanon, and of the heavy price they paid to check the Israeli invasion. Because of this steady relationship, the Druze have valued the role undertaken by Syria in Lebanon, while still stressing Lebanon's unquestionable sovereignty and independence, and the inalienable right of the Lebanese to run their own internal affairs without foreign interference. During the civil war, they considered the Syrian role as a balancing and stabilizing factor despite the disagreements that arose between a number of Druze and Syrian leaders at the onset of the war. Ultimately, the Druze appreciated Syria's support for the Lebanese national resistance and its role in laying down the foundations of the civil peace.

Nevertheless, because of the Druze commitment to Lebanon's sovereignty, independence and self-determination, they opposed Syrian interference in its internal political affairs and in all other aspects of its national life. This explains the fierce opposition of the major Druze political forces to the perpetuation of Syria's military presence in Lebanon in the aftermath of the liberation of the Israeli-occupied South in 2000, and their insistence on a redeployment of the Syrian armed forces in accordance with the relevant clauses of the Tā'if Accord. Following the assassination of Prime Minister Rafīq Harīrī, opposition to Syrian intervention in Lebanon's affairs gained momentum, as did the demands for the withdrawal of Syrian troops, the expulsion of their Intelligence Services and the cessation of all interference in Lebanon's national affairs.

An example of this Syrian interference in the internal affairs of the Lebanese religious communities was apparent in their opposition to the Druze leaders' accord on a law intended to manage their community's internal affairs. Had it been passed at the time, this law would have entitled the Druze community to elect its own council and appoint a new Sheikh al-'Aql. Certain forces exploited Syria's intervention to squander or delay the opportunity of electing the Druze boards responsible for the management of their internal affairs and the reorganization of their "household".

However, neither geographical nor historical facts alter their nature, and what is happening nowadays represents an exceptional phase in the history of the Druze relations with Syria. The Druze cannot dispense with their Syrian connection, provided this mutual relationship remains based on parity, respect and non-interference, and within the context of a balanced formula beneficial to both sides. For this reason the Druze Muwahhidun favoured the establishment of normal diplomatic relationships between Lebanon and Syria ensuring good neighbourly relations.

## The Druze and Israel

The Israeli occupiers of Palestine deprived the Palestinians of their basic rights, beginning with their inalienable right to establish their independent state – a focal point in their quest to safeguard their identity, take pride in it and live within its bounds like every other people on earth. However, unlike their Syrian and Lebanese brethren, the Druze Muwahhidun living in occupied Palestine were compelled to emphasize their "distinctness" through their refusal to establish any common ground with the Zionists. Although this "minority" in Palestine has benefited from "privileges" granted by the occupation, these privileges do not entail, in any way, relinquishing their Arab identity nor abandoning their solidarity with their Palestinian brothers. It is imperative to acknowledge the difficulties endured by the Druze minority as well as its efforts and endeavours to persevere and protect its identity and its land. The Druze in Palestine face a formidable challenge, as the state of Israel is trying hard to disassociate them from Islam and Arabism and to exclude them from the struggle for the Palestinian cause. The Israelis are bent on promoting the idea that the Druze are a distinct people, separate from other Palestinians and Arabs, as well as adherents to a different religious community.

The Druze reject all these attempts, and insist on reaffirming their Arab identity and their affiliation to Islam. Similarly, the Druze of the Israeli-occupied Golan Heights resist all attempts to absorb them within the Israeli society or merge them with Israel, and are striving to preserve their Syrian and national identity. The Druze of the occupied territories live to the rhythm of their Palestinian brethren and fellow citizens despite being subjected to harsh economic and political circumstances. It must be mentioned that a small minority cannot bear, on its own, the burden of the complex responsibility needed to resist the schemes of the Zionist state. Today, it is essential that the Arab world becomes more aware of the need to support the Druze minority in the Palestinian occupied lands and the Golan Heights as they face persistent attempts to absorb them within Israeli society or neutralize them and ultimately abolish their Arab identity.

It is unsustainable to claim that the Druze of occupied Palestine have yielded to the Zionist scheme. The Palestinian Druze poet Samīh al-Qāsim has brought to light the fact that the first armed resistance movement in Palestine, the "green palm" organization, was founded by Ahmad Tāfish from Beit Jann in 1929 in association with 27 Arab Druze militants. Samīh al-Qāsim also revealed the extent of the organization's participation in the Palestinian revolts of 1936 and 1948. Although the defeat of the Salvation Army at the hands of the Zionist forces stifled their rebellion, the flame of the mounting intifada and the ongoing Palestinian resistance provide the Druze of occupied Palestine with enough incentives to inflame their rage against the Israeli occupier.[2]

## The Druze Muwahhidun and the Challenges of Modernity

The Druze Muwahhidun, like all other Arabs, Lebanese and Muslims, are confronted with the challenges of modernity. The Middle East is witnessing an extremely difficult situation resulting from a sequence of wars, political instability and the proliferation of religious fundamentalism. The area is also suffering from a political deadlock due to the absence of democratic institutions, the systematic repression of freedoms and the lack – inter alia – of social, educational, and economic reforms. The Arab world, despite considering itself modernized and wealthy, is currently experiencing a phase of retrogression. Moreover, it is facing globalization in what has become an open clash to divide the world into two warring camps: the believers, and the heretics. This division is rekindling slogans, mottos and calls dating back to the Middle Ages. Islam is also passing through a critical phase by projecting an image incongruous with the true essence of its call and message. The regression of the forces of moderation, resulting in a progression of extremist and fundamentalist trends, is alienating Islam from its original nature which preaches tolerance, mercy and the recognition of the "differing other".

Certainly, the Druze of the Middle East are called upon to avoid seclusion and try to restore the historical role they played in the past, and to emancipate themselves from religious and political complexes. They are unable to confront modernity and keep up a dualistic discourse concerning their identity and beliefs. The last reform they undertook goes back more than 500 years. Since then they have not produced an imam of the stature and calibre of Emir al-Sayyid 'Abdallah al-Tannūkhī, nor have they managed to organize themselves in a way that enables them to confront the questions and issues that lead them into a deep state of religious loss. All Druze elders, religious sheikhs and wise men provide conflicting interpretations of the Druze religious creed. Nor does the Druze community in Lebanon have a history of unified interpretations. This loss and confusion is exacerbated by the absence of a single higher Druze religious reference comparable to al-Azhar in Cairo for the Sunnis, or the religious schools of Qom and Najaf for the Shi'is. Some Druze living in the diaspora, notably those in the USA, have recently tried to lift this confusion by living their faith in a free and contemporary way, and they have created internet sites explaining their understanding of Druze teachings.

The Druze, who have managed through all the difficult stages of their history to preserve their identity and their religious teachings, are now called upon to cope with the spirit of the age in which they live, just like any other religious community. Living in a closed circuit is definitely harmful. A minority with a rich heritage, such as the Druze Muwahhidun, has every right to be proud of its identity and to emancipate itself from all its complexes towards Islam and the Arabs.

## What Message Do the Druze Present Today?

In 1987, a proposal calling the Druze to establish their own "ecumenical" assembly was submitted to the annual congress of the American Druze Society held at Durango, Colorado (USA). The ultimate aim of this proposal was the unification of the Druze discourse, putting an end to all sorts of personal interpretations. In my view, this proposal represents the best approach to conceive, plan and reformulate Druze thinking while rejuvenating it in order to play a positive and effective role on the internal Lebanese, as well as the regional Middle Eastern, levels.[3]

The new Druze message presumes their contribution in a renewal process of Islamic thought and discourse, thus ensuring the safeguarding of their original identity. Only through this renewal will Islam be able to contribute to human felicity and to curtail the severity of the prejudices burdening it nowadays, mostly promoted by the raging conflicts between Muslims and non-Muslims in many parts of the world. It would also put an end to the radicalization of Islamic thought regardless of its source or background, bearing in mind that extremism breeds extremism.

On a national level, the Druze must keep up their struggle for a fairer distribution in the administration process of Lebanon's public affairs and for a more genuine co-existence based upon respect, justice and equality among all of its communities. They must also resist all extremist trends and contribute, keeping Lebanon faithful to its original message as a united country with a multi-confessional society, proving that cultural diversity is a source of enrichment and not a cause for conflict and confrontation. Lebanon's development – and that of all Arab countries – can only be achieved by the prevalence of concord among their various communities. The said communities must endeavour, together, to formulate a solidly founded vision of a true citizenry capable of preserving the "distinctness" of each and every community, and at the same time providing a margin for promoting what is common and destined to be shared to everybody's benefit in a single, mundane and all-encompassing state. Such a state should represent a guarantee of freedom and an appropriate frame for an equitable life for all Lebanese citizens.

## Conclusion

Emir Shakīb Arslān was not the sole proponent of the idea of re-integrating the Druze community within the Muslim fold. In fact, he represents a line of thinking within the Druze community. Several supporters of this trend ended up declaring themselves Sunni Muslims, repudiating their Druzism and even refusing to mention their sect on their identity cards. Shakīb Arslān's efforts were discontinued after his death, as the majority of the Druze Muwahhidun was not fully convinced by his arguments. In turn, Kamāl Jumblatt made further attempts to emphasize the Islamic character of the Druze, stressing, at the same time, their "distinctness". What is imperative nowadays is attaining a situation in which we all recognize each other and respect our particularities, uninhibited by fears and phobias, and to call upon all Muslims to recognize the Druze Muwahhidun and respect their status, and to urge the Sunni Muslims to accept other Muslim minorities as such and to respect their choice.

The Druze Muwahhidun also bear the responsibility of playing a pioneering role not only on the level of *inter*-religious Muslim–Christian dialogue, but also on the level of an *intra*-Muslim dialogue encompassing all Muslims. They must also rid themselves of their phobias and complexes in order to stand, confidently and steadfastly, as Muslims facing other Muslims in an honest and open dialogue. Their rich heritage should be their incentive to open up dialogue channels and communications with the all Muslims, especially the Sunnis who constitute their majority in the Middle East. But such an endeavour is not strictly a Druze responsibility, since the Shi'is face a similar situation in relation to Sunni extremism. In the 1990s, the late imam Muhammad Mahdī Shams al-Dīn, then Chairman of the Supreme Shi'i Council of Lebanon, formed a general secretariat for a spiritual Islamic summit in Lebanon, with the aim of activating this dialogue.

In the course of travels that I have undertaken within the context of the Arab team for Muslim–Christian dialogue, I regularly invited religious Druze Muwahhidun Sheikhs to participate in the conferences we used to hold. The favourable and welcoming reactions I received on these occasions are a good indication of how essential these dialogues are. Druze Sheikhs participated, for the first time, in conferences held outside Lebanon dedicated to Muslim–Christian dialogue. During the conference of July 2004, held in Cairo where I was accompanied by Sheikh Fandī Shujā'a and Sheikh Sāmī Abū al-Muna, I was approached by the Vice-President and General Secretary of the Worldwide Congress of Muslim "Ulemas" (Scholars), Dr. Muhammad Salīm al-'Awā – a prominent Muslim and brilliant thinker, widely recognized for his influence in Islamic circles, with a request to organize a Druze–Muslim conference that would be dedicated to the discussion of all issues of concern to both sides. An initiative along these lines could revive the vision of Shakīb Arslān and his efforts in search of Arab–Muslim unity. It could also open the door to a new dialogue that would contribute to the dissipation of premonitions, doubts and suspicions, and all reasons of wariness and phobia, paving the way for a solid, deeply rooted Muslim unity that would not only acknowledge the distinctness of every Muslim party, but also the plurality and diversity sanctioned by the Qur'anic verse: "If God had wished, he would have made you one community" (Q16:93) and a hadīth: "Diversity among my people is a blessing."

This idea of dissipating all premonitions, suspicions and reasons for wariness and phobia in order to launch a dialogue and embark on a discussion remains more than essential to the normalization of inter-Muslim relations and the facilitation of a Muslim–Christian dialogue, especially that such a dialogue is the only guarantee of a peaceful co-existence in the Arab Middle East. It would also be the answer to the Israeli discourse aiming at imposing a unilateral society devoid of any plurality or diversity. The main challenge at this level with regard to working jointly with the Muslims and Christians in laying down its foundations is securing a reciprocal acceptance of all agreed matters and mutual co-operation in solving them, and an acceptance of the differences and the belief in the necessity of holding a serious dialogue about them. This is the only way to help the Druze improve the way of living out their identity and "distinctness".

Finally, it must be pointed out that the discourse presented in this work is based on my personal understanding of the community to which I belong. It may be that some opinions and ideas or analyses are not universally shared but my intention has been to clearly set out my thoughts and opinions, as this is the essence of any dialogue. I leave to my reader the full freedom of expressing his/her thoughts and ideas. Any genuine dialogue should be based on the respect of the other party's opinion and the respect for oneself. It requires honesty, frankness, trust and a sincere desire to seek truth and justice. An ambiguous language and a contradictory or hypocritical approach to a dialogue is always a serious threat to its partners. I have tried my best to avoid these misgivings and remain truthful in word and deed, guided by the words of the great imam al-Shāfiʿī (may God have mercy on him): "My opinion is a verity that is susceptible to error, and your opinion is an error that is susceptible to truth."

## Notes

1 "Secular" in the sense of "civil", in the sense that religion has its place in the personal rather than the public sphere.

2 See ʿAbbās Halabī, *Al-hiwār wa-al-musālaha wa-al-silm* (2002): *Dawr al-Durūz fī Filistīn al-muhtalla ʿām 1948: azmat hawiyya am ʿuqda khusūsiyya*, pp. 161–165.

3 Cf. Appendix 5 for the text of the conference opening address.

# Appendix 1

## The Impact of European Influences on the Druze Community: "The New Look"[1]

### Introduction

My participation in this conference is, to me, a source of great personal joy and I do hope to present a meaningful contribution to our shared reflections on the theme of France and the Levant. In this respect, my participation underscores both the organizers' belief in the importance of the Druze representation in this forum and the special contribution that a Druze representative can provide in his evaluation of the impact of European influences on the peoples of the Levant in general and the Druze community in particular.

Definitely, any approach to the subject will not be fully comprehensive without assessing the impact of a number of recent events – particularly the events that occurred in the aftermath of the attack on the World Trade Center (11 September 2001) and the state of the ongoing political and human struggles, especially the Israeli–Palestinian confrontation in the Levant.

In the context of my remarks, and based on the Druze experiment, I will try to present a better understanding of the past, and project a clearer explanation of the present in order to formulate a new look of the future – all the more so since recent events tend to confirm Samuel Huntington's theory of the "Clash of Civilizations".

First of all, I would like to present a brief introduction about the Druze within the historical context of Islam in the region and the background of Arab–Islamic, as well as Mediterranean, civilization. Then I will speak about two historical events that bear a particular importance in the history of Lebanon and the Druze community: the rule of Emir Fakhr al-Dīn II, and the Druze–Maronite conflicts in 1840 and 1860. Both events illustrate the impact of foreign influences, especially that of France, on the history of the Levant. I will conclude with an analysis of France's relations with the Druze Muwahhidun in the aftermath of the First World War through a study of the reasons that led to the great Druze revolt against the French Mandate.

## The Druze

### Origin of the Word

The true descriptive name of the Druze is *al-muwahhidun* (Unitarians), and this is the only specific name mentioned in reference to them in the sacred texts of the Druze *Books of Wisdom*. The followers of the al-Muwahhidun faith subsequently became known as "Druze" in a period that followed their adherence to their faith, a name derived from Nashtakīn al-Darazī, one of the missionaries of al-Hākim bi-Amr Allāh, who was sent by the great Imam Hamza ibn 'Alī to Bilād al-Shām (present-day Syria, Lebanon, Jordan and Palestine) to propagate the message of *tawhīd,* first initiated in AH 408/1017 AD. The era of proselytization ended in AH 434/1044 AD).

### Geographical and Demographical Distribution

Historical research shows that the Druze Muwahhidun were an integral part of the population of Bilād al-Shām. This fact made their history inseparable from the history of these countries. The term "Druze land" is applied to several regions in which the Druze settled – namely:

- the geographical area that includes the region of the Sammāk mountains and the mountainous regions in between Hama, Aleppo and Antioch in northern Syria

- the central part of the range of mountains known as Mount Lebanon and the villages situated at the foot of Mount Hermon, which connect in the south with the province of Safad, at the foot of Mount Carmel in Palestine
- some inland areas in the suburb of Damascus
- the Lebanese coastal region of the Shūf, Matn and ʻAlay
- the Druze settlement in the region of Hawrān, which relates to a later date, specifically to the aftermath of the Battle of ʻAyn Dārā in 1711, which witnessed an armed clash between the Qaysi and Yamani clans.

Throughout their history, the Druze adopted a constant aim: on the regional level, the defense of Islam and Arab identity; on the Lebanese level, the fight for freedom from oppression and independence from subjugation.

### Druze Doctrine and Historical Beginnings

The teaching of *tawhīd,* or Druzism, originated in Cairo during the eleventh century AD, during the reign of the sixth Fatimid Caliph. Druze doctrine considers that "evil is an aberration from the truth, an alienation from Unitarianism and subservience to polytheism ... goodness, or supreme happiness emanates from uniting with the Only One and the aspiration to true union."[2]

In order to attain supreme happiness, man must seek the truth of the existence and act in accordance with it – that is, he should follow the path of piety and virtue in such a way that it becomes a natural disposition of his self and part of his intrinsic qualities. Thus, he will be able to overcome his egoism and seek union with the Absolute One.

The doctrine of Al-Muwahhidun recognizes equality between the sexes, rejecting all types of discrimination. All humans were created in the image of God and they are equal to each other and before God.

Druze teachings also call their followers to emancipate themselves from the bonds of selfishness and urge them to constantly seek the Ultimate Truth, and a better knowledge of the self and God, provided this knowledge is based on reason and logic and is harmonious with the ever-expanding realm of "science" in its broadest sense – that is, gnosis. The deeper this knowledge becomes, the more it is enriched with new data.

Druzism, besides being – basically – an Islamic sect, is also a mystical faith that invokes love to attain absolute Truth. It is therefore just as able to communicate with Christianity as it is with Islam.

## The Levant and Europe Before the First World War

### The Rule of the Druze emir Fakhr al-Dīn II in Lebanon

Following the Ottoman Turks' invasion of Bilād al-Shām in 1516, the Tannūkhī emirate – then loyal to the Mamluks – fell apart. Druze sovereignty subsequently passed to the Ma'an emirs, in the Shūf district. The history of the Ma'anite Druze emirate of Lebanon is replete with anti-Ottoman resistance. Their most prominent ruler was Emir Fakhr al-Dīn II (1572–1635), who successfully dealt with his opponents and extended his authority over a large area of Bilād al-Shām including parts of present-day Lebanon, Syria and Palestine. His expansion of his Emirate earned him the title "Sultān al-Barr" (Lord of the Land). To secure support for his struggle against the Ottomans, the Druze Emir entered into an alliance with 'Alī Bāshā Jumblatt, the governor of Aleppo and the ancestor of the present Jumblatt family in Lebanon.

Fakhr al-Dīn II attempted to create a modern independent state, free of sectarian, confessional and regional discrimination. To achieve this aim, he established political, economic and military relations with several European states.

Thanks to this ambitious policy, his realm of sovereignty extended beyond any of his predecessors, and even successors. But his aim to achieve independence from the Ottoman rule ended in failure when the Sultan organized a military expedition against him led by the rulers of a number of Ottoman dependencies in the Middle East known as "Wilayat". Their armies attacked him by land and sea and defeated him before holding him prisoner and sending him to Constantinople where he was condemned to death in 1635. His death put an end to any serious hope of achieving national autonomy in Lebanon.

Fakhr al-Dīn was an exceptional statesman in the modern sense of the word. He showed a keen concern for the prosperity, stability and development of his country and his people, and profited from a stay in Italy from 1613 to 1618, bringing to Lebanon several of the modern practices developed by the European Renaissance and attempting to implement many of them in Lebanon – particularly those related to urban development and architecture. He also brought from Europe several experts and engineers to help him in developing the major economic sectors in the country. But, according to some historians, Fakhr al-Dīn's true greatness lies in his avant-garde social policy, which ensured justice and equality for all his subjects. In my opinion, the example of Fakhr al-Dīn clearly negates the theory of the "Clash of Civilizations": here was an Easterner, a Muslim Druze, unburdened by any complex or sensitivity, engaging into alliances with European powers and successfully promoting an economic, social, political and cultural dialogue with them. Moreover, it was not with Europe that he clashed, but with the Muslim Ottoman Empire. As a secular statesman, Fakhr al-Dīn found that stronger ties drew him towards Christian Europe than to the Sublime Porte. Should we not therefore say that the purported clash between civilizations is in fact no more than a conflict of interests? Furthermore, Fakhr al-Dīn, the Druze, established in Lebanon a genuine partnership with the Christians and all other communities in what amounts to an example of co-existence, not clash, of civilizations.

### The Events of 1840 and 1860

The death of Fakhr al-Dīn II weakened the Druze who were forced to give up their political power to the Sunni Shihāb family, some of whose leaders would later convert to Christianity.

The nineteenth century witnessed a further decline in the political power of the Druze chieftains, particularly under the rule of Emir Bashīr Shihāb II, who used everything in his power to weaken their position. During his long reign, he succeeded in eliminating most of the chieftains of the Yazbak and Jumblatt clans. The conflict between Emir Bashīr II and the Druze reached its climax when Ibrahim Bāshā, son of Muhammad 'Alī Bāshā, the governor of Egypt, invaded Bilād al-Shām. Since Emir Bashīr II had conscripted many Maronites into Ibrahim Bāshā's Egyptian army to suppress a Druze rebellion in Wādī al-Taymt, the struggle turned into a confessional civil war between Druze and Maronites, and the conflict led to the infamous massacres of 1840 and 1860, which gave France the justification for its most overt and notorious intervention in the history of the Levant.

## French Intervention

The years 1840 and 1860 have a special connotation in the memories of the Lebanese and their contemporary history, given the way the consequences of their events subsequently engulfed the following period.

First of all, I will try to clarify the direct and indirect causes of these events, which tragically weighed on all Lebanese, regardless of their religious affiliation. Then I will attempt to explain the role played by France and its impact on Lebanon in general and the Druze community in particular.

The roots of these painful events should be traced back to Emir Bashīr II's attempts to weaken the political power of the Druze community by dividing it into feuding factions. Later, he resorted to utmost cruelty and exploited these divisions to weaken them even further and then to eliminate the chieftains of the Jumblatt and Nakad clans. By then, the interference of foreign powers in the internal affairs of the country had increased the internal tension, especially with the Ottomans securing the support of the British versus the French support of the new Egyptian dynasty, established by Muhammad 'Alī Bāshā and his family. This French support sought to achieve two aims: to weaken the Ottomans and leave them at the mercy of the British, on the one hand; and to profit from Muhammad ʿAlī Bāshā's ambition to extend his rule to Bilād al-Shām on the other. Had he succeeded, he would have fallen into the trap set by the French – by being indebted to them for his success – and France would have gained an extra advantage in its struggle with the British to secure a share in the control of the region.

To these external causes of the civil war must be added compelling internal factors of a rather social character – namely, the Maronite farmers' attempts to enfranchise themselves from the burdens of the Druze feudal system. This resulted in the aggravation of the conflict and the widening of its scope and turned it into a confessional struggle that eventually divided the country.

When the Maronites were defeated, France intervened militarily on their behalf directing a crucial blow to the large Druze feudal estates, ultimately precipitating their break up and fragmentation. In turn, the consequences of these events delivered a fatal blow to the notion of the Lebanese Emirate and had serious, even disastrous, repercussions on the future of the country, and the policy of confessional dissension initiated by Emir Bashīr Shihāb II put an end to the idea of the independent Lebanon envisaged by Emir Fakhr al-Dīn II. In fact, the year 1860 marked the end of the first Lebanese state.

Here it must be emphasized that internal factors alone did not justify the violence in Mount Lebanon, nor the scale, intensity or hostilities of the two warring factions. The real reason resides in the fact that the Druze–Maronite conflict represented a microcosm of the brewing conflict between the European and regional powers, which found in the Druze–Maronite dissensions a fertile ground for fuelling hatred and mutual accusations.

The Druze–Maronite conflict, and the support provided by France to the Maronites, might initially have given the impression of a clash of civilizations or cultures. But in fact, it was nothing more than a simple conflict of political and economic interests. Had not this Druze–Maronite dissension existed, the European and regional powers would have found a different battlefield and perhaps even invented phantom enemies. The (then) prevailing external circumstances were appropriate for exploiting the internal situation and fomenting resentments and sensitivities. Lebanon, at that time, became the scene of an open conflict in which the international powers aired out their disputes, and the withdrawal of Muhammad ʿAlī's forces from Bilād al-Shām left a political vacuum which the European countries sought to fill, using Lebanon as the axis of their policies in the Levant. France, Britain, Austria and Russia competed for hegemony over the Levant, and what is more effective than confessionalism as a practical means for achieving this aim?

France had a tradition of friendly relations with the Maronites and, after the departure of Muhammad ʿAlī and Emir Bashīr, found its interests threatened. Great Britain, which was trying to eliminate French influence in its quest to secure the route to India, found in Lebanon a suitable base from which to extend its control over the whole East. It was encouraged in this policy by the presence of its fleet all along the coast from Tripoli to Haifa, in the aftermath of its participation in the military operation that drove Ibrāhīm Bāshā's forces out of Bilād al-Shām. For Russia and Austria, it was in their interest to prevent France and Britain from gaining sole control over the region, so each of them tried to exert its influence. Russia established relations with the Greek Orthodox Church and declared its aim as safeguarding the interests of this church in the East, while Austria announced that it was trying to protect the interests of the Greek Catholics and the Maronites, thus entering into direct competition with France, which considered itself the "maternal protector" of Catholicism in the East and of the Maronites in Lebanon. Britain, thanks to its Catholic consul Richard Murphy, was able to attract several Maronite feudal chiefs to its side, but was unable to win over the Church and the clergy, who considered the British as enemies of the Catholic Church. Later, the activities of the Protestant Church increased the Maronite clergy's hostility towards the British, who then tried their best to win the Druze to their side.

## Notes

1 Opening speech at the conference "France and the Levant", held in Lyon, France, in May 2002.

2 G.A. Karam, *Dieu et l'Homme*, Lebanon, Editions Joquart, 1980, p. 411.

# Appendix 2

## Sheikh Halīm Taqī al-Dīn: A Man of Knowledge, Piety and Wisdom

Sheikh Halīm Taqī al-Dīn, one of our great Druze personalities, tragically succumbed to the hand of treachery while at the height of his maturity and the zenith of his intellectual contributions. His life was filled with memorable achievements.

He succumbed as a martyr of Muslim unity.

Sheikh Halim moved from the judicial body to the political realm in the noblest possible way. Before becoming a judge, he practised law and teaching. His experience in private and public functions shaped the human aspect of his personality. He was brought up in a well-known Druze family under the care of his father, the late judge and outstanding poet Sheikh Ahmad Taqī al-Dīn. His elaborate upbringing left its mark on all his fields of activity. Wherever he was active, he held a distinctive position.

I met Sheikh Halīm Taqī al-Dīn before I had heard of his brilliant reputation or his unabated activities. The occasion of the meeting was the gathering of a group of Druze dignitaries to establish the Druze Council for Research and Development in the aftermath of the assassination of the great leader Kamāl Jumblatt. Without hesitation Sheikh Halīm Taqī al-Dīn joined this group realizing the importance of creating a think tank in close contact with Kamāl Jumblatt's successor – namely, his son Walīd – especially at this tragic turn of events in Lebanon, and the necessity of assisting Walīd Jumblatt in filling the enormous gap left by the tragic departure of his father. Moreover, the repercussions of Kamāl Jumblatt's assassination on Druze–Christian relations in Mount Lebanon emphasized the urgency of such assistance.

It is highly difficult to differentiate between Sheikh Halīm's words and activities as a judge and as a political activist. President Nabīh Birrī – while not yet Speaker of the House of Parliament – rightly summarized his virtues by describing him, at a funeral ceremony held in his memory at the American University of Beirut, as: "compassionate (*halīm*), pious (*taqī*) and a man of religion (*dīn*)".

Throughout the meetings of the Druze Council for Research and Development, Halīm Taqī al-Dīn was the dynamic sponsor of many activities and proposals, and the person who pressed for their implementation. He was an eloquent speaker, clear in his goals, and a deep thinker concerned only with what would benefit his society and his country.

He was a prolific author and published a number of books. He is credited with organizing and structuring the Druze judicial system over which he presided. His keenness on organizing this system was matched only by his keenness on providing justice to his fellow Druze in the easiest and clearest ways. He gave the Druze personal justice system the best illustration of how courts can be an example of probity and order, making it possible for the litigants, the lawyers and the whole judicial community to seek justice without relying on connections or special pleading.

He was a model of honesty and fairness, and his verdicts were legal essays that became, with time, references and sources for precedents and interpretation of Druze personal status law. He was able to explain crucial legal matters in several books that he published, including: *Qadā' al-muwahhidīn al-Durūz* (The Druze Judiciary), *Al-ahwāl al-shakhsiyya 'ind al-Durūz wa-awjih al-tibyān ma'a al-sunna wa-al-shī'a: masdaran wa-ijtihādan* (Druze Personal Status and Aspects of Divergence from the Sunna and Shi'a in Sources and Interpretations) and *Al-wasiyya wa-al-mīrāth 'ind al-Durūz, wa-mi'at mithāl fī taqsīm al-irth, wa-muqārana ma'a al-madhāhib al-islāmiyya al-ukhrā* (Druze Wills and Inheritance: One Hundeed Examples of the Division of an Inheritance Compared with Other Islamic Schools). His last essay was jointly published with

Sheikh Mursal Nasr, who succeeded him as head of the Druze judiciary, and I had the privilege of writing its introduction.

I closely followed Sheikh Halīm's endeavours to ensure the independence of the Druze judicial system and to distance it from any political influence or outside interference in order to gain Druze public trust in their judges. As a member of the judiciary hierarchy in Lebanon, I felt proud, on several occasions, of the Druze judiciary body, especially as its reputation for uprightness and professionalism was spreading in stark contrast to the performances of some other religious and legal courts in Lebanon – all of this due to Sheikh Halim Taqī al-Dīn's straightforward and live conscience. He wanted the Druze judicial system to reflect the ideals of its tutors: to be just, conscientious and completely independent.

Sheikh Halīm Taqī al-Dīn was not solely a judge, lawyer and interpreter of legal texts. He was also a man of religion who respectfully wore the religious robe in his capacity of Prime Druze Judge and because he considered his position to be at the very core of the Druze spiritual institution.

The religious man within Halīm Taqī al-Dīn was not isolated from his environment in search of self-salvation. To the contrary, he projected the image of a new type of religious man convinced that his ultimate concern was working within his community for the benefit of all its members. He possessed a deep and yet open faith, unburdened by the restraints of the past, being both a learned man and a man of action – two characteristics that completed each other in his endeavour to bring about his community's contentment. He sought the inspiration of his Druze teachings in his efforts to determine his verdicts in certain litigations where legal texts were sometimes deemed to be insufficient to ensure the prevalence of justice.

But Sheikh Halīm Taqī al-Dīn's life achievement came at the climax of the armed conflict in Lebanon. At that time he acted as a messenger of entente among all Lebanese factions, urging the renunciation of violence.

His words and views relayed his deep belief in Lebanon's unity on all levels – state, people and institutions – a belief that was also reflected in his attitude towards his own community and the Islamic realm in general.

In fact, Sheikh Halīm Taqī al-Dīn played an outstanding role towards achieving unity within the Islamic communities of Lebanon, considering this unity a prerequisite to the unification of all Lebanese, Muslims and Christians. He enthusiastically adhered to the idea of an Islamic inner understanding as he considered that a few differences in religious interpretations cannot frustrate the case of the common source.

In this endeavour I accompanied Sheikh Halīm Taqī al-Dīn, along with a group of friends who shared his ideas and unabated efforts with other Muslim activists. He was an outstanding pillar of the Islamic Spiritual Summit, and held endless meetings with the late Mufti, Sheikh Hasan Khālid, and the late Imam, Muhammad Mahdī Shams al-Dīn. He never hesitated in joining them in calls for an end to schism, for reconciliation and for a dialogue among the various factions of the Lebanese society in the wake of the destructive war that split the country in half and intensified following the Israeli invasion of Lebanon that resulted in what was called the "War of the Mountain". He played an outstanding role in day-to-day events and was a major contributor to the formulation of the Islamic fundamental principles that engendered an important section of the entente eventually reached by the Lebanese in what came to be known as the National Agreement Charter.

Sheikh Halīm wanted to alter several biased concepts about the Druze held by many of their Muslim co-religionists, especially their skeptical approach to their Islam. He pursued this goal by sharing with them their religious festivities and occasions, and even their prayers. When he told us once that he intended to participate in the *'īd al-fitr* prayers – prayers to be held at the municipal arena in Beirut in 1983 – he asked us to accompany him to this public event.

I will never forget how we met in the office of a dear friend at the *An-Nahār* newspaper, Marwān Hamāda – also from Sheikh Halīm's home town, B'aqlīn – in order to allow Sheikh Halīm to coach us in the performance of the prayer's rituals – as he has always done with a number of devout Druze men of religion.

The prayers were a public occasion in which the Sunni Mufti, the late Hasan Khālid and several Muslim notables took part. It was also an occasion for Sheikh Halīm to demonstrate his deep belief in Muslim unity, both as a subject of faith and a matter of political behaviorism. It may be said, in retrospect, that the two main watersheds of his public career were his contribution to the basics of the Islamic Fundamentals in Lebanon and his participation in the prayers on *'īd al-fitr.*

With the escalation of the armed confrontations in the Mountain following the Lebanese Forces' incursion in Druze villages, we joined Sheikh Halīm Taqī al-Dīn in calling for a march in Beirut that was organized under the umbrella of the Permanent Office of Druze Institutions. He was one of the principal participants in the march, which began at the Druze Religious Centre in Beirut, later to converge on the Government's Serail (*al-sanā'i*), the seat of the Prime Minister. The foremost demand of the marchers was the deployment of the Lebanese army in the Mountain in order to prevent a sedition that actually happened soon afterwards and resulted in tragic consequences for the ongoing co-existence between Druze and Christians in the Mountain.

It was Sheikh Taqī al-Dīn's conviction to maintain the pattern of Druze–Christian co-existence in the Mountain in the belief that its status could be preserved through the deployment of the Lebanese Army in the area. But the political authorities ignored his plea and the events resulted in uncontrolled consequences until the great historical reconciliation in the Mountain achieved by the historical visit of Patriarch Mār Nasallāh Butrus Safīr to al-Muktāra and his meeting with Walīd Jumblatt.

Sheikh Halīm was an outstanding contributor to this initiative, leading the call for an end to violence and for the achievement of unity. This may have been one of the motives behind his tragic assassination. In those difficult days an overwhelming attitude prevailed in favour of keeping Lebanon prey to division, schism, war and violence. Anyone calling for restraint, reconciliation and unity was either targeted or assassinated, as happened to Sheikh Halīm's companion in this endeavour, the late Mufti Hasan Khālid and, before him, the imam Mūsā al-Sadr.

Sheikh Halīm's funeral was held at the Druze Communal Centre in Beirut and prayers were led by the Sunni Mufti Sheikh Hasan Khālid with the Shi'i Imam Muhammad Mahdī Shams al-Dīn standing at his side. We accompanied the funeral procession to B'aqlīn following rubble-strewn paths, as the main road between Beirut and the Shouf District was unfit for traffic, and laid his body to rest in peace in the midst of Ba'qlin – not far from the resting place of another Druze martyr, Kamāl Jumblatt.

I will never forget that this was the only occasion on which I witnessed the Druze *Sheikh al'aq'l,* the late Sheikh Muhammad Abū Shaqrā, conducting the prayers in person.

The chronology of these events bears testimony to the man who sacrificed his life in the service of his country, his community and Muslim unity. He was a truly pious, compassionate man.

May God have mercy on Sheikh Halīm Taqī al-Dīn.

# Appendix 3
# Mysticism in the Druze Faith

Dr. Sāmī Nasīb Makārem's book *Al-'irfān fī maslak al-tawhīd (al-Durūziyya)* (Mysticism in the Unitarian Faith), published by the Druze Heritage Institute in London (2006) aims, according to the author, to acquaint the reader with the creed of the Druzes, especially its elements of Islamic mysticism, and to convey the true teachings of Al-Tawhīd to its adherents.

Dr. Makarem's approach to the subject is candid, coherent, thoughtful and perspective. The text is written elegantly in rhetorical style, and draws on sources as varied as the mystical tenets of the Druze doctrines, the Qur'an, the Hadith, the teachings of the spiritual leaders of the Tawhīd faith, and the select sayings of notable scholars and venerable mystics. The book promotes communication and understanding between the different faiths and religions and, in this respect, it espouses a purely spiritual outlook, permeated with the love of God that the author confirms is the pinnacle of the Tawhīd creed.

In light of Makarem's long list of publications specializing in spirituality, Islamic mysticism, Sufism and Druzism, his latest title may be considered the crowning achievement of his prolific academic record. It stands as a shining beacon against the general ignorance of the truth of his faith and the distortions resulting from the reluctance of the learned Muwahhidun to elucidate their religious doctrine. This reluctance has left the door open for the lesser informed to distort and denigrate the realities of the Druze doctrine and its humanitarian and spiritual aims.

Who is more suitable to perform the task of rectifying the general perception of the faith than a scholar whose life and learning were devoted to exploring the spiritual and mystical realm within which the Druze Tawhīd message evolved? Who is more initiated in the deep intrinsic workings of the faith or more capable of demonstrating that the practice of religious dissimulation ("*Taqiyya*") is not exclusive to esoteric groups, as he proved in his previous book *Al-taqiyya fī al-Islām*.

The author states the object of his book in the introduction: he aims to reveal "the connections between the Druze faith and mysticism". During the process, he hopes to mend the prevailing erroneous views resulting from superficial or invalid understandings of "Al Tawhīd" and mysticism while "respecting the secrecy of some ancient manuscripts as well as the sanctity of foundational tenets of Tawhīd due to what they contain of mystical insights that may not be revealed save to the devout few who have comprehended them, endured, experienced or believed them, and ascertained them before deciding to grapple with their heights". Here Makarem bears witness to the saying of Abū Hāmid al-Ghazālī in *Mishkāt al-anwār*: "The chests of the free are the burial grounds of secrets."

The book consists of an introduction, six chapters and an appendix containing the prayers and invocations of a number of mystic masters, sources, references and an index of Qur'anic verses.

It would be difficult to mention all the important topics covered by the book for fear of subsetting what are in fact coherent subjects through which the author gradates from a preliminary introduction to the Sharī'a, the "way" (*tarīqa*), the "truth" (*haqīqa*) and the "mirror" (mir'āt), to the mystical foundations of Druzism, its seven pillars, and finally mercy, compassion and love.

The author begins with a historical chronology of the evolution of Druzism set it in its general Islamic context as a Muslim sect evolving from Ismā'īlī Shi'ism under the tutorship of the Caliph al-Hākim bi-Amr Allāh, the sixth Fatimid Caliph (408/1017). His rule was basically founded upon esoteric (that is, mystical) knowledge seeking to interpret the word of God within the context of the prevailing circumstances and reach, through Shari, a level of the "way" (*tarīqa*), then gradate (*tarīqa*) to attain Truth, in essence and practice.

This knowledge is not revealed in its entirety, for knowledge is neither a credit nor a liability. One gains knowledge according to one's intrinsic and ethical aptitude to grasp it.

Resurrection, in the Druze understanding, is the fulfilment of (Sharī'a) through the "way" (*tarīqa*) and the fulfilment of the "way" by attaining the Truth.

The Qur'an differentiates between the level of Islam, as an act of acceptance, and the level of faith, as an act of belief to which the Hadith added excellence or perfection in the practice of faith (*al-Ihsan*).

In dealing with unity in multiplicity and multiplicity in unity, the author points out that in Druze belief man does not attain the level of reliance on God, surrender to His Will or submit to His Justice except through the love of His and His praise. This higher level of faith is the perfection in worship, as mentioned in the Hadith, and the path to Unitarism, as noted in the writing of imam 'Alī (may God honour him), and certitude as referred to in the sayings of imam Muhammad al-Bāqir and imam Ja'far al-Sādiq. This is the true level of "Tawhīd", and the first principle of belief in "al-Tawhīd" is the chosen Prophet's saying, "Thou shalt worship God as if you see Him." This level can only be attained by love, and the true "Muwahid" achieves purity in the love of God, as the Druze believe. Knowledge, in their view, is attained by combining the principles of Tawhīd and its practice with a pure love of God – a love devoid of ego and emancipated from any motive but the love of God. That is why supplication to God – that is, sincerity in prayers – becomes one of the necessities of Tawhīd. What benefit is expected from knowledge, endeavour, vision and "*waqfa*" if they were not for God, through God and from God? This is what was meant by the Druze faith in its reference to self-conceit as a source of dualism – that is, a deviation from the One and Only God and consequently a way of living in delusion, nothingness, chaos and contradiction.

Love, according to the Druze faith, is not merely a mental and intellectual condition, nor purely an emotional or aesthetic one, or a spiritual or sensual state only. All of these are aspects of One

Truth: our own essence, as the human essence is solely realized through God and becomes one of His manifestations purified by His love. This is the mystery of love. The One God can only be truly loved with a love that is in its gentleness akin to the gentleness of the divine beloved. The Druze believe that this divine grace is not a divine act happening at a specific time, but a divine concern as inevitable as the inevitability of His existence. Thus the virtuous "Sheikh" considers the divine existence a grace and it is up to each individual to accept it or deny it.

The author refers to a passage from *Fusūs al-hikam* on the manifestation of God, who is Existence "per se", and mentions God's manifestation in the mirror of the hearts of those who have attained spiritual maturity, and can perceive the truth of existence and are certain in their knowledge that existence, as a manifestation of God, does not exist by itself, but through God and in God and for the One God. The universe is a reflection of Him, akin to the reflection of an original entity as an image-copy in a mirror: "God assuaged His Self and called it the Truth, stepped up His Self and called it Creation."

Contemplation, to the onlooker, is commensurate with his mystical awareness, otherwise he would be struck down. But this ascertained vision with which the mystical lover is blessed is only a reflection of the Divine Emanation, just as an image in a mirror is a reflection of the original entity facing it. Nevertheless, the image in the mirror is only a likeness that does not fully embody the original entity, and can only serve to make it closer to understanding. This communion between the mystery of the contemplator and the mystery of the truth is a proportional reaction longing for the transient knowledge of the mystic in his awareness of his relativity and his orbiting around the One God. It is the response of the word to the meaning. It is the connection of this human mystery with the Divine mystery – which are in fact one mystery, even if they seem as two, for this is the unity of the meaning and its expression. Humanity is a language emanating from all people, from their plurality and not their individuality, and plurality is

> what is witnessed by God's zealots. The more the mirror is purified of its Ego, the more the onlooker is more prepared, more [of a]

> recipient and more knowledgeable. This person, transformed into love, acknowledges that the relation of Existence to the One God is akin to the relation of a circle to its point of compass and "if He decreeth a matter, he saith: 'Be' and it Becomes" (Q2:117). Love, in the Druze faith, is sensing unity with the point of the compass in its enamoured orbiting around this central point ... and the true Druze hates no one. Even an evil person, no matter how deeply he sinks into evil, acquits himself of his evilness ... and how can we hate him when his existence is an act of God? But it is his duty to resist and struggle lest he succumb to oppression or capitulates to aggression, or surrenders to evil, out of love for goodness and in support of it.
>
> Knowledge of the raison d'être and knowledge of the reason of existence of all creatures is God's prerogative, will and decree. "If He intends something, His command is, 'Be', and it Becomes" (Q36:82).

The author mentions the seven pillars of Tawhīd: truthfulness, protecting the rights of fellow humans, guiding them to righteousness, directing them to justice, assisting them in achieving what is just and righteous, talking to them in the best discourse. No one attains true Tawhīd except through abandoning the worship of nothingness, renouncing the path of twilight and darkness and alienation from true existence. Once this is achieved he attains freedom from the Satanism that hinders his way towards Truth. If he achieves these qualities he enters into a state of satisfaction, for he would have realized that God, in His Oneness, is the ultimate Goodness, and that He is Truth, Goodness and Beauty, and thus surrenders himself to Him, aware that in the Kingdom of God, the raison d'être of all beings and the sole Being has no substitute nor limit.

This is the call of the author to his fellow Druze to cognize the pure essence of their creed, listen to advice and follow the wisest, as to each nation its own charters and norms.

It is a call to all of us to grasp the venue through which the jewels of revelation were bestowed on us from the higher world and acknowledge how God chose us to be the recipients of the true existence, perpetually longing for perfection, enamored with its beauty and constantly probing, filled with satisfaction, the horizons of contemplation.

It may be that this book compliments its readers with the *mantle* of knowledge and imbues them with true religious knowledge, illuminating the hearts of the mystics with the light of God.

This is the resumé of a book full of precious gems, deep knowledge and the enlightenment of a religious discipline that many who are ignorant of it have tried to distort; many despots have tried to denigrate the historic background of its adepts.

I offer my warm congratulations to its author for his capacity to comprehend and his desire to ensure that knowledge does not remain lost, but rather illuminates the world as a beacon that guides the believers, for the best provision in life is piety.

# Appendix 4

# Kamāl Jumblatt: A Man for Dialogue with the Younger Generation

The 30th anniversary of the death of Kamāl Jumblatt was a revered occasion dedicated to the memory of a patriotic Arab leader who sacrificed his life defending Lebanon's sovereignty, independence and right of free decision.

Many aspects of the life of this great departed figure became better known due to Walīd Jumblatt's sponsoring of the publication and distribution of his numerous books, writings and manuscripts dealing with his political and national struggle. In this respect the Progressive Socialist Party's publishing instrument, "aldar al-taqaddumiya", played a commendable role.

These publications made it possible for the post-Kamāl Jumblatt generation to become more acquainted with him and his political struggle. In spite of the abundance of books dealing with his intellect and his personality, many aspects of his intellect and his exceptional personality remain open to research and investigation. He harmoniously combined in his personality nobility with modesty, intellectualism with spiritualism, strength with humility, high social status and the ability to easily mix with the most ordinary people, never lacking shrewdness and an acute sense of humour.

I was one of those who had the honour of knowing him personally, and I was close to him when, in the early years of my involvement in public affairs, I was still a university student. In this respect, I feel entitled to reveal some of the details of this relationship, which began in 1969 and lasted until his tragic death.

Kamāl Jumblatt was a beacon of knowledge and an idealist who made every young person long to be close to him and understand him, first of all through his political stance, and especially his concern to assess the pulse of a wide stratum of his society – the younger generation in particular. He was a leader whose prominent family background, rooted in political life for hundreds of years, did not impede his ascendancy to the level of popular leadership transcending religious and regional divides. He held office as a minister and Parliamentarian in his quest to participate in his country's political process of decision-making as representative of an Arab segment that played, and continues to play, a prominent role in achieving what Fr. Yoakim Mubarak used to call "the Lebanese idea", and what the late Pope John Paul II subsequently referred to when he defined Lebanon as a "message in plurality and freedom".

To Jumblatt, his Parliamentary message was simply to "spread around him a deep understanding and respect for the human entity as an end in itself, and for the general freedoms upon which it rests: personal freedom, freedom of discussion, freedom of assembly, the right of forming associations, the right of work, the right of life … the Parliamentary representative should hold in his mind and heart, and spread around him and among his fellow countrymen, the principles of the natural right to life and liberty and the pursuit of happiness, principles that are beyond the control of the state and human authority in general … and should protect these rights."[1]

The Druze had lost their prominent political role in the wake of the transfer of power from the Ma'n to the Shihābī dynasty. Then, as a result of French support for the Maronites in the nineteenth century and the Ottoman's policy of accommodation with the Western powers throughout what was described as the "reign of the consuls", Druze influence gradually deteriorated and, by the time of the declaration of the French Mandate, it had become weaker and less spirited. Druze weakness and despondency increased throughout the French Mandate as a result of the biased policy adopted by the mandatory power towards the Maronites at the expense of the Muslim components of the population. Furthermore, the declaration of the state of Greater Lebanon aggravated their political weakness by introducing into it a demographic element. When, on the eve of Lebanon's independence and throughout the independence period, Kamāl Jumblatt assumed the political leadership from his departed cousin, Hikmat Jumblatt, under the auspices of his revered mother, Nazira Jumblatt, the Druze were in a state of degradation on all fronts. As these combined factors resulted in a particularly unusual state of Druze political decline, Kamāl Jumblatt played a conspicuously prominent part in restoring the lost role of the Druze, a role greatly exceeding the weight of the community he represents.

Walīd Jumblatt may also be destined to follow this pattern despite the fact that the Ta'if Accord superseded the Sunni–Maronite political duality of the 1943 National Pact with the aim of guaranteeing the involvement of all Lebanese religious communities in this concordial agreement. At the time, those who held a decision-making position in Lebanon – and particularly the Syrians, who assumed a mandatory authority over the country in the early years of the implementation of the Ta'if Accord – were intent on classifying the Lebanese religious communities into two categories: the larger communities, referred to on several occasions as the "major communities"; and the marginal communities, among whom were the Druze. Today, Walīd Jumblatt plays a role akin to that previously played by Kamāl Jumblatt in exceeding in its importance the role of the community he represents – and this in tandem with the unique personality of both leaders expressed by each of them in their own way and style.

Among the principal events that shaped Kamāl Jumblatt's thinking and left a mark on Lebanon's political life were his foundation of the Progressive Socialist Party (PSP) in 1949, the "white revolution" against the regime of President Bishāra al-Khūrī in 1952, and the rebellion against the regime of President Camille Chamoun in 1958 and the ensuing power struggle to prevent the renewal of his presidency.

The presidency of Fu'ād Shihāb, who strived to build the institutional infrastructure of Lebanon upon legal modern bases, offered Kamāl Jumblatt the opportunity to excel as a responsible statesman engaged in the building of state institutions. During Charles Helou's presidency, the rising hegemony of the Secret Service Bureau and the fear of dragging Lebanon into an axis with one of the (then) striving totalitarian regimes in the area – thus abolishing democratic life and a peaceful co-existence of Lebanon's communities – was enough to convince Kamāl Jumblatt, the freedom lover, to back the candidacy of the late Sulaiman Franjieh to the Lebanese presidency, assuming that he would be capable of putting an end to the interference of the Military in politics.

Within the context of his official activities as deputy and minister, Kamāl Jumblatt noticed that the Lebanese official institutions were failing in the performance of their role as co-ordinators of Lebanon's political life. As Lebanon gradually slid towards civil war, Kamāl Jumblatt founded, and subsequently led, the "National Movement", which included in its ranks parties, political forces and personalities sharing a common non-confessional popular base, thus hoping to formulate a historic bloc transcending religious factions and regional divides, and capable of rescuing Lebanon from sinking in a bitter confessional quagmire, a bloc akin to the "destouri" (constitutional) and "ketla watania" (patriotic bloc) that brought about Lebanon's independence from France, and the historic bloc that joined together the "Nahj" and "Hilf" supporters in ending the meddling of the (Secret Service) Agencies in Lebanon's political life.

Thus, the "National Movement" offered the Lebanese a patriotic base untainted by sectarianism, whose aim was to reform the confessional political system and put an end to any odd practices that hindered democratic life and replace it with confrontations in the streets. Kamāl Jumblatt once said: "Had I been free to choose, I would have left politics aside and completely banished it from my mind."

Walīd Jumblatt undertook to reassess this period, as did the Progressive Socialist Party. In fact, we should all be called upon to critically reassess this chapter in Lebanon's history in order to allow the future generations to draw the right conclusions from it and prevent their country from slipping again into confrontations and conflicts, as is still happening.

The lesson to learn from the chronology of these events is that when Kamāl Jumblatt was given, during the regime of President Fu'ād Shihāb, the opportunity to participate in the building of state institutions, he proved to be an able statesman. And when he noticed, later on, that political power was falling into a level of "political banality" – as he used to describe the members of the political class – he confronted them as a formidable nationalist and popular leader.

I was introduced to Kamāl Jumblatt when he was Minister of the Interior. I was in his office in the "Serail" – the great Serail that housed (before its restoration and renovation) all the offices of the Ministry of the Interior – and this is when I offered him, in my capacity as a student representative, an invitation to deliver a lecture at the College of Law at the Jesuit University of Beirut. At the time, the university was not much in favour of giving Kamāl Jumblatt a platform for his thoughts, as it had become a stronghold for his political opponents known as the "Hilf" (Alliance). However, a number of young open-minded students – few as they were in those days – approached me with a request to invite him, assuming that I knew him well – being a Druze myself.

Not wishing to disappoint them, I did not reveal the fact that, at the time, I did not know Kamāl Jumblatt. So, I arranged to meet him through one of his assistants and paid him a visit at his office in the Ministry. This visit offered me the opportunity to get to know him, and the personal interest he showed in me encouraged me to pursue this relationship and ask him whether I could accompany him, on the day of the lecture, from his home in "Furn al-Hatab" (Beirut) to the university. And so it was.

There, Kamāl Jumblatt, the statesman, gave a lecture in which he focused on public freedoms, the role of the young in continuing to build their nation, the importance of avoiding partisanship and extremism, and the significance of adhering to democratic means, especially in the inter-dealings of the younger generation. How in need we are for a lesson of this kind in our present situation!

I continued to visit Kamāl Jumblatt, sometimes accompanied by a few friends from university. In 1972, at the height of his dispute with the leaders of the "Alliance" and Prime Minister Sā'ib Sallām, the student union of the university invited him to give another lecture.

On the day set for this lecture, I noticed an unusual busyness in the university among the activists of some political cells, and the presence of security elements in the area. Then pictures of Prime Minister Sā'ib Sallām, President Sulaiman Franjieh and Camille Chamoun, and the leader of the Phalangist Party, Pierre al-Gemayel, began to be displayed within the university campus. I then realized that this tense political climate was bound to affect the atmosphere of the lecture. I discussed this eventuality with some of the leaders of the student movement representing the main parties on the campus, but was assured that we were only witnessing a "limited" protest that would not affect the lecture. I informed Kamāl Jumblatt's associates of what was happening and they asked me to put him in the picture with what was taking place. I explained the situation to him, but he replied: "I've been invited and I can't turn down the invitation."

The Lebanese leader arrived at the appointed time while the area around the university was thronged with students carrying pictures of Kamāl Jumblatt's political opponents. The university's great hall was packed with people. Kamāl Jumblatt entered to the sound of hostile shouting alongside some supportive chanting. When the president of the student union began to speak, the shouts of disapproval and objections grew louder. He called on the lecturer to begin his address. The late great man made his way towards the platform. The students tried to stop him and when he continued walking towards it, they squatted on the ground to prevent him from moving further forward. We repeatedly tried to open a way for him, but in vain. I remember one of those accompanying him telling him: "If you wish us to, we can get rid of them, sir", to which he replied: "They're students and they must be treated in the best of ways", warning them against the use of force in any way.

Having been prevented from reaching the platform, Kamāl Jumblatt returned to his seat in the front row of the hall and asked me to bring the microphone to him so that he could address the students from that position. But as he began to speak, someone cut the cable and the microphone stopped working. At that point, we decided that the situation had become impossible, and it was advisable to leave the hall and move on to the "Social Welfare League" at Verdun Street (Beirut).

A large crowd of students followed us, denouncing the disruptive activities of their colleagues. There, they listened to Jumblatt speaking, clearly and maturely, and heard him expressing his desire, without any bitter feeling or malice, to open up a dialogue with the youngsters who rejected his ideas and whom he called "the neo-rejectionists", being the politician who believed that the basic essence of modern democracy is man's freedom in the genuine sense of the word, and equality by nature (*l'égalité naturelle*).

On several occasions, Kamāl Jumblatt had further meetings with his political opponents. One such meeting was held on the eve of the eruption of the bloody events of April 1975, when a friend of mine invited a number of the Christian political elite opposed to Kamāl Jumblatt's policies to a get-together at his home.

In view of the tense atmosphere accompanying the discussions, the oft-repeated collapse of previous dialogues and the occasional use of harsh terms, I was wary of being blamed for arranging such hostile gatherings. However, as I was pondering these thoughts, I realized that Kamāl Jumblatt was quite satisfied with what occurred during the meetings, assuming that it "broke the ice".

In this context, I must also recall another aspect of my personal relationship with Kamāl Jumblatt. When I became president of the Social Welfare League (a body comprising Druze university students) we organized a series of lectures and seminars under the broad title of "Religious knowledge for all Druze".

Kamāl Jumblatt was one of the most prominent participants in this series of lectures, which were delivered at the Society's seat and the Druze community's headquarters in Beirut. I have kept the recordings of him delivering these lectures in which he proved himself unparalleled in his spiritualism and his acquaintance with human and philosophical knowledge, referring at length to several philosophers and quoting them with great ease – especially in the context of defining their role in, and influence over, the doctrine of Unitarianism

(Al-Tawhīd) "for there exists the relationship between what Druze Unitarianism directly adopted from Egypt and what it drew from the Greeks wisemen".

Thus Kamāl Jumblatt, a man of calm and attentive dialogue, was both visionary and firm in his attitudes, modest when dealing with the younger generation whom he constantly called upon to play their part in public life the way he urged the elite to play its part too: a man shunning violence, even though he sometimes preferred it to "surrender and weakness".

In his view, knowledge and action complement each other, along with the example of the early Druze ascetics who considered that complementing knowledge with action was their aim and message. He believed that

> seeking the face of truth is deeper and fuller and closer to the oneness of truth in this visible existence, thus forecasting a new mental and spiritual age that would eliminate from souls the issues of infidelity and atonement and drive Christianity, with the deeply integrated love emanating from its evangelical roots, to converge with the renewed Islam open to its early past, the rule of its caliphs and the tolerance of its Qur'an ... then all conduits of discrimination and apartheid will deeply disappear from souls ... for the vehicle of the issues of infidelity and atonement would have departed unable to return.

To hear him is to attend a school in morality, nationalism and leadership.

Years after he departed, and with the passing of this dark period in Lebanon's history, the Lebanese began to realize the reasons that commanded his departure – that is, the control of all of Lebanon, its seat of decision-making and the dismantling of its leading nationalist elite. The assassination of Kamāl Jumblatt was considered to be the end of an era of objection and resistance and of the attempts to establish a progressive, liberal, open system of government and, ultimately, the beginning of an era of subjugation and weakness.

As a new spring dawned in Lebanon in the aftermath of the tragic death of Prime Minister Rafīq Harīrī and the coming together of the Lebanese on 14 March 2005, Kamāl Jumblatt's call for the protection of Lebanon's Arab identity – the safeguarding of its sovereignty, independence and self-decision on the basis of freedom, democracy and co-existence – was re-instated. In his concern for the younger generation, he nurtured the ambition of transforming Lebanon into a country in which young Lebanese could excel and live an honourable life open to the cultures of both East and West. He was also keen to preserve the harmonious co-existence of all Lebanese communities and their distinctiveness, allocating to religion its own exclusive niche and to the joint common state the reins of public affairs engaged in the initial stages of abolishing political sectarianism and eventually reaching a stage of full secularization, but, in his view, a secularism not aimed at religion – as some interpret it – but at respect for religions and beliefs.

Kamāl Jumblatt's struggle over many years – a struggle he baptized with his pure blood – revolved around the project of establishing a state upon the bases of diversity and the preservation of distinctiveness, shunning sectarianism and its tragic consequences of dividing and weakening the unique Lebanese society. Kamāl Jumblatt opened up the chapter of tragedies in Lebanon but every day his ideas are revived in their quest to prevail and Lebanon's spring flourishes anew, although at the prohibitive price paid in blood by Kamāl Jumblatt, along with a long procession of other martyrs.

May God have mercy on Kamāl Jumblatt. How much we miss him these days, he who once pondered: "Is there a more honourable achievement than crossing over the bridge of death to a life aimed at resuscitating others and giving their cause the power to vanquish and, in time, establish an example of steadfastness and sacrifice in the souls of the combatant?" This is the last will and testament of Kamāl Jumblatt. May it be a lesson for future generations.

## Notes

1 A conference of Kamāl Jumblatt at the "Lebanese Forum", 18 November 1946 under the title "رسالتي كنائب" "My mission as a deputy".

# Appendix 5

## Meeting of the American Druze Society in Durango:[1] An Address on Behalf of the Permanent Office for Druze Organizations

My honourable friends, the President of the American Druze Society, directors and members of its branches, and assembled guests:

I take pride in standing before this gathering to speak on behalf of the Permanent Office for Druze Organizations in Lebanon.

First, I would like to relay to your esteemed assembly the greetings of your brethren and sisters in Lebanon, greetings to your flourishing Society and your convention, which has become a sought after destination for Druze from all over the world in view of its achievements in serving our community in the United States of America and its welcome co-operation in promoting the general Druze goals in Lebanon and elsewhere, especially throughout the disastrous years of the Lebanese war, which reached its climax in the years 1982, 1983 and 1984.

In Beirut, we were virtually in daily contact with your Society's representatives, liaising with them and admiring their efforts and vitality. This exceptional relationship went on throughout the following years and we deem it necessary to continue in the future.

Brothers and sisters. God's will made it possible for us to attend this convention in Durango, Colorado, in this great, hospitable country – that is: 'Afīf Khodr and Ziyād Hamādeh, representing the Permanent Office, 'Isām Makārim representing the Welfare Institution, and Jihād al-Zuhairi representing the leader Walīd Jumblatt.

Myself, even though I attend this gathering for the first time, I am no stranger to your activities. Together with my colleagues of the

Druze Council for Research and Development I have had the honour of co-operating with the American Druze Society and similar Druze societies throughout the world and of inviting them to the International Druze Conference that was due to convene in 1981.

Following the disastrous Israeli invasion of Lebanon in 1982, the Permanent Office for Druze Organizations took upon itself to send delegates, on a yearly basis, to represent it in your convention. Today, I am proud to be among you and to be delegated to address you on its behalf.

The idea of holding conferences has always been close to our hearts since it provides a framework for meetings and dialogues and for pondering upon our problems and their practical solutions. That is in addition to the basic axiom of keeping up the brotherly relationship between us, preserving our friendship and passing it to the younger generations.

Your annual convention represents an example for emulation, and our endeavour has always been promoting institutionalized thinking upon sound foundations in order to channel the vital efforts of the Druze Muwahhidun through the framework of a permanent international conference, with a permanent general secretariat comprising an organizational structure that provides their institutions, associations, federations and vital activities with the opportunity to express their thoughts with the aim of uniting their voice and formulating a united stand *vis-à-vis* the rest of the world. As members of the Druze faith, we were given, 1,000 years ago, the responsibility of preserving the religious, ethical and social principles that our forefathers called for and in doing so we should proceed through consultation and joint activity.

Although the proposal for a permanent conference has been deferred due to particular circumstances – well known to many of you at the time – despite the success of the preparatory conference in February 1980, we are still pursuing our efforts to base this idea on solid grounds.

We deal with the issues arising from the worldwide dispersion of the Druze not as a political matter, but as a cultural and social issue. The Druze' only policy is to defend Arab rights and uphold their cause in conferences and meetings and through their personal efforts, as our history amply illustrates.

Today we find ourselves confronting a problem imposed on us by new circumstances in our life. We are no longer a clan assigned the duty of protecting Islam's gateways from foreign invasions, but a community dispersed all over the world entrusted with the duty of preserving its national and cultural heritage in ways that do not contradict with the social systems of our countries of settlement. We are no longer a small closed society harbouring its own beliefs, no matter how sublime they are. We have become a community that must stand up to the challenges of modernity and relay its thoughts to the world within the context of contemporary ideas. Our success in this endeavour greatly depends upon our ability to work, collectively, in an institutionalized manner and through democratic dialogues and organized activities.

The Druze survival in the East and their ability to accomplish, over the centuries, and despite their small number, outstanding military and cultural achievements, was made possible by their reliance on reason, logic, consultation and on an exceptional spirit of sacrifice that cannot be the product of ignorance or hesitation, but the outcome of a determined faith in their rights and a genuine identification with their Arabism that won them the admiration of historians and poets. Druze military victories in recent years were the direct result of the social cohesion between their leadership and the popular base.

As I have mentioned in previous addresses – some at past conferences – the Druze have devoted their victories to the nation and Lebanon, hoping to liberalize the Lebanese regime and promote its status from an undemocratic, authoritarian state to a more progressive one that takes into consideration the longing of its citizens for a free, emancipated home state built on justice and equality. We have full faith in the present Druze leadership, represented by Walīd Jumblatt, and in the continuation of his struggle to achieve this aim.

We were drawn to your convention by the desire to see your Society take a leading role in bringing about institutionalized forums in the Druze diaspora worldwide. If we call upon your conference to work for the achievement of this aim, it is because your existence in this affluent country, with its high standards of freedom and democracy, offers you the opportunities of freedom of speech and expression. This being the case in this country, we definitely expect your Society to take the initiative, without delay, in re-opening the files previously submitted to you by the Druze Council for Research and Development within the context of preparing the Druze international conference previously planned for the summer of 1981. The council, and then the Permanent Office for Druze Organizations, have been promoting these ideas.

As to the subjects that need to be researched with due care, they are:

- The religious issue, with the aim of putting its doctrines within the reach of all Druze in general, and not only a chosen few, in order to preserve the Druze identity in the midst of the turbulent circumstances we live through today.
- The historic issue, by making the history of the Druze Muwahhidun easier to comprehend by the younger generation by presenting our fathers', and forefathers', achievements as examples in heroism and self-sacrifice, thus dispelling the fallacies propagated by some biased historians about their role in the setting up of their country and the upholding of its existence and independence.
- The organizational issue, in order to set up the relevant framework for the institutionalized activities I referred to earlier, by way of a permanent general secretariat convening the various federations, institutions and associations, in the homeland and the diaspora, under one organizational umbrella capable of channelling our efforts, facilitating our communications, and confronting our internal and external foes. To achieve this goal, we hope that your convention recommends the formation of a preparatory committee for such a conference, setting out its aims, schedule and proposed executive arm.
- The socio-economic issue, already tackled by your brethren in the homeland in their quest to manage the dire consequences of the war through relying on institutions caring for the families of the dead, disabled, wounded and sick. Here we would like to emphasize the pressing need to reach a decision on practical

steps to support the Druze Organization for Social Care, which, in our view, is a beacon of hope in helping those who suffered from Lebanon's long ongoing disaster, and also providing for the completion of the Druze health centre in 'Ayn Wazayn.

- The cultural-media file, which the Permanent Office for Druze Organizations is following up through commenting on everything said or written through their daily monitoring of Lebanese, Arab and world events and their documentation. The Druze Council for Research and Development also plays its part in promoting intellectual activities by waging a cultural campaign and publishing highly informative books. In this regard and, from this platform, we call on your convention, to support the Permanent Office's special fund for this activity in order to allow the Office to actively pursue this mission.
- The political and military file. Although your Society is not directly concerned with it, each and every one of us shoulders, on a personal level, the responsibility of supporting our politico–military position by all available means, not only with material means, but [also] by explaining the general Druze position that is, under the leadership of Walīd Jumblatt and the PSP (Progressive Socialist Party), which is in concert with the united Muslim position and that of all the nationalist forces. Nothing is more indicative of the importance of this matter than Walīd Jumblatt's repeated visits to you and his numerous communications with you, both individually and as a Society, and the repeated requests of the Permanent Office to forge a suitable framework for our future activities, taking into consideration the available resources within the context of the laws and structures that regulate your existence and responsibilities as Druze citizens directly concerned with what is happening in your country of origin. Therefore, we hope your Society will positively respond to every initiative undertaken by the Druze leadership, not because we aim at sparing you the effort, but in order to channel your activities within a process conducive to fulfilling the hopes pinned on you and on your contacts in the

> decision-making capital of the world regarding the situation of your brethren in the mother country and its outcome that will undoubtedly affect your future and that of your children.

Furthermore, we were acquainted, today and by your previous conventions, with the religious concerns you face in your endeavour to maintain your identity, and the fact that you have opened the door for discussing numerous opinions and religious interpretations brought from outside or inside your circles. We firmly believe that free discussions are bound to clarify thoughts. However, a matter of such importance cannot be decided on an individual basis by one person or one body no matter how high his or their status is in the mother country or abroad. Rather, it should be globally agreed upon through a precise "ecclesiastical" formula capable of unifying the religious doctrines and putting an end to personal interpretations. Any uncoordinated activity in this regard will only add dissension in our midst, a development none of us intends – God forbidding. Therefore, we call on you to continue your co-operation and dialogue and remain receptive to any initiative, keeping everything within its appropriate limits until the time is ripe to prepare the global "ecclesiastical" formula which, alone, bears the right to develop and unify religious outlooks.

Our aim is unity, and union is our guiding principle. Our community has never assaulted the others but has always been a thorn in the eye of its foes and a spear in their side. In the war inflicted on us, your brethren, the righteous martyrs, paid with their lives, youth and future the price exacted from them in order to preserve a homeland for you and dignity for your community. Their battle was fought in self-defence and for the protection of their land and honour.

Brothers and sisters, I have spoken at length because our internal affairs and our concerns demand seizing every opportunity to explain our situation in your country of origin still preoccupied by the burden of self-defence, setting aside, for the time being, all aspects of the normal civil life you enjoy in this great country, the beacon of freedom, democracy and justice, even though these values are not practised in our Middle Eastern region. I am certain Lebanon will eventually emerge victorious over all obstacles hindering its ambitions, progress and democratic development. It is always in the nature of countries to rise up again from the ashes, like the phoenix. And in your country are men of will, and their will shall be granted. God Almighty supports their hopes.

May peace, mercy and God's blessing be with you.

## Note

1 This address was given at the annual convention of the American Druze Society in Durango, Colorado in 1987.

# Appendix 6

## An Address of the Druze Representative to the Synod Convened to Discuss Lebanon[1]

Your Holiness
Reverend fathers
Brothers and sisters

It is an honour to represent the Druze community at your venerable gathering convened in response to the invitation of His Holiness Pope John Paul II, revered by all Lebanese, regardless of their religious affiliation, as a spiritual leader and a great friend of theirs. It is not a mere coincidence that the Vatican attaches a great importance to renewal in Lebanon. His Holiness highlighted the importance of Lebanon by granting it the status of "a mission". Indeed, Lebanon is more than a country – it is a mission with human dimensions.

Since this Synod was first called, in 1991, I have closely followed its preparatory activities over a period of months, not unaware of the importance of the invitation addressed to all those of good intention. In fact, the invitation was not addressed to the Lebanese in general, nor to the Christians in particular, but to all those of good intention. It is therefore a matter of human dimension.

Within the time allocated to me, I will touch on three subjects: the consolidation of the national entente, the reassessment of the Christian role in Lebanon, and the resumption of the Druze–Christian relationship.

## Consolidation of the National Entente

We earnestly share this revival of the Lebanese awareness of their cause, and the belief in a diversified Lebanon, alongside the reassertion of the principle compatriotic belonging that must underpin the allegiance of all Lebanese to their country.

Despite everything we experienced and all you have heard of or seen in Lebanon, the points of agreement between the Lebanese by far transcend the points of diversion. All Lebanese suffer from common economic and social problems and share, sometimes unconsciously, the same aspirations. Therefore, they form a "single entity" in dealing with the daily necessities of life, healthcare and economic problems, even though they may differ in the way they administer legal matters concerning their personal status.

The Tā'if Accord offered a transitional base for the establishment of a new political system in Lebanon. We therefore deem it is useful to participate in an overall political discussion aimed at formulating an electoral law capable of satisfying the ambitions of all Lebanese sects in taking into consideration their particularities. We invite all Lebanese, particularly the Christians, to participate in the forthcoming Parliamentary elections in order to prevent the country from reverting to the situation that arose as a consequence of boycotting the 1992 elections.

We hope that, at the earliest opportunity, it will be possible to treat the Lebanese differences within the context of a House of Senate representing all Lebanese sects, Muslim and Christian communities alike, on an equal basis.

As to the points of agreement, they could be dealt with in the framework of a Parliament that would ensure national, non-confessional representation, and where the people's representatives are elected on a national, non-confessional, basis. This system would offer the Lebanese minorities an additional element of assurance and would constitute a step forward in the march to abolish confessionalism from Lebanon's political life.

We believe that this step is essential as a transition from a purely confessional system to a system capable of protecting national harmony and injecting Lebanon with the needed immunity to overcome its internal ailments. This transition cannot be achieved without the active participation of all Lebanese, and the Christians in particular.

## The Reassessment of the Christian Role in Lebanon

We welcome the initiative of renewing the Christian Church in Lebanon. Such a renewal is a necessity confirmed by the invitation of His Holiness the Pope to convene this Synod. Regrettably, some political formations and some trends within the Church itself have contributed driving the Lebanese Christians, and consequently all Lebanese, to a stalemate. Obviously, this was not the only factor behind Lebanon's tragedy.

It is useless to present the "balance sheet" of a political trend that led the country to a real tragedy, as you all know. Needless to say that extremism breeds extremism and justifies its opposition, and by feeding on each other extremism results in expulsions, migrations, massacres and misery ...

This mass madness – and I hope you will understand my frankness – has led some parties to wage a war of slander and factual distortion impinging on the sacred theological beliefs of other communities, particularly the beliefs of the Druze. Books were written, and publications circulated profaning Druze teachings and their relation to Islam and depicting them as a community on a contradictory course with its fellow Muslims. Needless to reiterate, on this occasion, that the Druze are Muslims. We still believe that this political perversion would never have gained the full support of all Christians.

This suicidal situation which Lebanon endured for about 20 years requires a genuine awakening of Christian – and Lebanese – awareness in general. This emphasizes the importance of His Holiness's initiative in inviting all of us to engage in an assessment of this issue.

We, as Druze, believe – and this belief emanates from a long era of living together (myself, I was a student at St. Joseph's University of Beirut) – that this political behaviour was incompatible with the spiritual, social, political and cultural heritage of our Christian brethren in Lebanon.

We consider the presence of Christians in Lebanon is essential for both the Arab world and Lebanon. Their role and their participation in the Arab cultural revival is undeniable. I would even say that we regard the position and role of the Christians as imperative in the revival of Lebanon. Our shared history has promoted a mutual bond of friendship and concord between the Druze and Christians, a bond which proved difficult to maintain sometimes, but never a case for divorce.

## The Resumption of the Druze–Christian Relationship

I do not hide the fact that the Druze are a minority. This word, dear to the hearts of our Christian fellow citizens, is also a source of anxiety to us. Therefore, we share with them common aspirations.

We have witnessed periods of harmonious relations in our history. The outcome of these periods was greater and more important than any of the periods of crisis. Without going far in quoting the past – the aim of this gathering being building for the future – I would like to remind you of some stages worthy of consideration, which may help us understand how confessionalism grew within the context of the relationships of the various eastern communities.

As an example, Emir Fakhr al-Dīn, who was brought up, to a large extent, in the fold of a Maronite family (the al-Khāzin clan) introduced the Christians to the Druze Mountain. When he was forced to abdicate, he found refuge with the Medici family in Tuscany. When the last of the Druze Maʿn emires died, the Druze notables met together and appointed a member of the Shihābī clan to succeed him, an emir who did not belong to the Druze sect ... and there are many such examples of tolerance and co-operation.

The two conflicts that set the Druze and the Christians against each other (in 1860 and 1983) cannot erase the basic gains achieved by both communities.

However, in order to build the future, we should be objective and acknowledge the internal dimensions of the 1983 tragedy in the Mountain. I hope my words will not shock you if I mention that some Christians consciously and deliberately breached the (then) existing political equilibrium between Druze and Christians in the Mountain. The Druze waged a legitimate defensive war as the tragic events took place on the land of their ancestors where they have lived, generations after generations, in friendship and harmony with the Christians.

Today, the Druze leadership is endeavouring in all honesty and sincerity – with the support of the whole Druze community and the means provided by the Lebanese government – to achieve a speedy and honourable return to the mountains for all its displaced Christian inhabitants.

Today, the fears of the Druze, as a minority, are similar to those of the Christians. Their concerns are focused on preserving their distinct identity within a framework of complete freedom. Nevertheless, the status of the Druze as a minority did not develop as a phobia from the majority, and they reject any form of cultural, social or political isolationism.

The Druze have striven to affirm their Arab and Lebanese identity, alongside all Lebanese nationals. We believe that this sense of national allegiance helps us to overcome our minority status and share the political and cultural ambitions of the majority. From this perspective we are, with the Christians and Muslims, on the same battlefront against all forms of fundamentalism as we share their assessment of the dangers that threaten us, especially with regard to "Eastern fundamentalism" and Western atheistic secularism.

We, as Easterners, remain devoted to rational spiritualism.

## Conclusion

Within the complexities of the East we must adhere to simple ideas as the danger of deviation is extremely great. This is why we are not pessimistic.

We share with all other communities and all Lebanese a great faith in the future of Lebanon.

Lebanon, as the Synod working paper mentions, is not just a country. It is more than a country. It is space of freedom.

Finally, brothers and sisters, I say that God created us different from each other, although it would not have been difficult for Him to create us all alike. The challenge facing us is to use this diversity to enrich our lives rather than turning it into a source of conflict.

We are confident, and we would like you to share this confidence, that the right to differ is, like the right of similarity, a basic right. And as André Faroussar said, we must fight to uphold this right as an asset for civilization and a guarantee of peace among peoples.

## Note

1 At the Vatican in 1995.

# Appendix 7

## The Mighty Refuge of the Druze: Sheikh Abū Hasan 'Ārif Halāwī[1]

Sheikh Abū Hasan 'Ārif Halāwī is the cornerstone of the Druze spiritual establishment and its most prominent figure. He is the spiritual leader of the Druze of Lebanon, Syria, Palestine and the rest of the world.

It was due to his humility and chastity that he acquired his status at the head of this Arab social stratum. Through his simplicity he gained precedence over his peers.

He transformed his life into an ethical paradigm and a model of behaviour tempered only by his spirituality. He was a listener to all sayings but a follower of the best of them. He was a recipient of the essence of Unitarianism as revealed to him. He longed for perfection and did not confine it to himself but shared it with others, what was apparent or inconspicuous among the incidental and the essential, the pure and the complex, thus propagating, in the process, his inner light and reaching heights that allowed him to become a shining beacon of grace and simplicity.

It is no surprise to find the Druze of Lebanon, Syria, Palestine and the world gathering around a symbol of theirs reputed for his piety and serenity, nor his winning the consensus of Druze of all persuasions and all corners of the world ... feelings that he reciprocated with modesty, sympathy and faith, and the devotion of his life to truthfulness and the safeguarding of his brethren.

This great Sheikh, a religious symbol acquainted with God's ways, ascetic and chaste, used to project a perplexing image to all those who look at him, for in his nature was embedded loftiness and aloofness, and in his face a glow of a divine light, and in his thoughts rays of a gentle spirituality incarnated in his body, transforming him into a slim, light and simple man whose footsteps could hardly be heard, his shadow hardly noticed, except through the awareness of being in the presence of a devout Sheikh different from any other Sheikh or any other man.

Sheikh Abū Hasan ʿĀrif Halāwī was a unique phenomenon in the modern history of the Druze. He lived over 104 years in constant activity, bringing people together, getting them to speak with one voice and unite their ranks both in peace and war, and especially striving for the consolidation of their ascetic faith.

His love was profound, his chastity constant and his interest always defined: the need for solidarity in order to achieve the best course of action, and above all, the necessity of religious devoutness in order to guarantee an afterlife based on his deep belief that this Arab social stratum beholds a history and a heritage worth preserving with lives and blood.

To him, the mission of the Druze Muwahhidun was to safeguard Unitarianism (Tawhīd) until the Day of Judgement, and in politics uphold the flame of Islam and Arabism in order to remain faithful to the conduct of our fathers and ancestors.

The Druze hold a futuristic mission: the renewal of Islam through more openness to other faiths, and the provision of modernizing opportunities to enable it to survive and grow, and, internally, to preserve our neighbour. We all remember his role in upholding the state of co-existence throughout the years of hostilities, and his blessing on the return of the displaced (Christians) to the Mountain in order to reinstate the Lebanese national texture in all its elements.

This great Sheikh and exemplary imam left his mark on his era. He was a witness to major events experienced by his country and his community. Everyone felt that this noble Sheikh was an icon of protection from aggressive intrigues and a bulwark for the preservation of the dignity and existence of the Druze community.

Throughout his life he represented a noble spiritual heritage. His vision enriched his colleagues and inner circle with eternal, bequeathed values. He passed on to the new generations the wisdom of the elders who founded and spread the faith, and whose preaching encompassed the divine and the mundane. He is among the sanctified guardians of faith, a bearer of the Muwahhidun creed, a scion of divine grace, mysteriously in contact with the Divine Being. His head bears the crown of the Arabs and his cloak shelters the warmth of faith, endurance and the Muwahhidun's pride. He was an incarnation of the way of life set out by the Emir al-Sayyid 'Abdallah al-Tannūkhī, a virtual brother of al-Sheikh al-Fadel and a symbol of benevolence and abstention from wrongdoing, detached from everything but his endeavour to please Almighty God.

## Note

1 Published in *An-Nahār*, 16 November 2003.

# Appendix 8

# Muhammad Khalīl al-Bāshā: An Illuminating Personality[1]

The dearest thing to my heart would be to have an opportunity to write about the late scholar Muhammad al-Bāshā, may God have mercy on him. He was an old friend of my late father and I opened my eyes on his friendship, which grew deeper over the years to be transferred to us after my father's death, may God have mercy on him. The merits, qualities and talents of Muhammad al-Bāshā cannot be summed up in a few lines. He was a brilliant administrator who served for a long period in the Lebanese Civil Service. He was a model of generosity, uprightness and experience. Like other distinguished civil servants, he left a mark that neither the passing years, nor the events that struck the public sector – whether before or after the civil war – can erase.

Throughout his entire life, the late Muhammad al-Bāshā was bent on widening his scope of learning, pursuing knowledge, boosting his knowledge of philosophy and following up the study of languages. He acquired from his various sources of knowledge an exceptional wisdom and a clear vision, making his writings a definite guide to how best to synchronize the love of knowledge and the love of giving, as his output was prolific and diversified. He did not restrict his knowledge to one subject, or his research to one discipline, and his extensive output reflected his multitalented personality, with its tolerant nature, amiable presence, pleasant friendship, mild manners and ethical principles. His knowledge prodded his modesty, his command of the Arabic language made him an erudite writer. He was a religious person with an open mind. His openness was, in itself, an act of faith.

He wrote about illustrious and famous people – being himself one of them – in his compendium of Druze notables. He wrote about Unitarianism (Tawhīd) and its attributives, about reincarnation and its manifestations. He was a believer without having a closed mind, genuine like all the revivalists of the wisdom of his Druze fellows, a spiritual scion of the mystical wisdom of the elders. He researched and strove to achieve a greater understanding of this world. He elaborated new means for communicating his thoughts, relying mainly on original sources. He did not restrict himself to issues only related to his country and language, but was interested in wider scopes of knowledge, an interest that led him to translate books and conduct studies enriching to the Arab library. He perused the language and its dictionaries, revised several manuscripts, not least the Arslān family records, which contain a record of Arab and Lebanese history during the rule of Bilād al-Shām by the Druze emirs, and derived his own particular analysis from all that had been written.

I knew him intimately and lived closely alongside him. He was a success to his family, a Prince in his behaviour, a penetrating intellect blessed with the wisdom of an elder. Above all, he knew how to give generously, not keeping to himself what he knew, thus allowing the younger generation to benefit from his knowledge and the outcome of his research and studies.

May God have mercy on Sheikh Muhammad al-Bāshā. We miss him in these dark days as a beacon of light, an illuminating personality intent on giving, transparent in his spirituality, patient in his sufferings, and always beholding the joy that only believers can sense.

## Note

1 A personal testimony given on the occasion of a book published in his memory: *Dr. Khalīl al-Bāshā: his life and thought*, by Riyādh Husayn Ghannām (2003).

# Appendix 9

## In Commemoration of the Druze Emir al-Sayyid Jamāl al-Dīn ʿAbdallah al-Tannūkhī[1]

To start with, I would like to salute the vitality of your committee and its intense and tireless efforts to present everything new to its guests.

Welcoming your presence, I am doubly honoured to notice that the purpose of your meeting is to acquire more knowledge about the "others" who are different from yourselves.

In the context of this series of conferences that dealt with Lebanon's historical personalities, and in response to the organizing committee's request, I seize this opportunity to reflect upon a personality of utmost importance to both our historical legacy and our Druze conduct, that is Emir al-Sayyid Jamāl al-Dīn ʿAbdallah al-Tannūkhī.

It would have been easier for me to choose a topic about other prominent Lebanese Druze personalities. In this vein, historical figures such as Emir Fakhr al-Dīn II or Sultān Bāshā al-Atrash, or contemporary personalities such as Kamāl Jumblatt, immediately spring to mind.

However, the choice of Emir al-Tannūkhī is, to me, both a challenge and a dilemma. The challenge arises from the fact that most Lebanese, apart from the Druze – and sometimes even the Druze themselves – are not familiar with the personality I will be talking about, whereas the dilemma lies in my presentation of a non-academic work since I am not in the process of delivering a course. Moreover, this dilemma is compounded by the rarity of available French references and documents – the language of my address – dealing with the personality of the Tannūkhī emir or his period.

Given this situation, I have taken up this difficult challenge in the hope that this choice will enrich us all.

My approach will be as follows: first, I will deal with the personality of the Emir and the historical background of his birth and upbringing until the time he achieved fame. Second, I will talk about his work and the renaissance he brought about on the moral, legal and communal levels. Finally, I will try to evaluate this research based on the scale of their success or failure.

However, before presenting my subject, I must point out that two weeks ago, on the occasion of ʻĪd al-Adha, I conducted, with a number of Druze elders, an interesting dialogue focused upon the renovations the Emir brought about in the fields of Druze doctrine and ethical conduct. I noticed that our elders, who strictly adhere to the fundamentals of their faith, prefer using a different term than "renewal" in referring to Emir al-Thanukhi's contribution – to them he achieved a "revival" of the Druze doctrine. This "revival" was necessitated, from the Emir's point of view, by what he noticed, at the time, as signs of laxity in the Druze community's faith and ethical behaviour, 500 years after the doctrine's declaration. Therefore, he endeavoured to clarify the doctrine and stress the need to a commitment to follow its conduct. I will, therefore, use, from now on, the term "revival" rather than "renewal".

## First, the Emir Himself

The Emir al-Sayyid Jamāl al-Dīn ʻAbdallah al-Tannūkhī was born in ʻAbeyh in the ninth century AH (around AD 1417). He was the scion of a noble family whose roots go back to the Buhtur and Tannūkh clans. Al-Nuʻmān ibn Mundhar ibn Māʼ al-Samāʼ, one of his ancestors, was one of the greatest kings of Hīra, the descendants of Qahtān and ancestors of the Arabs. His mother, Princess Rīma, is a descendant of the same family. He was named ʻAbdallah and became known, later on, as Jamāl al-Dīn.

The Emir al-Sayyid was born to a purebred Arab family belonging to the upper social and political class in the political capital of the Buhturī-Tannūkhī Emirate. Despite being born into a noble Arab family, he grew up in the fold of his mother's family, in the aftermath of the death of his father at a tender age.

From childhood, he was remarkable for his sharp wit and exceptional ability to learn. He devoted his youth to studying the sciences and religious chronicles, thus gaining a good reputation among the clerics who discovered in him exemplary abilities and exceptional talents.

The Tannūkh dynasty ruled Lebanon for centuries in the Middle Ages, throughout difficult political circumstances. They were among the first to embrace the "Tawhīd" call and the Druze message.

In fact, the Tannūkh tribe comprised three Arab–Christian clans: Bahrā', Taghleb and Tannūkh from which descended the Tannūkhīs who, since the dawn of the Arab conquest, settled in northern Syria and in the vicinity of Beirut in western Lebanon. They converted to Islam in AH 165 (AD 741) and then embraced the Druze faith at the beginning of the eleventh century, and persevered in maintaining their Arab identity and their allegiance to Islam.

The "Tawhīd" teachings originated, in Fatimid Egypt, in the eleventh century (AH 408/1017 AD). This era, and the following one, were characterized by a politico–religious feud between the Fatimid Caliphate in Cairo and the Abbasid Caliphate in Baghdad, both vying for full control of the Arab world. Being at the core of this feud, Bilād al-Shām (modern Syria and Lebanon) bore the brunt of the clash of its ambitious mighty neighbours and, being an inevitable corridor spanning the midst of the Islamic world, it became, to the Fatimid Caliphate, a connecting bridge to Baghdad – a strategic geographic situation substantiated by the constant attempts of the Seljuks, the Crusaders (who landed in Syria towards the end of the eleventh century), the Moghouls, the Tatars and, eventually, the Mamluks, to dominate Bilād al-Shām.

This background depicts the critical situation of an Arab world plagued with chaos, wars and divisions, and this concise historical narrative provides a deeper understanding of the repercussions of such harsh circumstances for the Druze community, until then not independent in running its own affairs. Apart from the social consequences of this chaos, the Druze themselves adopted many concepts that were alien to their creed.

In the midst of these prevailing conditions, the Emir al-Sayyid was considered a divine messenger, and his stature grew in proportion to his wisdom and distinctiveness. People flocked to him from all corners seeking his guidance and advice. He encouraged the building and repairing of mosques, ordered the Qur'an to be recited according to the established rules of recitation, and called for the rejection of sinful behaviours and the acquisition of virtuous characters.

He devoted one day a week to preach to his disciples and lecture them about how the Druze way of conduct would qualify them, in turn, to propagate the faith and preach in their villages. He extended his extreme benevolence to other religious communities, too, as he believed that all human beings are the children of God.

His brilliant success and his wide scope of knowledge aroused the envy and resentment of the wicked. However, he did not seek to confront them; he chose instead to depart to Bilād al-Shām to spread there his wisdom and extend his guidance to jurists and scholars. He stayed in Bilād al-Shām for 12 years, and gained the respect and acknowledgement of everybody.

The Emir al-Sayyid possessed a wide-ranging library that included around 340 manuscripts. He himself was the author of several books. His most famous work was known as *The Commentaries of the Emir al-Sayyid*. It runs to 14 volumes.

Within the Druze community, the Emir holds the most pre-eminent position among those who bequeathed their belongings to charity foundations, for he was the founder of the Druze Endowments Committee.

## Second: The Emir's Endeavour to Revive the "Tawhīd" Way

Firstly, I will describe his contribution to the Druze Endowments Committee and then report on his endeavours to revive the Druze way of life.

## The Druze Endowments Committee

The increasing number of people keen to acquire knowledge caught the attention of the Emir. However, most of them were deprived of the basic means to pursue a decent living. This situation aroused his concern that they might fall prey to ignorance, corruption and illiteracy. He was torn between his will to satisfy their longing for knowledge (through setting up schools in villages despite the cost it would incur, including the teachers' salaries), and leaving the social and religious situation to deteriorate – which was unacceptable to him.

Appointed as the spiritual leader of his community, the Emir focused his attention on the values of the society within which he lived, convinced that all reforms must be channeled through education in schools and mosques, and through urging people to adopt a spiritual life.

In order to meet the enormous costs of this project, the Emir al-Sayyid donated his property to fund the project. He transferred ownership of his possessions to the Endowments Institution and specified in a legal document certified by the communal court that it would be the [sole] beneficiary. This document reflects unparalleled generosity, a complete disinterest in material considerations and a willingness for giving that is difficult to match.

For example, the Emir al-Sayyid expressed his wish to assign his various dwellings to accommodate the schools' students (especially the orphans among them), and to give the poor and destitute the right of benefiting from his property in meeting their needs. He indicated the purpose of his donations as being for the teaching of the Qur'an, the repair of mosques and the provision of water sources. He also defined the categories of individuals who owned the right to benefit from his donations and the specific conditions allowing them this right. They were: the destitute, the Muslim orphans regardless of their origins or allegiances, the widows who did not remarry, and the captives and prisoners.

## The Revival of the Druze Way of Life

As known, the Druze way of life is rooted in the belief of the "return" of the expected Isma'ili Mahdi, and related to the person and authority of the Caliph and Fatimid Imam al-Hākim bi-Amr Allah (AH 386–411/AD 996–1021).

In AH 408 (AD 1017) the Isma'ili Fatimid preacher al-Akhram launched the first campaign preaching the divinity of the ruler. The official preaching authority in Cairo refuted this idea, and some months after the emergence of his movement al-Akhram was assassinated.

In the year AH 410 (AD 1019) another preacher of Persian origin, Hamza ibn 'Alī, appeared. He assumed leadership of the movement and gave the doctrine its final divine theological form. Hamza promoted a powerful, coherent doctrine, assisted by a large number of followers and preachers in Cairo, and became the actual founder of the Tawhīd religious way.

In this context a third person, called al-Darazī, should be mentioned. He was a former disciple of Hamza but eventually became his teacher's rival and a competitor to his ambition to take over the leadership of the ruler's new way. Many of Hamza's followers joined him, although he was acting independently of his leaders and even in contradiction to them. He was the first person to publicly declare the divinity of the ruler. In AH 410 (AD 1019), he disappeared in mysterious circumstances, after being condemned by the official authorities, the Fatimid religious authorities and Hamza. It is widely assumed that he was assassinated by order of the Caliph.

The official religious establishment in Cairo did not desist, for a moment, from rebutting and refuting the new creed of "Tawhīd" (Unitarism). The followers of the way preached by Hamza were persecuted and suffered the cruelest forms of oppression. As this ambiguous situation persisted for several centuries, the Muwahhidun (Unitarians) became perplexed by the various interpretations disseminated by the followers of Hamza's original teaching.

At this particular level, and within this critical context, it became clear how essential the work of Emir al-Sayyid had become on an ethical level, the Druze personal status level and the organizational level of the Tawhīd way.

## The Ethical Level

The building and rehabilitation of mosques, as well as the establishment of schools open to all free of charge, contributed to a true educational renaissance. Where it was impossible to build new schools, the Emir al-Sayyid delegated his disciples to teach the illiterate, whether young or adults. He also directed them to meet with elders and officials in order to exchange information on matters related to the Tawhīd way and the spiritual knowledge.

The Emir al-Sayyid recommended certain principles of behaviour and was keen to observe them himself before the others. He forbade lying, swearing false oaths, ridiculing others, adultery, murder, alcohol, usury and, especially, the unquestioning obedience to rulers. He advised against wearing luxurious clothes and the excessive enjoyment of temporal possessions. He encouraged modest behaviour and the non-objection to God's will, especially at the death of a relative. In short, he laid the foundation of a religious tolerance promoting social justice.

At the religious level, he stressed throughout his lifetime and in all his writings the principle of justice. Because of him the Druze prided themselves on being seen as the sword of Islam. He set out a social system for the Druze community giving priority to "the welfare of the community" over all other concerns and interests, thus implementing the idea expressed by Prophet Muhammad himself.

The Druze Muwahhidun doctrine evolved from a sequence of divisions that plagued Islam. They consider themselves to be the repositories of the historical and religious legacy of the Shi'a and the Isma'ilis. They therefore acknowledge the Imam as the sole person entrusted with the divine message.

The role of the Imam was inferred from a number of ancient gnostic and mystical religions, particularly Christianity. To these religions, gnosticism represents the true knowledge of the divine truths and is based on the duality of good and evil. It is set upon the search for the true goodness, which can only be grasped through a life of purity, untarnished by materialism and the desires of the flesh.

Gnosticism also believes that the salvation of mankind is brought about through a perception of the divine truths unlike any knowledge attained by ordinary believers and, in fact, transcending it. In a consonance of thoughts with gnosticism – and in disparity with the Sunnis' respect for the apparent meaning of the word of the Qur'an and their commitment to it – the Shi'i schools of Islam, especially the Isma'ilis, developed the precept of considering that the true knowledge of divine truths is embedded in the hidden, or intrinsic, meaning of the Qur'an.

From the general outlook of Shi'ism and in particular Isma'ilism, only the Imam, and he alone, is qualified to interpret this intrinsic meaning, and beholds the qualities entitling him to read the Qur'an on several levels. In his capacity as mentor and guide to the knowledge of God, the Imam must pass on the divine message, and explain it to his disciples according to the spiritual level of each one of them and his ability to comprehend. For the Druze, the Emir al-Tannūkhī is that Imam and the reason why they add, when they mention his name, "may God sanctify his mystery".

## The Personal Status Level

The Emir al-Sayyid sent a cultural message to his contemporary Druze, urging them to "fulfil the binding condition passed on from the Imam": it is imperative for every Druze or Muwahid holding a responsibility towards a Druze woman to consider her as his equal and share with her all his belongings.

The Emir al-Sayyid, who lived in the midst of his community and was acquainted with its social circumstances, noticed that many of its members rejected the Imam's text and avoided implementing it, disregarding the rights of their wives and treating them irreverently regarding the due equality commanded by the Imam. Since no written text defining the relations between husband and wife and their obligations towards each other, was available, the Tannūkhī Emir undertook to formulate a legislation embodying justice and equality. He based the legislation on a religious foundation as an obligation imposed by God, and one of the true pillars of certainty – that is, the mutual acceptance and free choice on the part of both spouses. This condition became an essential condition for mutual understanding, agreement, harmony, love, affection, tolerance and forgiveness between husband and wife.

Without going into the details of marriage legislations, I would like to point out that this institution – that is, the family – is the basic framework for a man-to-woman relationship. Marriage embodies their commitment to respect their mutual obligations and their eagerness to fulfil them. Marriage contains within itself the legislation that defines the context of the relationship between both partners which, if neglected, exposes them to the oppression and hostile behaviour of the other partner, while marriage ceases to be a means of co-operation and partnership in bearing the burdens of married and social life.

In addition, the Emir addressed his concern to other subjects related to the personal status law. He defined the will as being all we order to be done. This should be mentioned in the will. Everything we leave behind, we can bequeath it in our lifetime or after our death. He left to the Druze individual complete choice and the absolute freedom to bequeath his possessions to whomever he desires, regardless of being a direct or indirect heir, a Druze Muwahhid or a member of another religion.

Given that the Emir, in his quest to set the right example, always observed his commands, he made it a point to bequeath a house [of his] and parcels of land, including a share in the olive harvest and olive oil it produced, to a family with no legal right to it – the Sarkis Christian family.

These examples demonstrate the far-reaching insight of Emir Al-Sayyid. Six hundred years ago he declared the equality of men and women at a time when European society, for example, did not consider women capable, at all, of shouldering any responsibility, and granted men complete freedom in matters of wills and legacies on a basis unparalleled in the legal systems of other religions and at a time when all religions forbade the bequeathed property from being passed on to members of another religion, unless it was reciprocated.

## The Level of Organizing the Tawhīd Way

The work of Emir al-Sayyid focused essentially on organizing and reviving the Tawhīd way of life. To avoid going into great detail, I will mention only the essential headings of his "revival" scheme:

- Laying down a spiritual scheme for assessing behaviour and knowledge, based on outward meanings.
- Clarifying the relationship of the Druze way with other schools of Islamic jurisprudence.
- Explaining the general concepts of Druze beliefs through his commentaries and interpretations.
- Establishing a system of global education through his methodology of interpretation.
- Confirming the Muwahid's, possible attainment of perfection within his worldly society and not in isolation from it.
- Emphasizing the importance of the Muwahid's inner balance *vis-à-vis* a strict outward behaviour.
- It has been mentioned, within the context of his biography, that the nations of his time used to differentiate between school education, learning by heart, and knowledge. This means that he released a cultural renaissance that solidly established the foundations of spiritual and social reforms.

## Conclusion

Nowadays, the Druze Muwahhidun consider Emir al-Sayyid a great imam and a companion of God. They honour him and elevate him as one of their holy custodians. Among his contemporaries, no one else shared the mental sharpness that qualified him to proselytize the message of *ijtihād*. He called for opening the door to *ijtihād* and its enfranchisement because he believed that every legislation should be interpreted in accord with the conditions of the time and place of its implementation – that is, according to the development of the customs and ideas of its period and environment.

Unfortunately, the Druze are not inclined, nowadays, to initiate new interpretations, and do not even accept this simple idea. Must we wait for the arrival of another new imam of the stature of Emir al-Sayyid to convince them to face modernity?

In my view, a religious community rich in its historical and spiritual legacy should not be fearful of the prospects of renewal.

Is it the case of a closed frame of thought buttressed by an Eastern mentality forcefully subjected to fundamentalist ideas that abort all attempts of renewal?

Or, is it not, above all, a question of minorities living in a complicated East that requires being dealt with by simplistic thoughts?

## Note

1 A lecture given on 15 January 2007 at the Jesuit Institute of Notre Dame de Jamhour - Lebanon.

# Appendix 10

## Tawfīq 'Assāf: 1,000 Men in One

Early in the aftermath of the Israeli massacre of Lebanese civilians in Qānā,[1] Sheikh Tawfīq 'Assāf departed from this world to meet his Lord, carrying with him the memory of the atrocities committed by the Israeli aggressors. Striking among those memories was the image of the fatal deceit of more than 100 innocent Lebanese civilians who believed that a UN quarter would be a bridge to a safe haven from the vileness and brutality of the enemy.

Inasmuch as he suffered from the sight of this horrendous massacre that will never be absent from the psyche of all Lebanese, his memory had also the joy of witnessing their solidarity in the face of the disaster.

It has been a year since the passing of this greatly missed personality[2] who was grieved and praised by all Lebanese regardless of their religious or regional affiliation. He rightly deserved his peace of mind as a man who fulfilled his duties as best as could be.

The day when his fellow villagers of 'Aytāt and its region rallied to meet his casket at Beirut's airport and carried it on the palms of their hands, they were in fact welcoming the return to his native village of a distinguished son. To them he was an exemplary human who embodied their ideal model of a man. He was the valuable supporter of his country in its hours of hardship. They reverently welcomed the return of the warrior who knew no rest throughout his life, fighting for the welfare of his countrymen, defending their causes and their right to a decent, honourable livelihood. The earth of his quiet village hugged his remains under an ancient oak tree that casts its shadow over the dear departed.

"How many men are worth a thousand ... and how many men pass by unnoticed?" What can we say to the son of a village whose country was not big enough for him, and who had to emigrate in order to achieve his ambitions in work and welfare.

While abroad, he was stirred, from his 30s onwards, by the turbulent events of Palestine. He took upon himself the support of the Palestinian struggle until he became known within his immediate circle as a standard bearer in defence of the Arab cause.

He was not away long before returning to his homeland, only to find it suffering from the legacy of the Mandate and the complexities of promoting the independent state. He decided, alongside other well-intentioned Lebanese, to participate in the urgent process of laying down the foundations of the economic revival of independent Lebanon. His contribution embraced all sectors of production – construction, trade, industry and finance. In every project he started and in every ongoing company, he represented the benevolent, compassionate father of the workers and employees. He held a deep understanding of the needs of the workers and labourers, and would deal with them with the humility, magnanimity and benevolence of the self-confident.

Throughout the 50 years he spent at the helm of the institutions he founded, none of his assistants remembers him but in praise and expression of loyalty.

His business ties did not distract him from his country's and nation's concerns. His advice was constantly sought by his Druze community, whose representation fell solely upon his shoulders in the most difficult circumstances, especially during the formulation of the National Accord at el-Taif in 1989. He remains his country's unknown soldier in the defence of its causes, especially in the darkest times, as witnessed in his refusal to be drawn into sanctioning the 17 May agreement and his fierce opposition to it. In his nation he embodied the genuine believer in the Arab cause and the brotherly relationship with Syria, and never deviated.

He was never approached for assistance without heeding the request. His door was always open to applicants. He was never asked for help that he did not deliver, both morally and materially. All the humanitarian, social, cultural, health and sports institutions that depended on him and his paradigm of donors regret his passing. He regularly extended a helping hand to them, even without being directly asked to, and gave as much as he could; he never defaulted on giving.

Dearest of men and of their model: we miss you. On the anniversary of your passing we recall the happy days you adorned with your presence and the examples you have set to future generations: a great heart, a preponderant mind, an unbending will solid as the rocks of Mount Lebanon and towering as its summits, forceful sometimes to the point of aggressiveness. As his great heart became exhausted and his body worn out, his will did not falter. He overburdened his body, frail with age and sickness, with duties that were beyond bearing. "When souls are great, bodies become weary of their ambitions."

He passed away on a desolate dark night, in the presence of his lifelong partner and companion, and his daughter whom he cherished and held in his affection and sentiments dearer than any father could have done.

May God have mercy on you, Sheikh Tawfīq. The consolation is the offspring you left behind. They carried on your banner in all the venues of your eventful life, enriched by your loving friends, and the blessed acts that tell the story of a young man who left his quiet village to the open arms of the world and mankind ... and succeeded.

## Notes

1 The First Qana massacre took place on April 18, 1996 near Qana, a village in Southern Lebanon, when the Israeli Forces hit a United Nations compound. Of 800 Lebanese civilians who had taken refuge in the compound, 106 were killed and around 116 injured.

2 Sheikh Tawfīq 'Assāf passed away in May 9, 1996.

# Appendix 11

# Beating the Odds: The Case of Druze Survival

*Linda Abbas Halabi*[1]

The survival of religious and heterodox minorities in the Middle East should not be taken for granted. Throughout history, many factors have contributed to the extinction of dozens of religious groups whose doctrine challenged the dominant Sunni Orthodox discourse in the region. In fact, referring to a famous hadith by the Prophet Muhammad who predicted that the Muslim umma would be divided into 73 groups, of which 72 were destined to hell, Thomas Scheffler found that less than a dozen minorities have managed to survive until this day (Scheffler 1995). In this context, the survival of the Druze in a hostile environment is nothing short of an accomplishment, and one well worth examining. After briefly introducing the Druze, their doctrine, and some important historical events that affected their development as a community, this paper aims to explain why the Druze were able to survive, and why they were able to play an important political role in the countries where they have a significant presence – that is, Lebanon, Syria, and Palestine/Israel – despite their small number and in contrast to other religious minorities in the region.

This paper argues that the Druze communities in Lebanon, Syria, and Palestine/Israel have survived by using a combination of measures both common to other minorities such as taqiyya and territorial isolation, and measures unique to them such as their military prowess and centralized leadership. A distinction must nonetheless be made when considering the Druze community in Lebanon, as these factors which successfully explain the survival of its sisters in Syria and

Palestine/Israel are not sufficient to explain the much larger role that the community has played in Lebanese politics. In Scheffler's words, the Druze in Lebanon were able "not only to maintain a critical mass but also to achieve a hegemonic role in a catchment area which far exceeded their economic and demographic weight" (Scheffler 1995). This paper concludes that the most important factor that accounts for the Druze's survival is each community's strong adaptability to their respective country's political context.

## A Brief Introduction to the Druze

The Druze religion constitutes one of the many heterodox and syncretistic religions of the Middle East who originated from Islam, and more specifically from Shiism. The Ismaelite sect, an offshoot of Shiism, established the Fatimid caliphate in North Africa with Cairo as its capital in the tenth century AD (El Halabi 2005, 39). The Druze doctrine was born during the reign of the sixth Fatimid Caliph al Hakim Bi Amr Allah, when a group of Ismaelites declared that al-Hakim had a divine nature (*ibid.*). After al Hakim mysteriously disappeared, the adepts of the new doctrine, who were named the Druze after one of their militant preachers, were persecuted and forced out of Egypt (El Halabi 2005, 40–41). The Druze Da'wa (preaching mission) encountered its biggest success in the area comprised of modern day Syria, Lebanon, Palestine/Israel and Jordan, and until this day the Druze remain concentrated there. The Da'wa persisted from AD 1017 to AD 1043, until continued persecution by the Sunnis finally convinced the Druze to close the door to new adepts. From this day on, only children born to a Druze father and mother were considered legitimate by the community (El Halabi 2005, 47).

The Druze consider themselves to be the recipients of the historic and religious heritage of Shiism and Ismaelism. Elements from monotheistic religions, Persian religions, and from Greek philosophy were also incorporated into the Druze religion (El Halabi 2005, 40–41). The Druze then engaged in the reinterpretation of the Qur'an in light of all these influences, proudly considering their doctrine to be the most perfected version of the message of Islam (El Halabi 2005, 35). In addition to the Qur'an, the Druze also possess their own sacred scriptures, the *Books of Wisdom* (El Halabi 2005, 43). Only those initiated into the religion have access to these scriptures.

A small community developed in the Galilee, while the core remained in Lebanon. The inhabitants of Lebanon's mountains were themselves the descendants of Arab tribes such as the Tannukh and Rabia (El Halabi 2005, 50–52). Factional struggle among the Druze was frequent, and in a decisive battle in the eighteenth century opposing the Qaysi and Yamani factions, the defeated Yamani were forced to flee Mount Lebanon and take refuge in the Mountains of Hawran, Syria. The modern-day Syrian Druze are the descendants of the Yamani faction. Today, there are around a million Druze in the world (El Halabi 2005, 54). The Druze constitute around 7 per cent of the population in Lebanon, 3–4 per cent of the population in Syria (*ibid.*) and a bit less than 2 per cent of the population in Israel. Their presence is quite insignificant in Jordan (around 15,000 people). A small Diaspora has also emerged mainly in the Americas and in the Gulf (El Halabi 2005, 53).

The Druze tend to be concentrated in the agricultural sector in Lebanon and Syria, but are increasingly being attracted to urban centres such as Beirut and Damascus. In Israel, the army remains the most important institution and source of employment for Druze males. In a study analysing the Israeli government's policies concerning the Druze, Lisa Hajjar highlighted the very low numbers of Druze youth attending university, particularly female Druze youth, as a result of Israel's education system, which is segregated along ethnic lines (Hajjar 1996).

## Explaining Druze Survival

Following this brief introduction, we will now examine the reasons behind the Druze's survival until this day. First, it is important to note that surviving minorities in the Middle East possess similar characteristics. Most minorities strictly enforce the policies of endogamy and exclusivity to strengthen their numbers and communal cohesion. Because they were persecuted and rejected by the Sunnis as heretics, most also resorted to taqiyya or to the "dissimulation" of their faith. Firro defines taqiyya as everyday political opportunism (Firro 1995), where the religious minority pretends to follow the Sunni majority or join the side of a conflict that is most likely to win. Layish argues taqiyya is used to deliberately blur a minority's uniqueness to create a relaxed atmosphere of unity and of belonging to the majority (Layish 1995). Another important strategy of survival used by many is territorial isolation. The Druze have resorted to this strategy since the time where they were forced out of Egypt after Al Hakim's death. They took refuge in the mountains of Lebanon, Syria, and in Galilee. This partly explains why to this day, the Druze remain mostly concentrated in rural areas.

Nevertheless, there are many factors that distinguish the Druze from other minorities. Notably, the Druze's military prowess has enabled them to drive away powerful enemies and hostile neighbours, as well as preserve their land. Many historians have written about the Druze's warring abilities. In the words of Kamāl Salibi, the Druze are a "community of mountain peasants organized for war" (Harik 1993, 53). During the Lebanese civil war (1975–1990), the Druze Progressive Socialist Party led by Walīd Jumblatt included only about 4,000 full-time fighters, a very small number compared to the other warring parties. However, unlike other groups, when the survival of the community was perceived to be threatened, the Druze had an astounding ability to mobilize thousands more fighters on very short notice (*ibid.*). For instance, during the War of the Mountain in the 1980s that opposed the Christians and the Druze, Israel's invasion of Lebanon in 1982 gave its (then) Christian ally, the Lebanese Forces, a favourable environment and an opportunity to defeat their historical adversaries, the Druze. As Judith Harik argued in another paper, the objective of the Lebanese Forces was to wrestle control over strategic mountain positions from the Druze, such as those overlooking the Beirut International Airport and the presidential palace in Baabda (Harik 1999, 159). The Lebanese Forces' attack was met with an overwhelming and "furious response" by the Druze. The Druze offensive crushed the Christian forces and resulted in a massive Christian exodus from the Mountain (*ibid.*).

Some have argued that the Druze's military prowess originates from certain precepts of the Druze faith which have translated into effective martial skills. For instance, Scheffler argues that the belief of being automatically reincarnated as a Druze after death allowed for riskier behaviour in warriors and soldiers (Scheffler 1995). Both the political and religious elites have used the community's expectations of suffering a period of trials before the Last Judgement for the collective mobilization of the Druze in times of crisis (*ibid.*). Moreover, the fear of losing their territory greatly increased their bravery on the battlefield. Losing their territory could mean the extinction of the community, as the territory guaranteed a space for endogamy and exclusivity to persist, and for the protection of the sheikhs, the guardians of the sacred faith (Roussel, HAL). This fear is justified when looking at other minorities, such as the Alevis in Turkey. Due to extensive flows of migrants from the Alevi regions into the cities as a result of modernization, the socio-religious organization of the Alevi community collapsed, and many feared in the 1970s that the Alevis were in danger of disappearing because a whole generation grew up without being initiated to the doctrine (Kehl-Bodrogi 1997, xiii).

Furthermore, the Druze's centralized political leadership contributes a great deal to their military superiority. Despite a history of factional struggles between rival clans, who sometimes ally themselves with external forces to defeat their Druze opponents (Scheffler 1995), at times of crisis in the 19th and 20th centuries, factions "repeatedly made common cause when the welfare of the community was at stake" (Harik 1993, 53). The extreme concentration of power in the hands of a few families, a situation which was legitimized by the religious clergy, created a highly disciplined and hierarchical social structure which allowed effective martial skills to develop (*ibid.*). Centralized leadership also translated into powerful political influence. Scheffler argues that the centralism was greatest when a clan succeeded in prevailing over rivals. The Jumblatt family changed the internal balance of power within the Druze community and preserved them from counterproductive rivalries (Scheffler 1995). According to Yusri Hazran, Kamāl Jumblatt's credentials in the Druze community were so high that during the 1972 Parliamentary elections, Majīd Arslān, a national hero and the leader of the Druze Yazbakiyya clan, had to run alongside Kamāl on a shared slate to secure his seat in Parliament (Hazran 2010).

In Lebanon, the creation of the Progressive Socialist Party by Kamāl Jumblatt institutionalized centralized leadership (Scheffler 1995), and allowed Jumblatt to anchor his supporters in a modern political frame (Hazran 2010). During the civil war, all high school students in Druze areas were required to study the PSP's military text and take part in civil defence and paramilitary training (Harik 1993, 55). Harik found that the Druze viewed strong and centralized leadership as an absolute imperative. Jumblatt's command of the armed forces, and dominance of channels through which money was distributed to the Druze, made allegiance to his rival fruitless (Harik 1993, 57). In Syria and Israel, the Druze's leadership is also very centralized. Harik concludes that the marshalling of human resources helped the Druze turn small numbers into a military asset (Harik 1993, 66).

Another factor that helped the Druze survive in the twentieth century was the Arab world's embrace of pan-Arabism. Pan-Arabism as a political ideology was developed by Egypt's immensely popular Nasser and it stressed values such as secularism, socialism, and the importance of Arab unity. The emphasis on secularism appealed to many minorities as an alternative to Sunni religious domination (Firro 1995). When Syria and Lebanon became nation states, the Druze adopted pan-Arabism as their political ideology (Firro 1995). Since they spoke Arabic and were ethnically Arab, they didn't need taqiyya to be considered part of the Arab world (*ibid.*).

## The Druze Role in Nation-Building Processes

All of these strategies and attributes were shared equally by the three Druze communities in Lebanon, Syria, and Palestine/Israel.

However, the different Druze communities also had to adapt to the circumstances of their respective countries. Each country's unique nation-building process prompted the Druze to behave differently in each case.

### Syria

In Syria, the Druze's embrace of pan-Arabism was instrumental in securing Druze interests on the national level. The Mandate period specifically provided a historic opportunity for the Druze of Hawran to identify with Arab nationalism, in the form of the Great Syrian Revolt of 1925 which was led by the Druze Sultān Bāshā al-Atrash. Today this event is considered one of the first historical manifestations of Syrian nationalism. During this time, the French had divided Syria into five nations which were meant to become independent, but the new Syrian state kept the local elites of peripheral regions in power (Firro 1995). Because the Druze region of Hawran was originally meant to form an independent state, the concentration of the Druze population in the independent Syrian state played a determining role in turning Druze territory into a province whose interests then became represented on the national level (Roussel 2009). Roussel notes that the Atrash clan occupied all the important posts of administration of the province when the French left; thus dislodging them was really difficult (*ibid.*). These structures allowed the Druze leadership to remain strongly centralized.

After his death, the authoritarian Assad regime in Syria attempted to control the symbol of Sultān Bāshā al Atrash's figure to establish control over the Syrian Druze (Roussel, HAL). When Sultān died in 1982, he was acknowledged by all the Syrians and the rest of the Arab world as a hero. At his funeral, personalities such as Walīd Jumblatt, Yasser Arafat and Hafez Assad attended, and people from all over Syria came to pay tribute to Sultān (*ibid.*). A year later, Sultān's son Mansour had called upon his community to commemorate the death of his father; however, that day became an opportunity for the frustrated Druze youth to protest against the government's oppression. They skipped school and defied the law which prohibited citizens to gather without permission and the regime in Damascus violently repressed them (*ibid.*). Sultān's memory became a "point of crystallization of the discontent of the community in this decade of the 1980s [my translation]" (*ibid.*). In 1987, after negotiations with the Atrash clan, the regime decided to allow Sultān's death to be commemorated only on 17 April, the national independence day of Syria instead of the day of Sultān's actual death on 26 March (Roussel, HAL). In exchange, the state promised to build a mausoleum in his name (*ibid.*). This was in fact a great victory for the Druze in the long run. The commemoration of Sultān's death on Independence Day ties Sultān's image to Syria's independence (*ibid.*). It serves as a reminder of the contributions the Druze made for their country.

## Lebanon

In contrast to Syria and Israel, the Druze in Lebanon have not only managed to survive and play a role in the nation-building process, but the Lebanese Druze's political weight is considerably larger than their demographic size would suggest. During the time of the Ottoman Empire, the Druze community in Lebanon was able to stretch its influence outside its territory and become a major player in national politics. In fact, the Druze who ruled Mount Lebanon for hundreds of years see themselves as the real founders of the historical Lebanese entity (Hazran 2010).

Scheffler argues that it was the geostrategic position and social structure of the Druze in Lebanon that shaped their political rise (Scheffler 1995). Lebanon is an interface periphery society caught between several centres (*ibid.*). In reality, Lebanon's mountains were neither marginal nor inaccessible. They commanded important lines of communication between the Syrian hinterland and the Mediterranean coast, therefore they could not be a matter of indifference to the surrounding state centres (*ibid.*). Lebanon's topography was also never a serious military obstacle (*ibid.*). Hence, because of the geostrategic importance of the area for surrounding centres, the Druze needed to effectively use external alliances to guarantee their superiority in Mount Lebanon. For instance, the Druze Emir Fakhr al-Dīn ruled an area stretching from Antioch to Galilee. He owed his success to "far-reaching intrigues in which bribing influential officials in Istanbul was just as important as contacts with Ottoman governors in the Levant and Christian leaders in Italy" (Scheffler 1995).

The Druze were open for negotiation and alliance with everyone regardless of ideological affinities; thus they possessed the comparative advantage of never being identified with a single external power (*ibid.*). Whenever their political power was challenged, they found ways to reassert control over their territory and consolidate their national influence. For instance, France, a staunch supporter of the Lebanese Christian Maronites, imposed itself as the superpower in the region since 1860 and later established the Grand Liban in 1920 (*ibid.*). The Druze were opposed to the creation of the Grand Liban because they identified it with the political interests of their rivals the Maronites (*ibid.*). The balance of power shifted, allowing the Maronites and the Sunnis to emerge as the most important actors due to their demographic weight and their relative wealth compared to the others, especially the Druze and the Shiites (*ibid.*). The Druze leadership adapted to these changes and played a decisive role in achieving Lebanon's independence. The French had imprisoned most of the Lebanese cabinet in 1943 for unilaterally declaring Lebanon's independence. Two members of the Lebanese cabinet, Druze leader Majīd Arslān and Greek Orthodox Christian leader Habīb Abu Shahla, managed to escape and took refuge in the Druze village of Bshamun in Arslān's stronghold (Hazran 2010). Arslān's armed men formed the National Guard and he was able to mobilize the Druze to protect the Lebanese government (*ibid.*). He was consequently named "the hero of the independence" (*ibid.*).

After France was forced to recognize Lebanon's independence, Lebanon's first president and prime minister created the National Pact, which stipulated that any position of power in the country must be attributed on a confessional basis and in consideration of the demographic weight of each community. The President could only be a Maronite, the Prime Minister only a Sunni and the Speaker of Parliament only Shiite (*ibid.*). Arslān supported the National Pact as he believed that "it was the best way to secure peaceful co-existence between the different Lebanese communities and to get them equitable shares in the administration; it would also protect the smaller communities from the despotism of the larger ones" (*ibid.*).

However, Kamāl Jumblatt remained opposed to the new Lebanese state's structure which he saw as entrenching Sunni–Maronite domination on the Druze. He created the PSP with two objectives: abolishing the confessional system and creating a secular political system, and Hazran argues that both demands were aimed at "revitalizing the historical role of the Druze in Lebanon, under the guise of progressivism and revolutionarism" (Hazran 2010). In a survey done right before the second civil war, Harik notes that the Druze felt socially estranged and alienated from the system, but remained politically active because they were aware of their underprivileged status (Harik 1993, 56). Hazran explains the Druze's political alienation by arguing that the Druze were always discontented with their stratification within the Lebanese confessional system because they believed that their role in the political system and the amount of representative power they were given never reflected their great contributions to help create the Lebanese polity and defending it throughout history (Hazran 2010). The Druze's centralized leadership under Kamāl and then Walīd Jumblatt, the careful blending of external alliances during the war, and the Druze's military prowess allowed the Druze to achieve a political victory at the end of the civil war. The Taif agreement of 1991 considerably weakened the Maronites and promised the establishment of a Lebanese senate whose leader would be a Druze. However, this state of alienation remained after the Taif agreement. Harik conducted research in 1992–1993 where she found that 90 per cent of respondents wanted confessionalism to end so that Druze could compete for key governmental positions (Harik 1993, 59–60). The Lebanese Druze's heightened awareness of their historical heritage has kept them in a state of constant political alienation, despite the fact that their situation is much more enviable than the situation of their brethren in Syria and Israel.

**Israel**

In contrast, in Israel, the Druze had to overcome many more challenges to protect their land, culture, and faith. Israel, as a Jewish state, is an ethnocracy which aims to serve the interests and needs of the dominant charter settler group (Yiftachel et al. 1998). The Israeli state's biggest fear is the coalescing of Arab minorities into one group that would be Arab in national identity and Muslim in religion (Firro 2003). Thus, to "divide and rule" the different Arab minorities has been the official Israeli state policy since 1949 to counter the powerful appeal of pan-Arabism (*ibid.*).

According to Firro, these efforts to divide Arabs in Israel have focused primarily on the Druze by fostering Druze particularism, and the deliberate spread of the notion that Druze ethnicity and identity makes them distinct from other Arabs (*ibid.*). Driving a wedge between the Druze and other Arabs has allowed Zionists to create "good Arabs" and "bad Arabs" and to co-opt the Druze elite. Such a wedge serves Israel "as a foil for an ongoing policy of dispossession and control" (*ibid.*). The first step towards achieving this goal was the creation of the Minorities Unit in 1948, a special army unit of the IDF that aggressively recruited Druze villagers. Its true purpose was to use the Druze as "a sharp knife blade to stab the back of Arab unity" (*ibid.*). It was followed by the conscription law of 1956 (*ibid.*) and the recognition in 1957 of the Druze as a distinct community with the establishment of separate Druze religious courts to settle matters of personal status in 1963 (Layish 1995). The state then began issuing identity cards to the Druze on which "nationality: Arab" was replaced by "nationality: Druze" (Firro 2003).

The Israeli state also used the shrine of Nabi Shayb, an important prophet for the Druze, as the site for the first swearing-in ceremony, when new Druze recruits were asked to pledge allegiance to the Jewish state (*ibid.*). This act was used to symbolize the "newly discovered historical connections between the sons of Shuayb and the sons of Israel". It allowed the state to co-opt the leading Druze Tarif family by investing money to renovate the shrine and giving the Tarif family guardianship of the site (*ibid.*). Firro argues that what resulted from these policies was the creation of a new Druze identity which was part reconstruction and part invention (*ibid.*). For instance, the Israeli state created new feasts for the Druze such as ʻId al Kadir and ʻId Sablan, while not allowing the Druze to celebrate ʻId al Fitr which is traditionally the only holiday the Druze celebrate but one that is also shared with other Muslims (*ibid.*).

These policies allowed the state to expropriate Druze land, and thus led to the Druze's occupational restructuring, which had negative consequences for Druze collective identity (Firro 2003). By 1962, the Druze had lost more than two thirds of their land, and they received less than 0.05 per cent of Israel's water supply for agriculture (*ibid.*). About 40 per cent of the Druze male labour force became employed in the army and less than 1 per cent of the Druze work force still cultivated family owned land (*ibid.*). Given the structure of the Druze labour market, high levels of education were not required, thus a "vicious circle of inadequate education and low-level jobs created a complete dependency of the Druze on the Israeli authorities" (*ibid.*). Yiftachel and Segal provide a theoretical explanation for the Druze's occupational restructuring. They argue that Israel's economy is that of a capitalist settler state, and in consequence indigenous people's culture is antithetic to its logic. Indigenous cultures revolve around the spiritual bond to the land, an agrarian lifestyle and "other non-Western patterns of caste, family and authority" (Yiftachel et al. 1998). It was therefore imperative for Israel to de-territorialize these indigenous communities and make them dependent on capitalist and centralist systems for their survival as "an effective method of annihilating competing modes of production and governance" (*ibid.*).

Firro concludes that Israel's policy towards the Druze was successful as it was able to use traditional features of Druze particularism to transform them into a new kind of particularism made to fit the reality of the Jewish state (Firro 2003). Yet, Firro argues that this would not have been possible without the transformation of the community's occupational structure and their inclusion into the military (*ibid.*). Despite the Druze's loss of their land and the Israeli attempts to mutilate their culture, the fate of the Druze community was marginally better than some other Arab minorities in Israel. The Druze leaders saw the military as a means to assure the state's support for communal needs (*ibid.*).

However, the institutionalized discrimination of the Israeli state towards minorities still applied to the Druze, and by the late 1950s the community massively protested against the government's unequal treatment, its efforts to separate it from other Arab communities, unrest fuelled by economic and social changes affecting the community, and the collapse of agriculture as a result of the intensification of the policy of land confiscation (*ibid.*). The Druze youth became increasingly radicalized, alarming the Israeli authorities (*ibid.*). Yiftachel and Segal attribute this radicalization to the nature of the ethnocentric settler state itself. This type of state encroaches on territorial and symbolic resources of the previous inhabitants of land thereby creating structural conditions of embedded conflict (Yiftachel et al. 1998).

A clear instance of confrontation between the Druze and the Israeli state is over the Bet Jan issue. The Israeli state used the excuse of environmental protection to create a National Park reserve around the Druze village of Bet Jan and confiscate land from the Druze while allowing the IDF to establish two bases in 1969 which ignored environmental regulations (*ibid.*). This situation made the Druze aware of their inequality, and with the election of a new militant mayor in 1985, the villagers of Bet Jan went on strike in front of the Prime Minister's office in Jerusalem and established a lobby in Knesset to force change (*ibid.*). Police forces even fought Druze citizens after villagers established temporary settlements in the forbidden National Park (*ibid.*). The whole Druze community in Israel united behind the village of Bet Jan and the rest of the Arabs in Israel used Bet Jan as a symbol of the oppression of the Druze and Arabs as a whole under the Israeli state (*ibid.*).

Yiftachel and Segal then conclude that the Bet Jan case demonstrates that policies of territorial control over the homeland of ethnic minorities cannot be self-sustaining in democratizing regimes, because minorities will use the democratic rights, procedures, and institutions of the settler societies as the foundation of their campaign against the state (*ibid.*). Events happening in Israel in recent years have proved their conclusions to be correct. In her article published on ynetnews.com on 18 January 2008, Sharon Roffe-Ofir reported that a survey conducted in 2008 revealed that the Druze's love for the state of Israel has declined noticeably since the previous year. The article also noted that the number of Druze youth who refuse to serve in the army is growing. The article quoted the Environment Minister of the time Gideon Ezra who was surprised to see that "whereas in the past most Druze would vote for Jewish, Zionist parties, now many Druze are voting for Arab parties". Druze Member of Knesset Naffa concluded that "Druze people are beginning to realize that they are first and foremost Arabs, and we are entitled to equal rights by virtue of being Israeli citizens and not only because we serve in the IDF". Another article published on 2 February 2009 by Hana Levi Julian on israelinationalnews.com projected that more Druze candidates would likely be elected to Israel's Parliament in the 2010 elections, both Druze who belonged to Zionist parties and Druze who saw themselves as Arabs.

### The Golan Heights

In the occupied Syrian Golan, the Druze inhabitants used different tactics to protect their community from assimilation. In 1967, Israel annexed the Syrian region of the Golan and redesigned its borders to ensure that most of the population would be Druze (Hajjar 1996). The state offered the Golani Druze the possibility to receive Israeli citizenship for favoured treatment, with the ulterior motive of making the Golan a *de facto* annexation (Kennedy 1984). However, those who accepted citizenship were immediately shunned by the community (*ibid.*). In 1981, the Israeli state formally annexed the Golan. The Golani Druze consequently refused to work in northern Israel and many village leaders were imprisoned without trial (*ibid.*). The Golani Druze engaged in a campaign of non-violent resistance by violating curfews to harvest their crops, massing in town squares, and organizing co-operative economic structures (*ibid.*).

In 1982, the Israeli state moved to repressive violence, and 15,000 Israeli soldiers sealed the Golan Heights from Israel, the Israeli press, lawyers, and international observers. They cut off electricity and water, destroyed several homes and injured several people, some of whom died because of a lack of access to nearby hospitals. The Israeli army went door to door to confiscate Syrian papers and left Israeli papers instead (*ibid.*). The Golani Druze did not back down, and continue to resist to this day by carrying on with their daily lives without any kind of legal identification whatsoever (*ibid.*). A Golani lawyer, J. Kuttab, explained the courage of the Golani Druze, as without an identification card, it is impossible to cash cheques at the bank, travel, register births and marriages among other things (*ibid.*). Nevertheless, the use of non-violent resistance tactics has so far prevented the Israeli state from using excessive destructive force to compel the Golani Druze into accepting Israeli citizenship. Such a strategy has therefore ensured their physical security for now. Their economic security is however severely threatened by their resistance campaign. Their situation must continue to be observed carefully.

## Conclusion

The case of Israel is a case where the dominant group, the Jewish Zionists, thought they could understand "Druzeness" and use it to serve their political interests (Hajjar 1996). The Zionists believed that the meaning of Druzeness could be generalized from the Druze experience inside Israel. Hence, they assumed the Syrian Druze in the Golan would become loyal to Israel as did their co-religionists in Galilee. Yet, the Golani Druze have refused to see themselves as part of a Druze collectivity which would override their status as Syrian citizens living under Israeli occupation (*ibid.*). In fact, the Galilee and Golani communities have cool relations and don't encourage intermarriage, and their differing views on religious and national identity derive from differing modern histories (*ibid.*). Their experience highlights the separate development of the Lebanese, Syrian, and Israeli Druze communities as a strength that has allowed all three to survive in their respective environments. Hajjar similarly concludes that Druze particularism draws its meaning and strength from the political context (*ibid.*). In contrast, many Israeli scholars misperceived Druzeness and attributed every instance where the Druze co-operated with the Muslims as a manifestation of taqiyya, and thus considered taqiyya the essence of Druze existence (Firro 2003). The experience of the Golani Druze has proved them wrong.

The Druze experience validates the importance of the Darwinian notion of a group's adaptability to change as an essential feature to ensure the group's survival. Although they resorted to similar strategies such as endogamy and exclusivity, territorial concentration and isolation, and developed similar attributes such as their military prowess and centralized leadership, the three Druze communities in the Middle East have managed to survive most importantly because of their adaptability to their respective country's political context.

## Reference List

El Halabi, Abbas (2005) *Les Druzes: vivre avec l'avenir.* Beirut: Editions Dar An-Nahar.

Firro, Kais (1995) The attitudes of Druzes and Alawis *vis-à-vis* Islam and nationalism in Syria and Lebanon. Paper presented at the International Symposium "Alevism in Turkey and comparable syncretistic religious communities in the Near East in the past and present", 14–17 April, in Berlin, Germany.

Firro, Kais (2003) Reshaping Druze particularism in Israel. *Journal of Palestine Studies* 30, no. 3 (4 December), http://caliber.ucpress.net/doi/abs/10.1525/jps.2001.30.3.40 (accessed 1 November 2010).

Hajjar, Lisa (1996) Making identity policy: Israel's interventions among the Druze. *Middle East report* 200, (July–September 1996), http://www.jstor.org/stable/3013259 (accessed 1 November 2010).

Harik, Judith (1993) Perceptions of community and state among Lebanon's Druze youth. *Middle East Journal* 47: 41–62.

Harik, Judith (1999) The return of the displaced and Christian–Muslim integration in Postwar Lebanon. *Islam and Christian–Muslim Relations* 10: 159–175.

Hazran, Yusri (2010) Kamāl Jumblatt, the Druze community and the Lebanon state, 1949 to 1977. *The Muslim World* 100, no. 1 (19 January), http://onlinelibrary.wiley.com/doi/10.1111/j.1478-1913.2009.01311.x/full (accessed 12 October 2010).

Hyper Articles en Ligne (HAL), http://halshs.archives-ouvertes.fr/halshs-00431704/fr/ (accessed 1 November 2010).

Hyper Articles en Ligne (HAL), http://hal.archives-ouvertes.fr/halshs-00353068/ (accessed 1 November 2010).

Kehl-Bodrogi, Kristina. Barbara Kellner-Heinkele, Anke Otter-Beaujean, comp. and ed. (1997) *Syncretistic religious communities in the Near East, collected papers of the international symposium "Alevism in Turkey and comparable syncretistic religious communities in the Near East in the past and present" Berlin 14–17 April 1995.* Leiden, Brill.

Kennedy, Scott, R. (1984) Druze of the Golan: A case of non-violent resistance. *Journal of Palestine Studies* 13, no. 2 (Winter 1984), http://www.jstor.org/stable/2536896 (accessed 1 November 2010).

Layish, Aharon (1995) The status of Islamic law in the Druze family in a non-Muslim state as reflected in judicial practice. Paper presented at the International Symposium "Alevism in Turkey and comparable syncretistic religious communities in the Near East in the past and present", 14–17 April, in Berlin, Germany.

Roussel, Cyril (2006) Sultān al Atrash, un symbole identitaire entre iconographie officielle et communautaire. *Villes et territoires du Moyen Orient* 2.

Scheffler, Thomas (1995) Survival and leadership at an interface periphery: The Druzes in Lebanon. Paper presented at the International Symposium "Alevism in Turkey and comparable syncretistic religious communities in the Near East in the past and present", 14–17 April, in Berlin, Germany.

Yiftachel, Oren. Michaly Segal (1998) Jews and Druze in Israel: state control and ethnic resistance. *Ethnic and racial studies* 21, no. 3 http://web.ebscohost.com/ehost/detail?vid=1&hid=113&sid=558c178c-b2e6-47dc-9f97-9cd4bc6932d2%40sessionmgr104&bdata=JnNpdGU9ZWhvc3QtbGl2ZQ%3d%3d#db=sih&AN=629653 (accessed 1 November 2010).

## Note

1 The original version of this paper was written to fulfil a course requirement for POLI 340 "Developing Areas: Middle East" due November 2010 at McGill University in Montreal, Canada. The content was then edited in August 2012 for the purpose of including it in this book.

# Appendix 12[1]

**Beyrouth le 20 novembre 1995**

**S.E. Le Nonce Apostolique**
**Monseigneur Pablo Puente**

Suite à votre demande, nous vous prions de prendre note que Monsieur Abbas Al Halaby assistera comme représentant de la Communauté Druze au Synode qui se tiendra le 26 Novembre 1995 au Vatican en réponse à l'invitation de sa Sainteté le Pape Jean-Paul II.

Nous saisissons cette occasion pour vous renouveler l'assurance de notre haute considération

**Walid Jumblatt**

W Jumblatt

## Note

1 Mandate from Mr. Walīd Jumblatt to Mr. Abbas Halabi as representative of the Druze Community to the Synod for Lebanon signed on the 20th of November 1995.

# Appendix 13[1]

**Beyrouth le 20 novembre 1995**

**S.E. Le Nonce Apostolique**
**Monseigneur Pablo Puente**

Suite à votre demande, nous vous prions de prendre note que Monsieur Abbas Al Halaby assistera comme répresentant de la Communauté Druze au Synode qui se tiendra le 26 Novembre 1995 au Vatican en réponse à l'invitation de sa Sainteté le Pape Jean-Paul II.

Nous saisissons cette occasion pour vous renouveler l'assurance de notre haute considération

**Talal Arslane**

## Note

1 Mandate from Mr. Talāl Arslān to Mr. Abbas Halabi as representative of the Druze Community to the Synod for Lebanon signed on the 20th of November 1995.

# Bibliography


Abou Zeki, Nadine (2006) *Introduction aux épîtres de la sagesse: L'ésotérisme druze à la lumière de la doctrine de Cankara,* Edition l'Harmattan.

Abu-Izzeddin, Nejla, M. (1993) *The Druzes: A New Study of their History, Faith and Society,* Leyden - USA (2nd edition corrections).

Betts, Robert Brenton (1988) *The Druze,* New Haven.

Cheikho, Louis (1935) *Bayrūt: tārīkhuhā wa-āthāruhā* (*Beirut: its history and antiquities*), Beyrouth, Imprimerie des Pères Jésuites (in Arabic).

Dupont, Marie (1994) Fils d'Abraham: *les Druzes,* Edition Brepols.

Fandi, Talāl and Abi-Shakra, Ziyad (2001) *The Druze Heritage. An Annotated Bibliography,* Beyrouth (with an introduction by de Kamāl Salibi).

Hatem, Jad (2006) *Dieu en guise d'homme dans le Druzisme,* Edition de l'Orient.

Hichi Sélim, Hassan (1973) *La communauté druze: son origine et son histoire,* Beyrouth.

Hitti, Philipp Khuri (1928) *The Origins of the Druze People and Religion: With Extracts from their Sacred Writings,* Kindle Editions, New York.

Joumblatt, Kamāl (1978) *Pour le Liban, For Lebanon* (propos recueillis par Philippe LAPOUSTERLE), Paris, Stock.

Kais, Firro (1992) *A History of the Druzes,* Leyden, New York and Köln.

Khuri, Fuad (2004) *Being a Druze,* Druze Heritage Foundation.

Makarem, Sami Nasib (1966) *Adwā' 'alā maslak al-tawhīd* (Lights on the Druze spiritual way), Preface by Kamāl Jumblatt, Beirut, 1966.

Makarem, Sami Nasib (1974) *The Druze Faith,* Delmar.

Makarem, Sami Nasib (2004) *Al-taqiyya fī al-Islām,* London, Druze Heritage Foundation publications.

Makarem, Sami Nasib (2006) *Al-'irfān fī maslak al-tawhīd* (*al-duruziyya*), London, Druze Heritage Foundation publications.

Muakasa, Sahar (2004) *Comprehensive Bibliography of the Druze religion,* PHD, Druze Research and Publications Institute.

Najjar, Abdallah, *The Druze,* American Druze Society.

Narcisse, Bouronm (1930) *Les Druzes: Histoire du Liban et de la montagne haouranaise,* The Druze: History of Lebanon and the Mountain of Haouran, Berger-Levrault publications, Paris.

Nissim, Dana (2003) *The Druze in the Middle East, their Faith, Leadership, Identity and Status,* Sussex Academic Press, Brighton, Portland.

Nuwayhad, Ajjāj (1963) *Al-Tannūkhī, al-amīr Jamāl al-Dīn 'Abdallah',* Beirut, Dār al-Sahāfa.

Ramadan, Tariq Muhammad (2006) *Vie du prophète,* Edition Presse du Châtelet.

Sāsīn, Fāris and Sallām, Nawwāf (1999) *Lubnān: Al-qarn fī suwar* (*1900–2000*), Beirut: Dār al-Nahār.

Sheikh Halīm Taqī al-Dīn, *Al-ahwāl al-shakhsiyya 'ind al-Durūz,* Sivi publishers. 1981, Beirut.

Sheikh Halīm Taqī al-Dīn and Sheikh Mursal Nasr, *Al-wasiyya wa-al-mīrāth 'ind al-muwahhidīn al-Durūz* (with an introduction by Samī Makārim), Development and Research Druze Council, Beirut, 1983.

Shink, Bernadette (1994) *Kamal Gunbulat. Das arabisch-islamische Erbe und die Rolle der Drusen in seiner Konzeption der libanesischen Geschichte* (Kamāl Jumblatt. The Arab Muslim Legacy and the Role of the Druze in their Understanding of Lebanese History), Berlin, Schwarz; Arabic edition (Beirut: Dār al-Nahār, 2000).

The Tawhīd Faith: Fundamental Beliefs, prepared and edited by Committee on Religious Affairs, American Druze Society.

**المراجع:**

- أبو اسماعيل سليم (1945)، **التشيّع الفاطمي الإسماعيلي– الدروز–وجودهم مذهبهم وتوطنهم**، مؤسسة التاريخ الدرزي.
- أبو حزام الشيخ د. أنور (1995)، **إسلام الموحدين**، دار اليمامة.
- أبو زكي د. فؤاد (1997)، **الأمير السيد جمال الدين عبدالله التنوخي سيرته وأدبه.**
- أبو صالح د.عباس بالاشتراك مع مكارم د.سامي، **تاريخ الموحدين الدروز السياسي في المشرق العربي**، منشورات المجلس الدرزي للبحوث والإنماء.
- أبو مصلح حافظ وملاعب فارس حليم ويحيى أنيس (1999)، **التنوخيون: تاريخ وحضارة**، المركز العربي للأبحاث والتوثيق.
- الأطرش فؤاد (1974)، **الدروز: مؤامرات وتاريخ وحقائق.**
- أبي راشد حنا (1991)، **حوران الدامية**، مطبعة الفكر العربي، بيروت، طبعة ثانية.
- الباشا د.محمد خليل (1994)، **الإنسان وتقلبه في الآفاق**، مؤسسة نوفل، بيروت.
- الباشا د. محمد خليل (1982)، **التقمّص وأسرار الحياة والموت في ضوء النص والعلم والاختبار**، دار النهار.
- الباشا د. محمد خليل و غنّام د.رياض حسين (2000)، **السجل الأرسلاني**، مكتبة نوفل.
- الباشا د. محمد خليل (1990)، **معجم أعلام الدروز**، الدار التقدمية، بيروت.
- البعيني د. حسن أمين (1991)، **دروز سورية ولبنان في عهد الانتداب الفرنسي**، المركز العربي للأبحاث والتوثيق.
- البعيني نجيب (1992)، **أمير البيان شكيب أرسلان ومعاصروه**، الدار الجامعية.
- البعيني يوسف سليم (1992)، **أهل التوحيد "الدروز" وخصائص مذهبهم الدينية والاجتماعية**، 5 أجزاء.
- تقي الدين أديل حمدان، **الشيخ حليم تقي الدين.**
- تقي الدين د.حليم (1981)، **الأحوال الشخصية عند الموحدين الدروز وأوجه التباين مع السنة والشيعة مصدراً واجتهاداً.**

- مكارم د.سامي (2006) ، **أضواء على مسلك التوحيد (الدرزية)**، دار صادر، بيروت.
- مكارم د.سامي 2006 ، **العرفان في مسلك التوحيد (الدرزية)**، مؤسسة التراث الدرزي، لندن.
- المولى د. سعود (1990)، **الأمير شكيب ارسلان: بنو معروف أهل العروبة والإسلام**، منشورات المجلس الدرزي للبحوث والإنماء.
- النجار عبدالله (06 آذار 1974)، **إمامة العقل في مذهب الموحدين الدروز**، محاضرة في رابطة العمل الاجتماعي.
- النجار عبدالله، **مذهب الموحدّين الدروز**.
- نصر الشيح مرسل (2004)، **معالم الحلال والحرام عند الموحدين "الدروز"**.
- نصر الشيخ مرسل (1416هـ)، **الموحدون الدروز في الإسلام**، الدار الإسلامية، بيروت.
- نويهض عجاج (1963)، **التنوخي الأمير جمال الدين عبدالله والشيخ محمد أبو هلال المعروف بالشيخ الفاضل**، دار الصحافة، طبعة ثانية.
- هشّي د. سليم حسن (1985)، **دروز بيروت: تاريخهم ومآسيهم**، دار لحد خاطر، بيروت.
- اليحيى أنيس (2001)، **الشيخ بشير جنبلاط وتحقيق وصيته**، دار الفنون، بيروت.

**تاريخ الدروز في آخر عهد المماليك حسب رواية حمزة بن أحمد بن سباط في كتاب صدق الأخبار**، دار العودة، بيروت.

- أبو صالح د. عباس (1984)، التاريخ السياسي للإمارة الشهابية في جبل لبنان، **منشورات المجلس الدرزي للبحوث والإنماء**، بيروت، 1984.
- سجل **سرائر الأول والآخر**.
- **الصحف الموسومة بالشريعة الروحانية في علوم اللطيف والبسيط والكثيف**.
- **مجموعة قصص النبيين – منشأ السيد الأمير قدس الله سرّه**، مجموعة للشيخ الفاضل رضي الله عنه.
- **مذكرّات لسلطان باشا الأطرش القائد العام للثورة السورية الكبرى 1925–1927**.
- **مشيخة العقل**، لباب العلوم، 1980.
- **مناهل الحكماء والأولياء ومآثر الأعلام الموحدين**، منشورات المركز العربي للأبحاث والتوثيق، 1997.

- تقي الدين حليم ونصر مرسل (1983)، **الوصية والميراث عند الموحدين الدروز ومنه مثال في تقسيم الإرث ومقارنة مع المذاهب الإسلامية الأخرى.**
- تقي الدين حليم (1979)، **قضاء الموحدين الدروز في ماضيه وحاضره.**
- تقي الدين زين الدين عبد الغفار (1999)، **النقط والدوائر**، دار إشارات للطباعة والنشر.
- جنبلاط كمال، **حقيقة الثورة اللبنانية**، دار النشر العربية.
- حسين د. محمد كامل (1962)، **طائفة الدروز: تاريخها وعقائدها، دار المعارف بمصر.**
- حمزة نديم نايف (1984)، **التنوخيون أجداد الموحدون الدروز ودورهم في جبل لبنان**، دار النهار للنشر.
- زهر الدين د.صالح (1994)، **تاريخ المسلمين الموحدين الدروز**، المركز العربي للأبحاث والتوثيق.
- شيلبر بريجيت (2004)، **أنتفاضات جبل الدروز"حوران": 1850- 1949**، دار النهار، بيروت.
- الصدّي نبيه محمد (1993)، **مذهب التوحيد "الدرزية" في مقالات عدّة**، دار العلم بدمشق.
- طليع القاضي أمين (1971)، **مشيخة العقل والقضاء المذهبي الدرزي عبر التاريخ**، المطبعة الأنطونية في بيروت.
- عابد د.مفيدة (2001)، **التنوخيون في لبنان: مواقفهم السياسية وتحالفاتهم العسكرية ودورهم الديني والحضاري**، مطابع دويك.
- عبد الخالق نايف (1993)، **شمائل المسلمين الدروز ودلائل الآيات والرموز**، مكتبة الجيل الطالع.
- العريضي الشيخ أبو صالح فرحان سعيد، **مناقب الأعيان**، منشورات مدرسة الإشراق، عاليه.
- عنان محمد عبد الله (1983)، **الحاكم بأمر الله وأسرار الدعوة الفاطمية**، مكتبة الخانجي في القاهرة ودار الرفاعي في الرياض.
- غيث الشيخ بهجت (1998) ، **معارج الروح في مرايا التوحيد**، منشورات الضحى.
- فلاح سلمان حمود (1980) ، **فصول في تاريخ الدروز**، دار الصالح للطباعة والنشر.
- مكارم د.سامي نسيب (1966) ، **أضواء على مسلك التوحيد**، دار الصهاد، بيروت.
- مكارم د.سامي (1980) ، **مسلك التوحيد**، بيروت.
- مكارم د. سامي (2004) ، **التقية في الإسلام**، منشورات مؤسسة التراث الدرزي، لندن.

# Index